W0399497

Carl-Auer

Dirk Rohr
European Association for Counselling
International Association for Counselling

Counselling in Europe

Training, Standards, Research, 'Culture' & Information about 39 Countries

2021

Cover: Uwe Göbel
Printed in Germany
Printed by CPI books GmbH, Leck

First edition, 2021
ISBN 978-3-8497-9047-9 (softcover)
ISBN 978-3-8497-9048-6 (ePUB)

Bibliografic information published by Die Deutsche Nationalbibliothek:
Die Deutsche Nationalbibliothek lists this publication in
Die Deutsche Nationalbibliografie; detailed bibliografic data available
on Internet http://dnb.d-nb.de

Published by Carl-Auer Verlag: www.carl-auer.com
Please order our catalogue or subscribe to our newsletter.

Carl-Auer Verlag GmbH
Vangerowstraße 14 . 69115 Heidelberg
Tel. +49 6221 6438-0 . Fax +49 6221 6438-22

Germany

Content

Introduction 9

1 About Counselling 13

2 European Association for Counselling (EAC) 19

2.1 Introduction and Background to the Development of EAC Training Standards 19

2.2 Training Standards Guidelines 20

2.3 Definition of Counselling 22

2.4 Charter for Ethical Practice 22

2.5 Accredited Membership 26

2.6 Core Competencies for Counsellors in Europe 26

2.7 Training Standards 27

2.8 Counselling Training: Recommended Programme 29

2.9 Counselling Supervision 30

2.10 Procedure for the Award of the European Certificate of Counsellor Accreditation (ECCac) 32

2.11 Developing the EAC Accreditation Scheme 34

3 International Association for Counselling (IAC) 35

3.1 Aims and Functions 36

3.2 Strategy 37

3.3 Activity Framework (2021) 38

3.4 World Mapping Project 40

3.5 IAC Membership 40

3.6 Country Ambassadors 41

3.7 Continuing Education 41

3.8 Round Tables 42

3.9 Journal 44

3.10 Events 45
3.11 e-Newsletters 46

4 About Counselling in 39 European Countries 47
4.1 Introduction World Mapping Project 47
4.2 Methodological framework 49
4.3 Information on the 39 countries 50

5 Europeanwide Associations 141
5.1 Counselling and psychotherapy 141
5.2 Our Research 143
5.3 Presentation of selected associations 144
5.4 Presentation of the quantitative results 154
5.5 Future vision 156

6 A Comparison between the European and the American Standards of Counselling Training Programs 161
6.1 The Process of Counselling Globalization 162
6.2 Internalizing the Counselling Training Programs 162
6.3 Obstacles for Globalization 163
6.4 American 'Council for the Accreditation of Counselling and Related Educational Programs' (CACREP) 164
6.5 European Accreditation Systems 165
6.6 The Complexity of Development of the Global Code of Ethics 167
6.7 Conclusion 168

7 Teaching Counselling 171
7.1 Context of training in Counselling 171
7.2 Professionalisation – "Don't play what's there. Play what's not there" (Miles Davis) 183

8 Research in Counselling 197
8.1 Mixed-Methods Research in our Marte Meo Project 197
8.2 Mixed-Methods Research in our Genograms Project 202

8.3 European Qualifications Framework (EQF) for Lifelong Learning – A current research project in Germany 205
8.4 Further literature that is highly recommended..........................206

9 Integrating research knowledge and awareness into Counselling and psychotherapy training: an apprenticeship model (John McLeod) 209

10 'Transcultural Counselling', Racism, Power, and Discrimination 227

10.1 Preface 227
10.2 Introduction..228
10.3 Discrimination – what is it?...233
10.4 Racism and 'Culture' 234
10.5 Transcultural Approaches from a Racism-Critical Perspective 236
10.6 Components of training standards that are critical of power, discrimination, and racism...239
10.7 Conclusion and Outlook...240

Introduction

First of all I would like to point out that I am not a native speaker thus my English is by no means perfect. Nonetheless, I hope you will gain much information from this book and with it increase your knowledge and understanding about counselling.

I thank David Dutch (EAC) and Renate Luther for helping with the translation and Sofiia Molot for the editing process.

I am writing this book from various roles that I currently hold, and I would like to link the enumeration directly with heartfelt thanks to the many colleagues from the various institutions:

My team in the "Counselling Research Unit" at the University of Cologne, Germany include Annette Hummelsheim, Marc Höcker, Robert Baum, Clara Stein, and Bianca Rusch. I would especially like to thank Sofiia Molot, who played the most prominent part in bringing the book together, formatting it, etc.

Within that unit I lead the research group for "World Mapping: Europe" with Vivien Magyar, Leonie Ziehm, Nina Reiter, Nina Bergemann, Chiara Epifani, Sarah Krütt and Agnes Ottinger.

I head the "Centre for Advanced Teaching and Learning (ZHD)" at the University of Cologne, too. Together with Hendrik den Ouden and Miriam Gertzen I have developed expertise in Adult Education and Higher Education Didactics.

In addition to working at the university I am also director of the koelner-institut.de which offers non-university teaching of counselling. My special thanks there go to Christine Jablonski, Martina Masurek, Franziska Gnest, Jonas Lichtenberg, Robert Baum and last but not least the co-director, my wife, Kathrin Meiners.

In April 2019, I became President of the 'European Association for Counselling (EAC)'. I especially thank Eva Metallidi (Vice President), Ivana Paunovic (General Secretary), Carolina Welin (Treasurer), David and Brenda Dutch (Webmaster and Administrative Assistant) for their support and guidance.

In May 2019, I became a member of the Executive Council of the 'International Association for Counselling (IAC)'. From the Board of IAC, I especially thank Bill Borgen (President) and Naoise Kelly (CEO) for their contribution to Chapter 3, and Dione Mifsud (past president IAC) for our diverse cooperation (e. g. the University of Cologne and University of Malta).

I thank Carl-Auer Verlag publishing who have been responsible for bringing this book to life. My gratitude to Matthias Ohler, Ralf Holtzmann, Nora Wilmsmann, Sandra Lode, Klaus Müller and Beate Ulrich. I have been associated with them since January 2018 as series editor of the petrol-coloured series "Counselling, Coaching, Supervision."

From January 2020, I became a member of the International Advisory Board "Counselling and Psychotherapy Research Journal – Linking research with practice (CPR)". I thank CPR for their permission to reproduce excerpts from my publications. I thank Natalia Zapolsky for the collaboration – without her, chapter six would not exist. Concerning Chapter eight, Research in counselling, I thank my mentor Charles Deutsch, Harvard University, the Marte Meo Research Group, especially my wife Kathrin Meiners, also Sophia Nettersheim. The Genogram Research Group, Clara Stein, Mario Winter, Sven Kullack, and Ellen Aschermann and Kristin Spath. The Research Group "Counselling – European and German Qualifications Framework (EQF / DQR) for Lifelong Learning" Marc Weinhardt, Cornelia Maier-Gutheil, Tim Stanik, Marc Höcker.

The ninth chapter is a guest contribution from John McLeod. Thank you very much, John.

Chapter 10 deals with some essential ethical topics – e. g. transcultural. It is a short form of a book I am writing together with Ilja Gold and Eva Weinberg (Gold, Weinberg and Rohr 2021), including Interviews with Souzan AlSabah, Sandra Karangwa, Berivan Moğultay-Tokuş, Amma Yeboah and a preface from Eia Asen. I thank all of them.

Chapter 1, 7, 8 and 10 are partly already published in German. I think some of the thoughts are very interesting for an international audience. I thank the publisher and my co-authors for allowing this.

Book structure

The first chapter defines and explains counselling. Then, in chapter 2, the European Association for Counselling (EAC) and its training standards are presented. Chapter three describes the International Association for Counselling (IAC). Chapter four gives an overview about the brief history and background of counselling, the current regulatory status, the challenges and trends as well as additional information of 39 European countries. These are the European results of the World Mapping Project (IAC). Chapter 5 gives an overview of the selected European-wide associations. The American and the European Standards are compared in chapter 6, while Chapter 7 deals with teaching counselling.

I cover the importance of research in chapter 8. The following Chapter 9 features a guest contribution from Prof. John McLeod, "Integrating research knowledge and awareness into counselling and psychotherapy training: an apprenticeship model". Finally, Chapter 10 deals with power, discrimination and racism in counselling.

1 About Counselling

All countries differ significantly in economic opportunities, social policies, religious practices, political organisation, wealth, and much more. The world population reached the 1 billion mark in 1820, and less than two hundred years later (2011) the number of people had already increased to 7 billion. This excessive growth exacerbates problems related to employment, pollution, poverty, and depletion of natural resources.

The 20th century experienced two major world wars, advances in science and technology, the Cold War, and increasing concern for the environment. Steady growth in science and communications technology and changes in family structures in the 21st century raise both hopes and fears among the population (cf. Hohenshil, Amundson & Niles 2015, p. 3). The current time is characterised by the fast pace and constant change. Also, there is the problem of the Coronavirus, which spread worldwide, putting the entire population in a state of emergency. The stressors mentioned above lead to psychological strain on individuals and groups. Essential counselling functions are available in every culture globally. Yet in some countries they are more likely to be performed by families, friends, acquaintances, indigenous healers, shamans or non-specifically trained medical personnel. Against this background, there is a growing need to initiate, develop, and professionalise counselling services worldwide to promote society's mental health (cf. Hohenshil, Amundson & Niles 2015, p. 4).

Counselling is a discipline in its own right; it is a sub-discipline of various psychological, educational, social, labour, and organisational science or other disciplines. It is a cross-disciplinary, scientifically based concept of thought and action that different disciplines draw on and use according to their specific objectives and needs. From this starting point, I would like to use this book to help you understand that counselling is coming out of the shadow of a formerly predominantly therapeutic basic understanding. And not least due to international developments – is developing its own, scientifically based profile. Through specific counselling courses of study at universities and colleges and continuing education institutions. In no way should the previous diversity of counselling concepts and counselling formats be abandoned favouring a uniform counselling system. For it is precisely this diversity that represents a great resource in the fields of application and for the target groups of counselling.

With the social developments in recent decades, one can observe a rapidly increasing need for counselling in the most diverse everyday and professional life areas. It must guarantee that experienced-based, effective and efficient counselling based on theoretically and methodologically sound knowledge from an experienced perspective. A prerequisite for this is a scientifically elaborated, interdisciplinary counselling concept.

Counselling is in the field between individual therapeutic measures, social welfare activities and educational activities. It draws on knowledge from the following areas: medicine, psychology, psychagogy, psychotherapy, social work and sociology, and in exceptional cases, theology and legal sciences.

By synthesising and integrating psychodynamic, behavioural therapy, humanistic and systemic approaches, she develops ways of working for her specific work field.

Counselling in the psychosocial field deals with people who seek guidance, advice, support and help with various problems and questions of coping with their existence.

The counsellors are informed by the people seeking help with factual information about their personal life situation and the behavior of the people interacting with them and thus are allowed to work together with the person seeking help and clarify the concrete situation and resolve the conflict.

Counselling is a special get-together for a period of time. Its standards incorporate the individual's full intentionality. Then again, the counsellor gives complete privacy to the client. Counselling's objective is not to offer solid guidance, the advisor endeavors along with the individual looking for appeal, and help explain their troubles, issues, or clashes and attempts to give them both assistance in comprehension and direction as help in deciding. Opportunities for tackling problems are looked for together. Counselling is one form of empowerment.

One of the counselling objectives is to look for guidance and help more dependable and suitable and give that person more individual flexibility. Accomplishing this objective requires a fortifying of oneself. Accordingly Advising at the same time adds to the democratization of society" (BfgA, 1975, 4).

Counselling, as we can see, has a long history. First as a concept for action in social work, then as part of therapeutic action, counselling is on its way to becoming a discipline in its own right. It is here that it gains its ability to connect with international developments in counselling. Although the professionalization of counselling in Europe still seems to be borrowed from and linked to therapeutic schools and based on an internationally established academic profile.

Most recently there has been a great deal of progress in counsellings theorization in Europe (cf. Nestmann & Engel, 1997.

The Bologna Process at European universities, which favours an interdisciplinary approach without one discipline or another being able to claim dominance alone, is helpful in this regard.

Counselling has a long professional tradition but its independent academic formatting has only just gained momentum in Europe. To establish and maintain the international connection to the development of counselling, there is an urgent need for an expanded scientific positioning and establishing of direction (see chapter 8). This also applies to the professional discourses in the informal continuing education sector of the professional associations currently being sought, such as developments in the European Qualifications Framework for Lifelong Learning (EQF). A wide variety of cooperative ventures between universities, higher education institutions and continuing education and training institutes, between theory and practise are currently exemplary and could point to sustainable new developments.

The following visualisation attempts to delimit and narrow down the field of counselling (see Figure 1).

Its four axes express rather qualitative aspects (cf. Brandel-Nebehay & Russinger, 2005; Gregusch, 2013). Thus, they do not capture typically quantitative factors of counselling, such as the duration or frequency of sessions (one-time, several or up to fifty sessions; time from five minutes to one hundred and twenty minutes or more), the setting with the number of counselees (i. e. individual, couple, group or team counselling) or the specificity of the diagnostic process. Instead, the graph can be used to characterize concrete counselling via the range between the poles (1) specificity "Consulting" to "psychosocial counselling", (2) voluntariness in the use of counselling, "high voluntariness" to "low voluntariness", (3) formalisation of the setting, "formal" to "informal" setting (4) interests of the Counsellor, "own strong interests" to "no own interests" (if applicable, the term "convictions" would also fit here). I want to illustrate the four axes using the example of a freelance, practising Counsellor:

(1) On the axis of specificity from "Consulting" (or information-giving counselling, such as financial counselling or educational counselling) to the other pole: "psychosocial counselling" (or process counselling, Therapeutic Counselling, etc.), one would most likely make a point in the right quarter (since, for example, communication or conflict models or even psychoeducation are introduced and explained, it can also have parts of information-giving counselling).

(2) Voluntariness in the use of counselling: A very "high voluntariness" can be assumed here. At first glance, this axis may seem very clear-cut. Still, even in the coercive context of a correctional institution, there are voluntary counselling offers or, in the case of couples counselling, definitely 'involuntary' participants.

(3) Formalisation of the setting: In our example, we can speak of a 'formal' setting: Not as formal and bureaucratic as, e. g. psychotherapy, but also not as informal as the 'Counselling talk' between boss and employee.

(4) Interests of the Counsellor: Here, we would probably speak of 'not so strong own interests'. Maybe there is an institution with its expectations, mission statements, funding ideas, etc. – and yet no self-employed counsellor can have an interest in losing clients 'too quickly'.

Moreover, there are 'own convictions' of the Counsellor with regard to counselling per se: e. g. that a robust solution orientation is helpful or rather deep processing, that an intense confrontation e. g. in the sense of the provocative style is helpful or rather an empathic-appreciative listening is essential, that 'it is better not to separate' or 'that one does not stick to difficult couple relationships'. As in school, there are 'hidden curricula' in counselling.

If this visualiation invites professional (self-)reflection, it has already fulfilled its purpose, knowing that it is an inadmissible reduction of complexity (Rohr, 2017b).

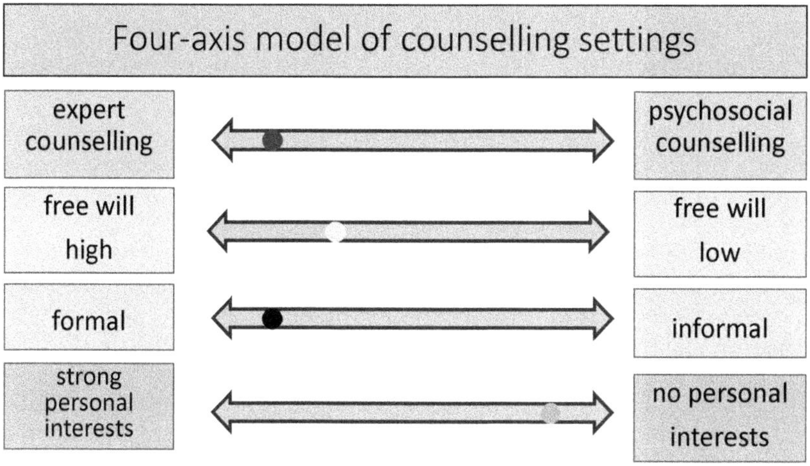

Figure 1: Four-axis model of counselling settings (Rohr 2017)

References

Brandl-Nebehay, A. & Russinger, U. (1995): Systemische Ansätze im Jugendamt – Pfade zwischen Beratung, Hilfe und Kontrolle. Zeitschrift Systemische Therapie 13/2: 90–104.

Bundeszentrale für gesundheitliche Aufklärung BZgA (1975): Beratungsführer. Köln.

Gregusch, P. (2013): Auf dem Weg zu einem Selbstverständnis von Beratung in der Sozialen Arbeit – Beratung als transprofessionelle und sozialarbeitsspezifische Methode. Bonn: socialnet Verlag.

Lumma, K. (Hrsg.) (1999): Counselling – Theorie und Praxis der Beratungspädagogik Humanistische Psychologie. 22. Jahrgang, Sonderausgabe 1/99. Eschweiler: IHP- Bücherdienst.

Nestmann, F. (2007b): Professionelle Beratung: Grundlagen, Verfahren, Indikatoren. In: Senf, W. & Broda, M. (Hrsg.): Praxis der Psychotherapie. Stuttgart: Thieme, S. 186–194.

Rohr, D. (Hrsg.) (2017b): Kontext – Zeitschrift für Systemische Therapie und Familientherapie. Schwerpunktheft Aus- und Weiterbildung in Beratung. 3/2017. Göttingen: Vandenhoeck & Ruprecht.

2 European Association for Counselling (EAC)[1]

Welcome to the European Association for Counselling!

Our vision is to strengthen counselling within Europe, to make counselling accessible for all – to empower people. We should improve the conditions of the daily work of all counsellors.

I hope that this document will serve as a guideline for you if you want to join us in our efforts to establish counselling as a European profession with clear goals, as formulated in the term's definition. In this chapter, we reaffirm the standards of excellence and continuous growth necessary if we, as counsellors, respond to the growing needs of people who are confronted with new educational, socio-political, cultural and economic realities.

This chapter also shows the progress of the European Association for Counselling. It follows the publication of the Charter of Ethics for Practical Counsellors and the Minimum Standards for the Training of European Counsellors. The European Certificate in counselling introduces a new level of qualification that genuinely reflects the status of counsellors receiving EAC accreditation and illustrates our acceptance of our different nationalities and cultures and the commonality of our efforts as European counsellors.

> "We are only as strong as we are united, and we are as weak as we are divided."

2.1 Introduction and Background to the Development of EAC Training Standards

The EAC has got a working group called 'Professional Training Standards and Accreditation Committee' (PTSAC).

This statement reflects the guiding philosophy for the work of the PTSAC.

The Professional Training Standards and Accreditation Committee's prime task is to acknowledge, respect, and address the tremendous differences

[1] Thanks to Eva Metallidi (Vice President), Ivana Paunovic (General Secretary), Carolina Welin (Treasurer), David and Brenda Dutch (Webmaster and Administrative Assistant)

within the countries in Europe and avoid all political efforts to make the EAC a representative of any single part of Europe.

The professional standards as developed should therefore be open to differences in:

- *dimensions of country / culture*
- *relationship between counselling and psychotherapy*
- *individual versus organisational counselling*
- *state-of-the-art developments*
- *the extent to which different theoretical orientations are valued*

2.2 Training Standards Guidelines

Establishing the standards to suit so many different countries proved to be a tricky balance. Some pushed for higher standards, and others wanted lower standards. It was clear that countries in which there were no agreed upon standards wanted lower standards. Eventually, the categories of European counsellor training standards were decided upon by the founding committee.

Over the years, there have been frequent discussions on this subject. And proposed training hours have been the subject of much debate, discussion and consultation. They reflect the need to incorporate the various 'levels' of counsellor under the European standards umbrella and promote the professional counsellor's mobility across National boundaries to enhance the career path working towards "*Counselling without Borders*".

We have been fortunate to have committee members representing different countries, modalities, and comprehensive experience of the counselling profession internationally.

EAC now offers accreditation as a European Counsellor. You will find the standards and procedures for the European Certificate of Counsellor Accreditation award on these pages.

The goal has been to attempt to honour accreditation in the setting of standards for counselling across Europe.

The European Association for Counselling
Synopsis of the History of Counselling

The emergence of the counselling profession could be said to be a twentieth-century phenomenon. Throughout the evolution of peoples, there have been healers for those who were emotionally traumatised. These included oracles, high priests, witch doctors, leaders in established religions and medical professionals. Because of the enormous sociological and cultural changes that swept Western Europe and the United States in particular, from the last half of the nineteenth century, the need for an additional and more specific professional response made itself felt. Professional family care started in the United States as early as 1877. Standardisation of the family social-work response had to come and was in place by 1911. It was in this Social Science working response that counselling techniques had their origins.

Theoretically, counselling training has its roots in philosophy, psychology and social science. It is broad-based and has drawn from a broad spectrum of scientific research. Buber's concept of the 'I-Thou' relationship has been one of the fundamental philosophical underpinnings. At the turn of the nineteenth and twentieth centuries, Freudian psychoanalysis and its variations spread north to Germany, south to Switzerland and across the Atlantic to the United States. The early twentieth-century behaviourism of Pavlov, Watson and Skinner was influential in forming therapies for addictions.

The first university course on couple counselling was established in 1937. In 1943 the first training manual in counselling for social workers was published. The decade of the 1930s saw the setting up of Hirschfeld marriage consultation bureaux in Germany, Austria, Switzerland, and the Netherlands and the Scandinavian countries. In the countries where Hitler gained control, he annexed these bureaux to his evil purposes. Fortunately, as first conceived, these bureaux's work continued in the United States, Britain, and Eastern European countries such as the Czech Republic, beyond Hitler's reach. The centre in Prague was closed down in the communist putsch in 1948 and re-established again in 1967. The work done includes premarital, marital, post-divorce, parenting, psychological problems, and psychological assistance in life crises and problems in relationships with colleagues, neighbours and friends.

There are several theoretical bases and specialisations, which deal with particular presenting problems. What do these variously described approaches have in common?

Counselling has a role in child development, education, physical and mental health, and minority populations. In its position in the coming century, it is possible to see the profession as the conduit of an intrapersonal and interpersonal revolution that can facilitate the human person's full development in a balanced society. This needs safe boundaries around such a task. A clear charter for ethical practice and accreditation guidelines and training must be agreed upon and disseminated across National boundaries. To this end, the European Association for Counselling sets out its criteria for those wishing to acquire the European Certificate in counselling.

The core value of the Charter is respect for human rights and differences. The attitudes that characterise the counselling approach are respect, integrity, authority, responsibility, autonomy, confidentiality, and competence. In the delivery of Practice, this leads to the skills of contracting, setting and maintaining boundaries, being explicit and open, monitoring the process and maintaining appropriate levels of privacy.

2.3 Definition of Counselling

Counselling: is an interactive learning process contracted between counsellor(s) and client(s), be they individuals, families, groups or institutions, which approach holistically, social, cultural, economic and or emotional issues.

Counselling may address and resolve specific problems, make decisions, cope with crisis, improve relationships, develop developmental issues, promote and develop personal awareness, work with feelings, thoughts, perceptions, and internal or external conflict. The overall aim is to provide clients with opportunities to work in self-defined ways, towards living in more satisfying and resourceful ways as individuals and as members of the broader society.

2.4 Charter for Ethical Practice

Introduction

The general ethical framework for EAC members is based on a set of philosophical principles.

Organisational and individual members of the EAC are expected to adhere to this Charter. The text takes into account issues that can be foreseen in the Practice of Counselling. Each member has to devise and monitor specific standards and rules, which consider and respect existing laws and their country's particular social and cultural norms. The principles outlined on these pages guide counselling and associated activities

Philosophical Principles

A counsellor's values are based totally on respect for frequent human rights cultural differences.

The values underpin a set of attitudes and skills, especially regarding the client's integrity, authority, and autonomy.

RESPECT is the unconditional acceptance of clients but not necessarily acceptance of all of their behaviour. Counsellors have a responsibility for making themselves aware of individual and cultural differences.

INTEGRITY honours the client's right to maintain their physical and emotional boundaries and the right not to be exploited in any way.

AUTHORITY recognises that entering a counselling relationship is vested in the client whether the counselling is by direct or indirect assignment.

AUTONOMY acknowledges the client's freedom to express themselves, their needs and their beliefs within the boundaries of a shared respect for universal human rights and individual and cultural differences.

PRIVACY protects the counselling relationship from uncontracted observation or inappropriate observation, interference or intrusion by others.

CONFIDENTIALITY respects personal information disclosed within a trust relationship and protected that information from inappropriate disclosure to others.

RESPONSIBILITY requires the counsellor to actively ensure the observance of the fundamental philosophical principles outlined above in the service provided through the counselling relationship.

COMPETENCE is the requirement for counsellors to ensure and maintain high standards of Practice in their work. Counsellors should provide only those services and use only those qualified techniques gained via education, training or experience.

Ethical Framework

In the counselling relationship, the counselling approach values the client's integrity, authority, and autonomy, expressed in a skilled and professional way.

Counsellors are responsible for the quality of work they do with clients by:

- They are acting according to professional standards of competence.
- They are maintaining confidentiality.
- They are open and explicit with clients about the counselling process.
- They Engage only in activity in which they have the expertise and in which they can act independently and objectively.
- They are remaining within the boundaries of the counselling role.
- Ensure they receive adequate Supervision of the counselling work.
- They continue their own personal and professional development as Counsellors.
- They are establishing, maintaining and monitoring a clear counselling contract.
- Information disclosed during counselling typically remains confidential to that professional relationship except when otherwise negotiated.

Confidentiality is an essential ethical requirement, and without high levels of confidentiality, counselling may be frustrated by the client's lack of trust and sense of safety. However, confidentiality is not absolute because counsellors need to consider the laws and the constraints of their society and their professional roles. Any limitations on confidentiality within the professional relationship should be made **explicit** at the time of contracting. Any subsequent conflicts with the principle of confidentiality must be handled clearly and **openly** with the client at the time of disclosure in a way that respects the client's right to privacy and safety. In circumstances where a breach of confidentiality may be required, the counsellor should endeavour to secure the client's written and informed consent.

Counsellors need to be open with themselves and with clients about the feasibility of working together in a professional relationship.

The professional relationship defined by an explicit and mutually agreed contract and ends with the contract's termination. However, specific professional responsibilities continue beyond the termination of the contract.

These include, but are not limited to, the following:

- maintenance of agreed-upon confidentiality
- avoidance of any exploitation of the former relationship
- consideration of any needed follow-up care

Counsellors need to be clear about any responsibilities, including those outlined above, involved in the professional relationship, which may conflict with the client's interests. Any duties to third parties must be explicit at the pre-counselling contract stage or as soon as they become a counselling factor. For example, a relationship can be the result of a counselling request by indirect assignment. In such cases, the counsellor needs to be explicit with both parties about the accountability involved to both the direct counselling client and the party requesting help, e. g. an employer who makes a request for counselling for an employee with burnout.

Research

Research into counselling should be by competent researchers who are familiar with the values of counselling. It requires full consideration of ethical issues and concern for the dignity and welfare of the participants. Researchers have a responsibility to behave in ways that are as consistent as possible with the core values of counselling. Research that violates those values is unethical. The fully informed consent of all parties is a fundamental ethical imperative in experimental research.

Conflicts between Ethical Principles

The complexity of ethical issues makes it likely that different moral principles and clauses within the Charter may cause specific circumstances. Sometimes, the Charter provisions may also clash with the expectations of, for example, Legal Professionals. By their very nature, the resolution of ethical dilemmas is not simple.

In particular, in cases when counsellors face a conflict between ethical principles, the intention should be to strive for the greatest good and the least harm for the client.

Members of EAC must comply with this Charter and must not work to lower ethical standards than those defined in this Charter. However, National Associations and Organisations are free to place higher stringent standards on their Nation-states members.

2.5 Accredited Membership

This membership category is open to EAC members awarded the European Certificate of Counsellor Accreditation. It is annually renewable and reviewed every five years. The member can apply for reaccreditation according to the guidelines of the EAC.

2.6 Core Competencies for Counsellors in Europe

Accredited European Counsellors will demonstrate their ability to:

- Continually develop multicultural awareness;
- Recognise cultural differences between counsellor and client at cultural / country level, and acknowledge and address these in a non-judgmental way;
- Adjust their style of communication to match that of the client;
- Set, maintain and review the appropriate structural and relational boundaries at different stages of the counselling process;
- Establish a contract or an explicit mutual working agreement regarding the aims of the counselling work;
- Develop awareness of the context in which the client and counsellor are functioning to create the best possible conditions; develop an understanding of how counselling influences the context;
- Address the client's issues in ways that contribute to the counselling process;

- Refine the aims of the counselling to move it forward;
- Facilitate the movement toward the client's insight, development and change;
- Facilitate the transfer of learning from the counselling relationship to the client's everyday life;
- Review the counselling process in terms of the client's experience;
- Bring the counselling to closure in a way that recognises the experience for both the client and the counsellor;
- Work consistently within a clear theoretical orientation;
- Recognise limits and boundaries, both professional and personal;
- Recognise client issues that need the attendance of another professional and refer the client appropriately;
- Be consistently aware of ethical issues and an appropriate approach to moral dilemmas;
- Evaluate the counselling process in terms of your learning as a counsellor;
- Recognise the need for ongoing Supervision and act accordingly.

2.7 Training Standards

Course Work

Refers to in-depth training in counselling, enabling the trainee counsellor to develop the core competencies outlined in the section entitled Training Programme. At best, this will generally be an integrated training within an established training programme, which employs an external examiner, has an appeals procedure and is recognised by the local National Association for Counselling. This training may include any primary academic degree already obtained.

Personal Development

The following are general guidelines for each training programme to be implemented according to their specific theoretical approach. The purpose of this component is to facilitate:

- Awareness of personal issues in work and how these might influence the counselling process;
- Ongoing development in:
    - intellectual understanding and knowledge
    - emotional maturity
    - acceptance of self and others;
- Experience of being in the client role, wherever possible within a formal professional counselling relationship;
- Development of a global perspective of self-concerning the world.

Counselling Practice

It will typically take place within a formalised and contracted counselling arrangement.

Training Requirements

- 450 hours of course work including personal development, theory and skills; A minimum of 50 hours of individual therapy consistent with the model of Practice;
- 100 hours of supervised counselling practice during training.
- An extra 450 hours under Supervision after qualification while working towards Professional accreditation.

The above will usually complete in a minimum of 3 and a maximum of 6 years.

Personal Commitment

From the start of training and post-qualification, Counsellors will:

- Sign their agreement to maintain the relevant codes of ethics and Practice;
- Hold professional liability insurance;
- Have ongoing counselling supervision or peer supervision as required;
- Ensure continuing personal and professional development.

2.8 Counselling Training: Recommended Programme

Each programme will have its methodology according to its philosophical and theoretical base. The following are guidelines for the establishment of a counsellor-training programme.

Length of training

This programme is a minimum period of 3 years and a maximum of 6 years, class contact of at least 450 hours.

Core Theory – to include

- Clear understanding of a core theoretical model of counselling
- Theories of personality
- Theories of change or client movement
- Models of human development
- Understanding of psychological dysfunction
- Understanding of ethics and professional Practice
- The history of counselling and a study of at least two other counselling approaches
- Study of cultural differences and awareness processes

Counselling Process

The programme will enable the trainee to:

- Establish a counselling relationship;
- Work within a clear theoretical frame;
- Heighten awareness of interpersonal dynamics;
- Develop their ability to understand and work with communication;
- Facilitate the client's understanding and self-awareness of the issue presented;
- Explore their ongoing professional development by review and evaluation;
- Become aware of and address personal and professional limitations and problems.

Counselling Practice

Training programmes must ensure that trainee counsellors pursue their supervised Practice in an appropriate environment. Usually, be in a formalised and contracted counselling arrangement. Training programmes must ensure that counselling supervision providers are experienced, accredited practitioners in the field and meet the EAC Accrediting Organisation guidelines in their own country.

In addition to these arrangements, clear contracts need to establish:

- Supervision arrangements;
- Ethics and Professional Practice;
- Administrative arrangements;
- Any financial arrangements;
- Liaison and referral to other professionals and services.

2.9 Counselling Supervision

Supervised Practice

Formal and contracted Supervision of counselling practice as defined below. EAC recognises that in some countries, practitioners will find it difficult at the moment to have Supervision from an accredited or professional counsellor. Supervision from a qualified professional in an allied field with an understanding of counselling as defined by EAC.

Definition of Counselling Supervision

- Counselling supervision is a contracted, professional relationship between two or more individuals engaged with counselling activities, which leads to reflection on the counselling situation and its structure;
- Supervision provides emotional support, containment and clear boundaries for the counsellor and the counselling work;
- Supervision encompasses an element of learning that includes elucidation of codes of ethics and Practice;
- Supervision responsibly monitors the working process between counsellor and client;

- The supervisory relationship and process of Supervision are congruent with the developmental needs of the supervisee;
- Supervisors are responsible for monitoring their ethical boundaries and abilities.

Description of Counselling Supervision

Counselling supervision enhances the counsellor's effectiveness in responding to the needs of the client. Towards this purpose, counselling supervision assists those involved in the counselling profession in:

- Becoming increasingly aware of their responses to their counselling work;
- Deepening their professional knowledge;
- Continuously developing their counselling and professional skills;
- Managing their caseload;
- Evaluating their professional Practice.
- Managing their self-care and the prevention of burnout and continuing support through personal development/therapy.

The supervisor offers a climate where the supervisee can feel understood, supported, and challenged and instructed and assisted in their counselling work. The supervisor's responsibility is to provide conditions that will help the supervisee consider their experiences as reflection, elucidation, and generating sources of knowledge.

Counselling supervision takes place both during the training programme and after completion of the programme. An independent supervisor of his own choice then supervises the counsellor. However, Supervision is evaluated along with the programme.

Models of Supervision

Adopted during the interim five-year period:

- One-to-one (supervisor-counsellor);
- Group supervision with counselling supervisor;
- Combination of the above modes of Supervision;

- Peer supervision could be acceptable for accredited practitioners with five year's post-accreditation experience. Subject to the requirements of the EAC or the guidelines of individual modalities.

Group Supervision equivalent to one-to-one Supervision.

The same person shouldn't undertake supervisory and managerial responsibilities. If this cannot be avoided, then the tasks and roles need to be clearly defined and contracted.

Peer group support with clear aims and boundaries can enhance good counselling practice. However, this does not replace Supervision.

2.10 Procedure for the Award of the European Certificate of Counsellor Accreditation (ECCac)

The Accreditation procedures will be monitored and developed by the Professional Training Standards and Accreditation Committee, PTSAC.

Relationship between the EAC Organisation and the Professional Training Standards and Accreditation Committee (PTSAC)

- The PTSAC will examine whether the training standards, accreditation and reaccreditation procedures of the Organisation meet EAC criteria.
- The PTSAC recognises that some Organisations have well-established procedures whilst others are in the early stages of development. Well-established Organisations that have comparable standards of training and accreditation should follow the methods below.
- The EAC Executive recognises that some Organisations are in the early stages of development.
- In these cases, the PTSAC will provide consultation to help Organisations meet the EAC standards of counsellor accreditation. Pro-forma has been designed to guide Organisations in the task.

EAC Accrediting Organisations Route to Accreditation with EAC

- Each EAC Accrediting Organisation will provide the PTSAC with copies of their standards and procedures for counsellor accreditation, codes of ethics, complaints procedures and the Proforma for application to the EAC Accrediting Organisations for accreditation with EAC.
- The criteria and procedures are in place and agreed upon by EAC for accreditation through the EAC and cannot be changed. The EAC Accrediting Organisation will be able to recommend candidates for the award of the European Certificate of Counsellor Accreditation.

Individual Accreditation Procedures

- Candidates apply to the EAC for the application form.
- The EAC sends the application form to the candidate to complete.
- The candidate sends the completed application form to the EAC.
- The PTSAC, in collaboration with the EAC Executive, will develop a system that will ascertain that the form's information is accurate and correct.
- A letter of confirmation will be sent to the candidate by the EAC Executive. An accreditation fee will also be required
- On receipt of the fee, the application is passed to the EAC Registration Board.
- When the Registration Board of EAC registers the candidate as an Accredited European Counsellor, the certificate is sent to the candidate.
- The EAC contacts unsuccessful candidates by a letter outlining the reasons for non-accreditation.
- All decisions of the Registration Board are final.

2.11 Developing the EAC Accreditation Scheme

The preceding pages outlined the first essential steps taken by EAC to establish an agreed set of standards for counsellor accreditation that can be owned and validated across the country, language and cultural boundaries.

So far, EAC has recognised a relatively small number of EAC Accrediting Organisations. However, we have many members in countries that do not yet have Accrediting Organisations. We intend to support the creation of new Accrediting Organisations for Counselling.

Special Case

EAC Members in countries without a National Association or Accrediting Body and whose modality is not covered by an EWO are invited to approach EAC for support in widening their national counselling network with a view to eventually developing an NA or Accrediting Body. In the meantime, they may apply for European Counsellor Accreditation under section 9.3.

The General Assembly, before implementation, must vote on any changes to accreditation procedures and training standards.

For more information as well as for current information (e. g. our webinar series) about EAC please look at https://eac.eu.com!

3 International Association for Counselling (IAC)[2]

The International Association for Counselling is an International Non-Governmental Organization and has consultative status with several organizations including UNESCO, WHO, ECOSOC, UNICEF, ILO and the Council of Europe.

IAC was founded by Professor Hans Hoxter in 1966 as the International Round Table for the Advancement of counselling. The name of the association was changed to the International Association for Counselling in 1997. Since its inception, the association has offered yearly conferences, consultations and / or digital educational and professional events in countries on all continents of the world. These events have brought together the perspectives of practitioners, educators, researchers and policy makers with the aim of increasing the quality and impact of counselling around the globe. One of the early developments of the association was the creation of the International Journal for the Advancement of counselling.

In an interview in late 2001, Professor Hoxtor predicted the increasing complexity of the issues that counsellors would face in the future, and what would be required of them:

> So, the question arises, how from now on how can we go ahead, how can we develop this whole field? The field has developed in a most spectacular way. Today there are people in certainly 120 countries who are committed to counselling as a major factor in emotional, intellectual and spiritual rehabilitation and growth ...so that is a great plus, a great achievement but there is so much to be done. The reason in part is that we are engaged in a society which is all the time trying to discover and develop new areas of understanding, new areas of spiritual and intellectual activity in the sense of the integration of the individual or the family in society, but we are today in a society we have to adapt to and live with, which is more challenged, more attacked from within and from without, than we have for the past hundred years. On the one hand I think that counselling offers huge opportunities for helping and supporting and understanding social and personal emotional needs, but it is based, in my opinion, on a major exercise in learning. I think that counsellors in the future

[2] Thanks to Bill Borgen (President) and Naoise Kelly (CEO)

> will have to develop their learning at a much higher level than we have done in the past (Borgen, 2003, p. 89).

With this perspective in mind, IAC has worked to fulfil scientific and educational and social justice aims to advance the understanding and practice of counselling wherever it is needed, developing or offered in the world, guided by the belief that counselling benefits individuals and groups, and society as a whole. With that broad perspective in view the association has been catalytic in promoting the development of counselling in areas of the world where counselling is less developed, and offers support and consultation to newly developing national and regional counselling associations (Borgen, 2006)

Participation in this association provides a unique opportunity to develop a global appreciation of the way counselling is being deployed to address humanitarian concerns including the promotion of human rights, and the delivery of education, health, and counselling services to individuals, families and groups to address a range of personal, interpersonal, career and social challenges.

3.1 Aims and Functions

IAC Vision: A world where counselling is available to all.
IAC Mission: To serve as an international leader and catalyst for counsellors and counselling associations by advancing culturally relevant counselling practice, research and policy to promote wellbeing, respect, social justice and peace worldwide.
IAC Core Values:

- **Respect**: For the dignity, value and human rights of individuals and communities
- **Integrity**: Honesty, accountability and ethical behaviour.
- **Excellence**: Demonstrated by the quality and professionalism of IAC's work.
- **Service**: To our membership and wider society.
- **Commitment**: To benefit humanity and improve people's lives.
- **Collaboration**: An inclusive culture that values diverse perspectives, the power of common vision, and equality among peers.

3.2 Strategy

In 2021, many countries and people are at a time of unprecedented strain. As a global community of counsellors it is crucial that we come together and work towards the IAC vision of "a world where counselling is available to all". Counselling is growing worldwide and it is important that counsellors have a leading, unifying voice that represents them internationally. Through our strategy, we have committed IAC to playing our part in advancing the field of counselling worldwide and promoting health, well-being, respect, social justice and peace. As counsellors and responsible individuals of the international community we have an unparalleled opportunity to succeed by working together through common principles and goals.

IAC seeks to advance counselling by uniting counsellors globally, serving as an international resource to individuals and associations in the following six Goal Areas, stated as:

1. Development of counselling: This is IAC's central goal and directly relates to our overall purpose. We will continue to advance the field of counselling through Practice, Education, Advocacy, Policy and Research initiatives.

2. Strengthening Partnership and Collaboration: We will strengthen and build connections with our International, National and Organisational partners.

3. Members and Services: We will increase our individual and organisational membership base across all world regions. We will enhance the representation, support and services provided to members.

4. Enhancing our Infrastructure: We will optimise IAC's structures and systems to ensure equal and inclusive representation from all world regions and cultures. As an Executive Council, our committee, sub-committees, and personnel will professionally deliver our services and aims.

5. Enhancing the Profile of counselling: Internationally, we will raise the profile of counselling by utilising our global connections, technology and relationships. IAC aims to serve as a strong and uniting global voice for counselling.

6. Connecting our Members: We will serve as a platform for counsellors worldwide to connect and share ideas on counselling, education and research with individuals, experts and organisations.

Our People: Our Executive Council (Governing Board) in 2021 are:

- President: Bill Borgen
- Treasurer: Blythe Shepard
- Secretary: Nate Perron
- Past President: Dione Mifsud
- Chief Executive: Naoise Kelly
- Membership Secretary: Ruth Falzon
- Regional Representative (Africa): Dominic Nsona
- Regional Representative (Asia): Anasuya Jegathevi Jegathesan
- Regional Representative (Caribbean): Anna Maria Mora
- Regional Representative (Oceania): Di Stow
- Regional Representative (Latin America): Desiree Carlson
- Regional Representative (Europe): Vacant
- Regional Representative (North America): Matt Lyons
- Regional Representative (Middle-East): Kabeer N.V.
- Member-at-Large: Amalia Madihie
- Member-at-Large: Kristen Dickins
- Member-at-Large: Dirk Rohr
- Consultant to the IAC Executive Council: Tommaso Valleri

The IAC Executive Council has regional representation from every world region.

3.3 Activity Framework (2021)

The IAC vision is of "A world where counselling is available to all". counselling changes lives for the better and reduces suffering. IAC's humanitarian movement advocates for more access to counselling worldwide. IAC lobbies and influences governments and international organisations to have counselling better recognised as a profession. In some countries there is no counselling at all. IAC helps to establish counselling structures, (e. g. National Associations or Education Programmes) in those countries. Technology is moving the global circle of counsellors ever closer.

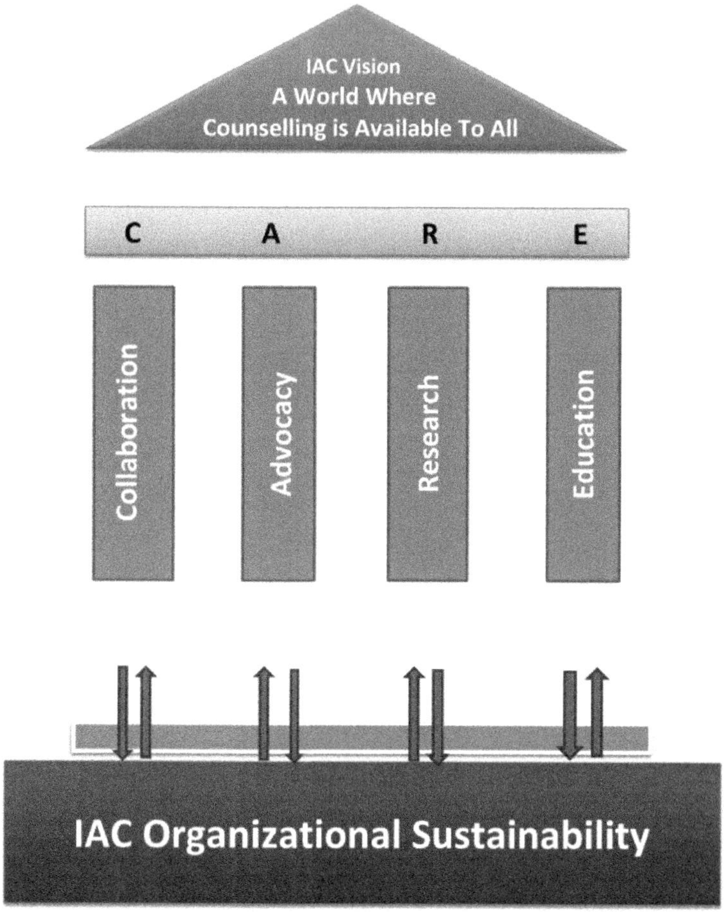

Figure 2: IAC Activity Framework (2021)

IAC embraces the modernisation of our profession and proudly serves at the forefront of connecting counsellors worldwide. Here are some of our main areas of work:

3.4 World Mapping Project

IAC is currently engaged in a major global counselling project entitled the 'World Mapping of the counselling Profession' (see chapter 4). The aim of the project is to compile data and information about the scale, standards and contexts of counselling activity in each of the world's 196 countries. Generating detailed knowledge about the counselling profession for each country will significantly raise public and professional awareness of counselling, enable enhanced advocacy (both national and international), and improve information sharing for individual counsellors and the wider profession. The World Health Organisation (WHO) views the IAC mapping activity as a positive development in gaining an accurate assessment of the numbers of mental health professionals worldwide. We have received financial and in-kind support from the American Counselling Association, the Canadian Counselling and Psychotherapy Association, Taylor's University, Malaysia, and the University of Cologne, Germany. The mapping information will enable IAC to better utilise its consultative status with the aforementioned United Nations (UN) organizations. These inter-governmental (UN) organisations make important high-level policy decisions on mental health, education, work, and social issues. These decisions have a strong and direct influence on the approaches that national governments take to these matters. In turn, the national policies directly affect counsellors and the counselling profession in all countries. The information will also increase the ability of those involved in counselling worldwide to connect with, inform and support each other in advocating for counselling, and enhancing counsellor education and counselling practice.

3.5 IAC Membership

IAC membership is available for individuals and groups and we invite you to consider joining IAC as a member. In doing so, you will be supporting the development of counselling worldwide. IAC membership creates an opportunity to demonstrate your commitment to inclusion, and communicates your values to clients, colleagues and others. IAC membership is open to groups (Associations, Education Institutes, and Services), and Individuals (e. g. IAC Professional Members, Students, Retired members) and carries with it multiple benefits including:

- IAC's Journal (International Journal for the Advancement of Counselling) – Quarterly journal and access to all back-issues since 1978.
- A Certificate of Membership
- A Free Webinar each year.
- IAC Newsletters: News, updates, articles, and events.
- An IAC Logo for use on your materials.
- Significant conference discounts and reports.

Becoming an IAC member supports our work and brings with it multiple professional benefits. Find all joining details on our website. We look forward to welcoming you to IAC, and to the global community of counsellors.

3.6 Country Ambassadors

In 2017 the IAC Executive Council (IAC EC) approved the establishment of a global network of IAC Country Ambassadors to represent and promote the Association. An IAC Country Ambassador is an IAC Member who represents IAC at country level and serves as a direct link to counselling in that country. There may be more than one Ambassador in any one country. This network helps deliver IAC's strategic and humanitarian aims for the development of counselling and the global promotion of the profession. It helps IAC to both broaden and deepen our connection to countries and regional networks.

The role of an IAC Ambassador is to increase awareness of IAC and its work, to promote membership, to act as a mentor to new and prospective members, and to help meet IAC's developmental aims for the profession worldwide. The IAC Ambassador will have an excellent understanding of IAC and its role within the global counselling community. The IAC Ambassador exerts influence in the country to promote IAC's work and ideals. IAC Ambassadors serve as official representatives of IAC in an enhanced volunteer capacity for a three-year term (with the potential to renew).

3.7 Continuing Education

IAC offers easy access to core counselling knowledge and instruction in a variety of online formats – from interactive, on-demand, and curated courses to live online education such as webinars. As an example, our prominent current (Spring, 2021) offering is 'Transcultural counselling' – a unique opportunity to learn online from world-renowned counselling experts. This 20-hour course is self-paced and creates the opportunity to increase your cross-cultural responsiveness in a flexible and supported learning environment. Participants receive a Certificate of Completion and fulfil 20 Continuing Education (CEU) Hours / Continuing Professional Development (CPD) Hours. The course has been priced with a view to increasing global accessibility and is suitable for counsellor educators who would like to strengthen this aspect of their programs, and for counsellors who wish to expand their practice and customize their approach, either internationally or when serving diverse clients locally.

Course Description: The transcultural course is designed for counsellors, counsellor educators, and students who wish to expand their practice and customize their approach, internationally or when serving their diverse client base locally. Benefits include:

- Gain fascinating insights into cross-cultural responsiveness
- Improve self-awareness of personal values and biases
- Add to your knowledge of the counselling profession worldwide
- Contributors from 20 countries

Course Objectives Upon successful completion of this course, students will be able to:

- Communicate key components of a transcultural counselling approach and relevant theoretical frameworks/models
- Apply learning from region-specific profiles to their own practice
- Reflect on their personal definitions of counselling and culture
- Set specific action items to guide future practice.
- Details and Registration can be seen on our website.

3.8 Round Tables

The International Association for Counselling (IAC) was born as the International Round Table for the Advancement of Counselling (IRTAC) in 1966. The concept of a round table for Counselling was the brainchild of IAC's founder and visionary Hans Hoxter. Professor Hoxter first viewed counselling as a force for peace and human well-being in the immediate aftermath of the second world war and when IRTAC was founded it gave a voice to all those counsellors and associations around the world who needed to meet, share and discuss with international colleagues.

The IAC round table concept presents us with scenarios where all counsellors and counselling associations irrespective of any kind of difference have opportunities to present, explain, understand and be heard and be understood. IAC is interested in becoming a vehicle for understanding, solidarity and opportunities for counsellors and their associations. During the Victoria, Canada conference (2014), the IAC Executive Council was presented with a plan to introduce several round tables for professionals to come together and belong to. The first batch of these include an **Associations' Round Table, an Ethics Round Table, an Indigenous Round Table, a Peace and Social Justice Round Table, a Projects Round Table, Counselling Practitioners' Roundtable and an International Research Round Table.**

The **Associations' Round Table** provides opportunities for the leaders of associations to meet physically during IAC conferences to discuss and share issues that can be similar or different to each other.

The **Ethics Round Table** should be made up by professionals, academics and students who are interested in understanding different ethical issues and dilemmas and how these are tackled in ways that make sense within particular international contexts. It should thus provide for opportunities to explore differences and similarities in what constitutes good practice in different contexts and should include windows for academic and professional exchanges within different contexts.

The **Counselling Practitioners' Round Table** creates an opportunity for practicing counsellors to learn and share the different experiences, approaches and standards adopted in different settings and countries. Too many times the counselling debate has been dominated by academics and researchers and this round table can be the repository of practitioners' experiences and field knowledge. The round table could also serve to create international awareness on the practitioner and help counsellors in different contexts to unite and strive for better standards and work conditions.

The purpose of the **IAC Indigenous Roundtable** is to: Establish a community of counsellors who are interested in clinical practice and research relevant to Indigenous people; To acknowledge the historical and political issues that impact Indigenous mental health; Share the practices of Indigenous people to promote holistic health and healing; and advocate for culturally appropriate counselling and research for Indigenous people internationally. The RoundTable provides ongoing support and recommendations to the IAC Executive Council in developing a plan of action for the enhancement of Indigenous Counselling internationally.

The **Research Round Table** substitutes the annual International Research Seminar held traditionally during an IAC conference. This round table gives the opportunity to counselling researchers and students to explore and research issues around counselling but particularly transcultural, contextual and social justice issues. This round table should attract top counselling researchers as well as budding researchers and students.

3.9 Journal

The International Journal for the Advancement of Counselling (IJAC) is published under the auspices of the International Association for Counselling. It promotes the exchange of information about counselling activities throughout the world. The journal contains over 1,200 conceptual, practical and research contributions that provide an international perspective on the following areas:

- theories and models of guidance and counselling
- counsellor education and supervision
- state of the art reports on guidance and counselling in specific settings
- special populations
- special applications
- counselling services in developing countries.

The International Journal for the Advancement of Counselling publishes original articles, major addresses and papers presented at the International Association for Counselling and other major international meetings, as well as thematic reviews and discussions related to guidance and counselling. The submission process for articles to go into the International Journal for the Advancement of Counselling (IJAC – published by Springer) can be seen on our website

3.10 Events

IAC welcomes collaboration with a wide range of organisations (e. g. Counselling Associations, Institutes, Universities, and Groups) looking to organise events. There are three types of IAC event:

- IAC Annual International Conference: Large, annual event, minimum of 400 participants, lasting 2–4 days.
- Regional Conferences: May also be large (200+ participants) events, but mainly focus on counselling issues in the specific world region. IAC has eight world regions: Africa; Asia; North America; Latin America; Middle-East; Europe; Caribbean; and Oceania.
- Country Events: Workshops, Symposia, One-day conferences. These vary in participant numbers and are normally one-day events. Whilst organised 'Under the auspices of', or 'In Conjunction With' IAC, some country events may have less direct input by IAC.
- Ongoing virtual symposia, webinars and other online events. With the advent of COVID, IAC has increased online offerings throughout the year in cooperation with other associations and educational institutions.

There are multiple educational, cultural, economic, and social benefits of hosting such events. IAC International conferences and regional events bring together scholars and practitioners from around the world interested in a specific theme related to counselling. Hosting an IAC event can create an expanded network of both global and regional counsellors, and creates a major opportunity to place a spotlight on specific regional, or thematic, issues related to counselling. Events such as these advance the development of counselling through education, research, information-sharing (and fun!).

Hosting such events also raises the profile of host organisations, and counselling activity in that country. This is of interest to all those concerned about counselling's development including practitioner's, educators, and government departments (e. g. of health, education, and social affairs), as well as many other stakeholders. International events create enthusiasm and excitement from association's members, students and partners.

3.11 e-Newsletters

These quarterly e-Newsletters aim to keep members updated on IAC activity and create an opportunity to share items of interest (e. g. counselling stories, articles, news) from around the globe.

If you would like further information on any aspect of our work, please do not hesitate to contact us at: ceo@iac-irtac.org.

Thank You

References

Borgen, W. A. (2003) Remembering Hans: His ongoing legacy for guidance and Counselling, International Journal for the Advancement of Counselling, 25, 83–89.

Borgen, W. A. (2006). Counselling and social justice: An international perspective. In C. C. Lee (Ed.). Counselling for social justice (2nd Ed) Austin, TX: Pro Ed. Inc., 161–180.

4 About Counselling in 39 European Countries

A research group at the University of Cologne collected information about the different European countries presented in this chapter.

My special thanks go to Sofiia Molot, Vivien Magyar, Leonie Ziehm, Nina Reiter, Nina Bergermann, Chiara Epifani, Sarah Krütt und Agnes Ottinger. This European project was part of the World Mapping of the Counselling Profession Project by IAC.

The International Association for Counselling (IAC) initiated the World Mapping of the Counselling Profession Project in 2017 to gain information about counselling worldwide (see chapter 3). The first areas of the world to be mapped were Latin America, Asia, and the Middle East in cooperation with the American Counselling Association (ACA), the Canadian Counselling and Psychotherapy Association (CCPA), and Taylor's University in Malaysia.

"The International Association for Counselling is pleased to acknowledge Dr Dirk Rohr's work, a member of the Executive Council of IAC. Along with his students at the University of Cologne, they have completed mapping the counselling profession in Europe. Referring to the IAC website (iac-irtac.org) keeps you up to date with what has been achieved so far as IAC continues with this important project. Once again, thanks to Dr Rohr and his students for their work." (Bill Borgen, President IAC)

4.1 Introduction World Mapping Project

Essential counselling functions are practiced in every culture globally. Still, in some countries, they are more likely to be provided by families, friends, acquaintances, indigenous healers, shamans or non-specifically trained medical personnel. Against this background, there is an increasing need to initiate, develop, and professionalise counselling services worldwide to promote societies' mental health (cf. Hohenshil, Amundson & Niles 2015, p. 4).

There is also increasing interest in recording the developmental status of professionalised counselling in individual countries through documentation. So far, not much is known about the number of practising counsellors, their training or the legal standards of different countries. In most countries, there are no state regulations, and the term "counsellor" is unprotected. This leads to enormous differences in quality and uncertainty on the clients' part to find their way through the confusing counselling landscape. This is why the International Association of Counselling (IAC) launched the World Mapping Project.

The World Mapping Project aims to generate knowledge about the development of the counselling profession and detailed facts about each country globally, as there is a significant lack of research on the counselling profession's global status. It provides a global overview of the entire world. It also aims to give counselling more recognition as a profession in its own right in the health sector.

> The aim of the World Mapping of the Counselling Profession Project is to compile data and information about the scale, standards and contexts of Counselling activity in each of the Worlds 196 countries. Generating detailed knowledge about each country's Counselling profession will significantly raise public and professional awareness of Counselling. Enable enhanced advocacy (both national and international), and improve information sharing for individual counsellors and the wider profession. The world Regions are (1) Latin America Region; (2) Caribbean Regions; (3) Africa; (4) Middle-East; (5) North America; (6) Oceania; (7) Asia; and (8) Europe. (International Association for Counselling, 2018).

The World Mapping Project is to be carried out worldwide for all countries. For Latin America, the research has already been completed and a document published.

The World Mapping Project aims to generate knowledge about the development of the guiding profession and detailed facts about each country globally, as there is a significant lack of research on the guidance profession's global status. This will provide a global overview of the entire world. It also aims to give counselling more recognition as a profession in its own right in the health sector.

In addition, a unique form of presentation of the results is presented online in an interactive map. This is a convenient and user-friendly design. Interested parties see a map on the IAC website and by moving the mouse over a country they can click on it and see the details. They immediately receive an overview of the most crucial guidance structures, organisations, and standards currently to be found in that country. For national and international associations and organisations, the project results are an opportunity to get in touch with others and possibly enter into new cooperations. Even the World Health Organisation (WHO) rates the initiative positively and supports the IAC in implementing the project.

4.2 Methodological framework

Country Researchers are those who are responsible for the actual research and for the exchange with the contact persons (cf. IAC, 2020c). These individuals are expected to have experience in scientific information retrieval and are encouraged to be creative in their research. This means that their work is about getting as accurate a picture as possible of counselling in their respective country by working primarily with scientific sources and scientific literature (cf. IAC, 2020b). In parallel, the writers take care of writing the report on the respective country, which is based on the results provided by the country researchers (cf. IAC, 2020d). The methods used in the pilot region Latin America, for example, include literature research, semi-structured online questionnaires, database queries, internet research and consultation with contact persons (cf. IAC, 2018). It also includes translations and the analysis and documentation of the information found.

Counsellors, counselling associations, organisations, universities and other (teaching) institutions were contacted, both in the field of counselling and psychology, as it turned out that the two fields were closely related in some countries. It should be emphasised that the research in some countries was complicated by an existing language barrier, as some associations and institutions were only present on the internet in their national language.

The main instrument of data collection was supposed to be the questionnaire. However, since the response rate was unfortunately very low or even non-existent, it became increasingly important for the group to also resort to literature. As time went on it became clear that it would not be possible to draw information exclusively from the results of the questionnaire and mail contact. Therefore, the research continued mainly on the basis of literature reviews, while in parallel continuing to try to contact and remind people about the survey. A mixture of both methods turned out to be effective and practicable.

Instruments used to gather information:

- Emails
- Online questionnaire
- Literature research
- Internet research
- Literature used for research in addition to the results of the questionnaire:
- Trade journals
- Government documents
- Research reports
- Websites of associations and organisations
- Websites of private counselling services
- Websites of universities and other teaching institutions
- Scholarly books and edited volumes
- Other available sources

In the following we present the information about the countries in an alphabetic order.

4.3 Information on the 39 countries

1. Albania

Brief history/ background of Counselling
Counselling is not an independent profession in Albania. Counselling linked with the psychology field of study and practice. Albania's first psychology major introduced in 1996 due to the socio-political transitions in post-communist Albania. During communism, psychiatry was the only field of study responsible for the treatment of the mentally ill. During communism, psychiatry was used as an additional instrument to control people's behaviour and treat what was considered 'deviant' behaviour by the totalitarian ideology.

Challenges and Trends
The mental health care system has not yet caught up with the European standard, although past political repression and persecution has

led to widespread mental disorders. Moreover, psychotherapeutic treatments are still only accessible to a fraction of the population. There is a need to establish formal procedures of training as it is done for example with psychotherapy. It is a grey area in determining implementation and who is monitoring counselling services in Albania.

During the last five years, there has been a significant change in the number of people asking for counselling services and the gap in monitoring the situation is wide. Most of the reliable services offering psychological counselling are by professionals who have studied abroad.

2. Andorra

Challenges and Trends

Currently, some providers are engaged in psychotherapy and counselling. However, there is no legal regulation of the profession. Universities do not offer training in this field and other training institutes have not been found. The area is very opaque.

Additional Information

Some counselling services, such as:

- Institut de la Ment. Online: https://www.institutdelament.com/
- SomSalut. Online: https://www.somsalutandorra.com/

Some psychological services, such as:

- Capsi – Centre Andorrà de Psicologia. Online: https://capsiandorra.com/

Andorra is a member of the "Small Countries Initiative." WHO started the initiative in 2013, and countries with a population of fewer than one million people can participate in the enterprise. The main goal is to promote a joint political commitment to develop good health practices in the local area. (cf. World Health Organization, 2020)

3. Armenia

Brief history/background of Counselling

The Republic of Armenia has a flawed health care system. Therefore, the counselling profession is not a focus for the government. Counselling is always combined with psychological assistance but is underrepresented in many health cares institutes.

There is no history of the counselling profession, as it still does not exist in Armenia.

Current Regulatory Status/Level of recognition

As counselling is always combined with psychology, you have to study psychology to become a psychological counsellor but this type of counselling is not available in Armenia (cf. "AYG" Centre for Psychological Services, 2020).

Challenges and Trends

The biggest challenge is to develop a counselling system in the Republic of Armenia and to improve the (mental) health care system.

Psychological counselling that exists in the country should be integrated into more institutions, as many hospitals and other healthcare institutions still do not have psychological services.

To improve the health care system requires trained professionals, but since there are not many universities (there are only 2) it is difficult to improve the system.

4. Austria

Brief history/background of Counselling

Vocational guidance initiatives existed in Austria even before the World War. Initially, private associations offered counselling. At the beginning of the 20th century, public associations and organizations also joined in. Women's associations also evolved and dealt with the topic of career counselling.

In 1919, public career counselling finally emerged in Austria, with career counselling centres. In 1921, the Berufsberatungsamt der Stadt

Wien was founded, becoming the largest and most powerful counselling centre. In addition to career counselling interviews, medical and psychotechnical examinations and consultations took place there.

In addition to career entry counselling, there was also continuing education and training. Finally, counselling centres for educational and life issues also developed in Austria. (cf. Gugitscher 2016, p.1ff.).

Since there was no legal regulation, anyone could pose as a psychologist* or counsellor* and offer alleged psychological treatment or counselling. The Professional Association of Austrian psychologists (BÖP) was founded in 1953. The association dealt with legal regulations, continuing education and the position and abuse of psychology from then on. The legal path was long but in 1991 the Psychologists Act finally came into force (cf. Berufsverband Österreichischer PsychologInnen, 2020), and in 1998, the Act on the Regulation of Life and Social Counselling (cf. Bundesgesetzblatt, 1998).

Current Regulatory Status/Level of Recognition

Social counselling has been regulated by law in Austria since 1998. This law requires an additional annual training of at least 16 hours and an annual individual or group supervision with a person who fulfils the Life and Social Counselors Certificate of Competence Ordinance (Lebens- und Sozialberater*innen-Befähigungsnachweisverordnung). Life and social Counsellors are not allowed to provide counselling if the client has a medical condition. In this case, they must refer the client to a doctor or psychologist. (cf. Federal Law Gazette, 1998).

In 2003, the legal definition was established for access requirements for life and social counselling. The law provides for attendance of a corresponding course in a certified training institution and individual self-awareness of at least 30 hours. Furthermore, professional activity of at least 750 hours under accompanied supervision must take place, or evidence certificates of a corresponding degree in an educational, medical, human or social science or psychological training or field of study. The exact requirements for admission and professional activity can be found in the Federal Law Gazette. (cf. Federal Law Gazette 2003).

Since 1991, there has been a "Psychotherapy" law that regulates the practice and training of psychotherapy. This law is one of the most progressive in Europe (cf. Cohen, 2002, p. 5) and describes the criteria that professionals must meet to bear the title of psychologist, clinical psychologist or psychotherapist as well as criteria for obtaining authorisation or licence to practice these professions. (cf. Van Broeck/Lietaer, p. 54).

Challenges and Trends

Who can practice psychotherapy is not clarified through the Psychotherapy Act. (cf. Cohen, 2002, p. 6)?

Also noted that some further training courses are too "verschult" (cf. ibid., p. 7).

For educational and vocational guidance to develop positively in Austria, there needs to be closer cooperation between the guidance services in the school and adult education and labour market sectors. (cf. Hofer, 2010, p. 5)

Austria is already very progressive in many areas and a role model for other countries, yet old and new difficulties and problems keep emerging that need to be solved. (cf. Cohen, 2002, p. 7f.).

Examination and review of the literature did not reveal specific challenges and trends.

Additional Information

Interested readers are advised to read the following articles for a more in-depth discussion of the counselling profession:

- Berufsverband Österreichischer PsychologInnen (2020). Geschichte des Berufsverbandes. Online: https://www.boep.or.at/berufsverband/ueber-den-boep/geschichte
- Bundesgesetzblatt (1998). 260. Verordnung: Standes- und Ausübungsregeln für das Gewerbe der Lebens- und Sozialberatung. Online: https://www.ris.bka.gv.at/Dokumente/BgblPdf/1998_260_2/1998_260_2.pdf
- Bundesgesetzblatt (2003). 140. Verordnung: Lebens- und Sozialberatungs-Verordnung. Online: https://www.ris.bka.gv.at/Dokumente/BgblPdf/2003_140_2/2003_140_2.pdf
- Cohen, M. L. (2002). Zur Situation systemischer Therapie in Europa. Zeitschrift für Systemische Therapie, 20 (2), S. 88–100.
- Gugitscher, K. (2016). Bildungs- und Berufsberatung in Österreich historisch betrachtet. Vom Fürsorgewesen über individualisierte Bildungsberatung zur lebensbegleitenden Beratung

und Kompetenzvermittlung. Magazin erwachsenenbildung.at, 29,1–14.
- Hofer, G. (2010). Bildungsberatung in der Arbeiterkammer Oberösterreich. AK-Angebote und Entwicklungsaspekte für die Beratung in Österreich. Magazin erwachsenenbildung.at, 9, 1–6.
- Van Broeck, N. & Lietaer, G. (2008). Psychology and Psychotherapy in Health Care: A Review of Legal Regulations in 17 European Countries. European Psychologist, Vol.13 (1), S. 53–63.

5. Azerbaijan

Brief history/background of Counselling
In Azerbaijan, the field of counselling is very new. Fifteen years ago, there was no such field as counselling or psychology and people did not care about them too much. Nowadays, the state guarantees citizens the right to receive timely and quality psychological assistance and tries to create conditions that ensure the Republic of the Azerbaijan population's psychological well-being and improve their quality of life. Optimization of mental development, adaption and integration of the person into society and rehabilitation support are becoming more critical.

Psychological assistance is either provided free of charge or on a paid basis. Citizens of the Republic of Azerbaijan in urgent cases, educated people in educational institutions, People detained and arrested or released from punishment, persons who have suffered from domestic violence and Servicemen serving in the Armed Forces have the right to free psychological assistance. Paid psychological aid is on a contract between the client and the institution (cf. Ministry of Justice of the Republic of Azerbaijan, 2020).

Counselling as a separate field is not standard in the Republic of Azerbaijan.

Current Regulator Status/Level of Recognition
The government regulates psychology and psychological counselling (which is the only form of counselling there really is). Following paragraph 1 of Part I of Article 94 of the Constitution of the Republic of

Azerbaijan, this Law determines the legal basis for the provision of psychological assistance in the Republic of Azerbaijan and the rights and responsibilities of persons receiving psychological assistance.

A psychologist is a person who meets the requirements established by this Law, received higher education in the field of psychology or received the speciality of a psychologist in the form of additional education under the Law of the Republic of Azerbaijan "On Education" and has the right to provide psychological assistance.

The Azerbaijan Republic legislation on psychological assistance consists of the Azerbaijan Republic's Constitution, this Law, other normative legal acts and international agreements. The Azerbaijan Republic is a party (cf. Ministry of Justice of the Republic of Azerbaijan, 2020).

Challenges and Trends

As psychology and counselling are relatively new in Azerbaijan, and was not known by many citizens of the Republic 15 years ago, many are not comfortable going to a counsellor or a psychologist. There is a framework given by the Ministry of Justice of the Republic of Azerbaijan on what is needed to become a psychological counsellor; there are not many educational or training institutes. Counselling on its own is not represented in Azerbaijan. It only exists in combination with psychology. Therefore, you need to have studied psychology to become a psychological counsellor. A simple Bachelor is not enough to become a successful Counsellor. Graduated students work in private psychological centres to improve their skills and knowledge (cf. Karimiva, 2020).

The most significant trend in Azerbaijan is the implementation of psychological counselling and awareness-raising activities and preparation and broadcasting of social advertisements and the hotline organisation.

Mostly counselling is combined with psychological assistance and is frequently practiced in educational and medical institutions (cf. Ministry of Justice of the Republic of Azerbaijan, 2020).

Rogerian therapy (person-centred communication) (c. Karimova, 2020) is a more specific trend about many personal development paths towards autonomy, supportive community, empathy, acceptance, and unity. The communication that emerges needs explored from the outside regarding its nature and characteristics. This occurs as a result of a persistent knowledge that any attempt to describe a continuously changing and thus in motion phenomenon can only contribute to an approximate explanation of its existence (cf. Motschnig/Nykl, 2014, p. 25f).

Another Trend is Cognitive Behaviour Therapy (CBT) (cf. Karimova, 2020), which encompasses a wide range of practices that incorporate both cognitive and behavioural conceptualizations and interventions with the goals of mental and behavioural change (cf. Iarussi, M. 2020, p. 34).

Additional Information

- Iarussi, M. (2020). Integrating Motivational Interviewing and Cognitive Behavior Therapy in Clinical Practice. New York: Routledge.
- Ministry of Justice of the Republic of Azerbaijan (2020). About psychological help. Online: http://www.e-qanun.az/framework/ 41280
- Motschnig, R. / Nykl, L. (2014). Person-Centred Communication: Theory, Skills and Practice. Maidenhead: McGraw-Hill Education.

6. Belarus

Brief history/background of Counselling

In Belarus the role of counselling psychologists in supporting the psychological health of the population is increasing. In this regard, there is a need to develop psychological counselling as one of the main areas of psychological assistance. Psychological counselling is a relatively young branch of psychology.

In Belarus, practical counselling psychology has developed much faster than theoretical. Vygotsky can rightfully be called the founder of counselling psychology in Belarus. His ideas became the fundamental basis for developing the system of psychological assistance in the post-Soviet space.

Since 1974, at the 7th Clinical Hospital in Minsk, a city consultation has appeared, in which the seven who applied could receive psychological assistance. In 1980, the Republican Centre for Consulting

"Marriage and Family" was opened, in which doctors and psychologists worked together. G.S. Abramova made a significant contribution to the development of counselling psychology in Belarus. She was the author of the first "Workshop on Psychological Counselling" and the tutorial "Introduction to Practical Psychology" (Olifirovich/ Kopteva, 2010).

Current Regulatory Status/Level of Recognition

The beginning of the 90s witnessed a regulatory framework for psychologists' activities in educational institutions. Temporary research teams formed on the initiative of the Ministry of Education made a significant contribution to its development (Ю.Н.Карандашев, О.С.Попова, Н.А.Цыркун). Their results formed the basis of many documents regulating the activities of psychologists.

An educational standard for practical psychology, the regulation on the social, pedagogical and psychological service of an educational institution, was developed. As part of the development of the psychology of education, psychological counselling was developing.

In Belarus, the question of practising consultants' qualifications is becoming more acute; the only answer to addressing this problem is developing a standard for accrediting vocational training programs.

Licensing and certification is the assurance that a consultants' professional level meets specific standards. The license gives the right to work independently. The certificate allows you to practice but does not give a specialist's title in this field, but only confirms that a counsellor's training meets specific standards (cf. Domoratsky, 2017, p. 135).

Challenges and Trends

There are still many problems in counselling. One is that there is no methodological and methodological basis for counselling of a psychologist. There is no unified conceptual model for training counselling psychologists that would consider fundamental research and applied developments in this area and the existing relationships between them. Also, there is no unity in defining the goals, objectives, forms, and work methods of counselling psychologists in the psychological environment itself.

Further, there is no internationally recognized professional organization dealing with professional qualifications and licensing of working psychologist-consultants and tracking ethical issues of relations in the "psychologist-client" system. There are difficulties in separating counselling as a personality-oriented psychotherapy focused on a clinically healthy person from psychotherapist's activities working with more severe and profound disorders. Last but not least, there are no programs for training and advanced training of counselling psychologists.

The presence of the above difficulties and problems has led to the fact that instead of seeking highly qualified help from counselling psychologists, the population is increasingly turning to alternative systems, including fortune-tellers, traditional healers, astrologers, spiritualists, psychics, Tarot card specialists, etc. Unfortunately, there are difficulties in separating the activities of a counsellor psychologist and a psychotherapist. We believe that psychological counselling and psychotherapy are two sides of psychological help, the content of which is to provide emotional, semantic and existential support for a person or group under challenging situations. Psychological counselling's role is associated mainly with situational problems that arise in clinically healthy individuals who are at the level of consciousness (Olifirovich & Kopteva, 2010).

Privately practising psychologists appeared, carrying out their activities within the framework of one of the theoretical directions. The most widespread areas in our country are gestalt therapy, family therapy, symbol drama. All the prerequisites for the development of counselling psychology in the Republic of Belarus exist. Psychological counselling primarily aimed at those who have problems in everyday life, such as having difficulties at work, in the family or making decisions, insecure, experiencing an age crisis, having low self-esteem, etc. (Domoratsky, 2017, p. 135).

Additional Information

- Belarusian Association of UNESCO Clubs (2020). Youth Centre for HIV VCT. "Know! Understand! Take action!". Online: https://belau.info/docs/anonsy_2020/Center20.pdf
- Domoratsky, V. A. (2017). Teaching short-term methods of Psychotherapy in a practice-oriented masters program. Psychological Counselling and psycho correction. Minsk: BGU centre.

- Olifirovich, N. I., & Kopteva, S. I. (2008). Counselling Psychology in Belarus: problems and development prospects. (4), 97–101.
- Zabrodin, Y. & Pakhalyan, V. (2017). Psychological Counselling. Moscow: Moscow State University of Psychology & Education.

7. Belgium

Brief history/background of Counselling

Since the 20th century, clinical psychology, psychotherapy, and counselling have been a part of the Belgian health care system. Counselling and psychotherapy evolved from inpatient psychiatric care by progressive-minded psychiatrists such as Dr Joseph Guislain.

The early 20th century also saw the first outpatient centres' establishment for 'mental hygiene' (Van Broeck, Stinckens & Lietaer, 2013, p. 262). The 'mentally ill' was transferred from the Ministry of Justice's authority to the Ministry of Health in 1948.

Mental health care became increasingly crucial between 1945 and 1975, as indicated by the development of psychiatric services in general hospitals. "In the 1980s and 1990s, the government decided to change the policy from investment in residential care in psychiatric hospital beds toward more resources from ambulatory mental health services for a larger amount of clients with various psychological problems" (Van Broeck, Stinckens & Lietaer 2013, p. 262). This shift focuses on the importance of mental health care workers such as psychologists, psychotherapists, and counselors.

Likewise, the formation of several professional associations of psychotherapy and counselling encourages the growth of these professions.

Initiatives that were taken in the early 1990s revolved around a legal framework for regulating the practice of these "non-medical mental healthcare practitioners" (ibid., p. 262), to protect the title of psychologist. The 'Ministry of Independent Professions' passed a law in 1993, it is only bound to essential training criteria (cf. Van Broeck, Lietaer, 2008, p. 55). "The authorization to carry the title of psychologist not associated with a regulation of the practice, control of quality, or respect of deontological rules. Subsequent law proposals in the last decade to extend the legal framework to the practice psychologists, psychotherapists and counsellors have remained without success" (Van Broeck, Stinckens & Lietaer, 2013, p. 262).

Current Regulatory Status/Level of Recognition

In Belgium, private training institutes organise training programs for counselling. Some universities offer postgraduate programs for counselling, but there is still no uniform academic training. There are hardly any prerequisites to participate in these programs. Only a bachelor's degree in human sciences is sufficient to enroll in a master's program in counselling (cf. Van Broeck, Stinckens & Lietaer, 2013, p. 262).

Counsellor education programs vary in length and scope of training. There are training programs that last 3 to 4 years to provide comprehensive counselling skills. On the other hand, there are also more specific training programs that require 3 to 6 months of training. This involves specializing in a particular counselling setting, such as secondary school, palliative services, or family work (cf. Van Broeck, Stinckens & Lietaer, 2013, p. 263). Furthermore, one can also focus on stress symptoms, burnout, grief, addiction, and types of counselling work such as psychoeducation, crisis intervention, or group dynamics.

Counsellors will join the "Flemish Association for Client-Centered and Experiential Psychotherapy and Counselling (VVCEPC)" after adding "Counselling" to their title in 2004 (Ibid., p. 263). This organisation ensures quality control through its certification processes. Counsellors must complete a postgraduate program that includes at least three years of part-time training. This includes at least 160 hours of theory, about 120 hours of supervision and about 120 hours of personal counselling experience.

"Since there is no legislation yet in Belgium for obtaining certification as a Counsellor, graduation from a program is not a general requirement. It is only a prerequisite for obtaining a counsellor membership in the VVCEPC. Because the professional activities of [...] counsellors in healthcare are not legally regulated in Belgium, there is no licensing system that authorises these professionals' practice and no register of authorised professionals. Further, there is no official accreditation process of training programs or training institutes, or a regulatory body that handles professional matters, complaints and malpractice" (Van Broeck, Stinckens & Lietaer, 2013, p. 264).

Efforts have been made in recent years to achieve regulatory frameworks for the health professions. To determine progress in defining training requirements, the Belgian Chamber of Deputies passed a law for psychotherapists. It came into force in 2018 (cf. Psychotherapist, 2020). However, no law was passed for the activity of counselling.

Challenges and Trends

A significant difficulty is the lack of legal regulations for the counselling profession. Quality control and control of ethical responsibility are not possible when professionals work without licensing and registration. Likewise, the lack of a legal definition is a hurdle for integration into the health care system (cf. Van Broeck, Stinckens & Lietaer, 2013, p. 266).

A challenge for the coming years is to achieve legal frameworks for the practice and training of Belgium's counselling profession.

"This framework should be explicit about the content of graduate and postgraduate training and impose ethical and deontological standards of practice. Once achieved, efforts have to be made to integrate the new professions in the healthcare system at different levels to enhance these services' quality and availability for the clients and patients who need them. It will be a real challenge to improve the accessibility and the quality of mental healthcare for the patients and at the same time avoid the negative side effects of a complex and overregulated set of rules (Van Broeck, Stinckens & Lietaer 2013, p. 267).

Projects that promote mental health development and target large groups through interventions and Internet-based programs are trending. Through social networks (e. g., Facebook and Twitter), target groups such as children and adolescents are reached and can contribute to the prevention of mental illness by developing and disseminating programs such as serious games (cf. Van Broeck, Stinckens & Lietaer, 2013, p. 267).

Additional Information

For a more in-depth examination of the counselling profession in Belgium, interested readers should read the following articles as well as books:

- Ministerium der Deutschsprachigen Gemeinschaft Belgiens (2020). Psychotherapeut. Online: http://www.ostbelgienlive.be/desktopdefault.aspx/tabid-6199/10665_read-58142/
- Van Broeck, N., Stinckens, N., Lietaer, G. (2013). Counselling and Psychotherapy in Belgium. In: Moodley, R., Gielen, U. P., & Wu, R. (Eds.). Handbook of Counselling and Psychotherapy in an international context, S. 261–270. Routledge.
- Van Broeck, N. & Lietaer, G. (2008). Psychology and Psychotherapy in health care: A review of legal regulations in 17 European countries. European Psychologist, 13(1), 53–63.

8. Bosnia and Herzegovina

Challenges and Trends

The healthcare system is deficient and a major overhaul is required. Insurance is sporadic, and in some cases, medication costs must be paid in full. Some mental health centres in Bosnia and Herzegovina are primarily concerned with treating traumatised individuals. However, they lack trained professionals, time, space and financial resources. Also, there are some non-governmental organizations and projects that provide psychosocial and medical assistance free of charge. All organizations are mainly concerned with the treatment of victims of war and torture. The need for psychological treatment and counselling is very great. Specialized personnel and training opportunities are very scarce, however. (cf. Scacchi, 2004, p. 6ff).

The International School of Sarajevo offers training in the field of psychology. On their website, they describe that after graduation, graduates can work in the following areas: Forensics, Counselling, therapy, psychiatric care centres, hospitals, research, marketing, school, business, social institutions, and in court (cf. International University of Sarajevo, 2020). As you can see, counselling is also listed. This means that there is an engagement with the topic in some way.

Additional Information

Interested readers are advised to read the following article for a more in-depth discussion of the counselling profession:

- Scacchi, J. (2004). Bosnien-Herzegowina. Behandlungsmöglichkeiten für schwer traumatisierte Personen. Online: https://www.ecoi.net/en/file/local/1196034/1006_1187252082_bosnien-behandlung-bei-traumatisierung.pdf

9. Bulgaria

Brief history/ background of Counselling

Counselling is not an independent activity in Bulgaria. Psychotherapists or social workers provide most counselling services.

Bulgarian psychotherapy roots started at the beginning of the 20th century. Developments and processes were almost completely stopped between the world wars and vanished in the times of communism. To be re-started and renewed again at the very end of the '70s and most of all at the beginning of '80s.

The Bulgarian Association for Psychotherapy (BAP) exists legally since 23.11.1993, registered as an NGO. The BAP also has psychotherapy sphere in general.

In schools, universities and other educational institutions, counselling services are often available (although they are not obliged to do so) not only the pupils and students but also the parents or teachers are involved in discussions, workshops or training courses. Specialists who advise in schools and other educational institutions include psychologists, educators, speech therapists, career consultants and pedagogical therapists.

Furthermore, the field of vocational guidance covers a wide range of counselling. The vocational guidance exercise requires many specific competencies, which can be acquired within several master's programmes and the global career development facilitator (GCDF).

One of the leading private providers of counselling training using an online platform is the Business Foundation for Education with the Prometheus project.

Current Regulatory Status/ Level of Recognition

Counselling in the field of health is not a regulated profession.

Challenges and Trends

It is challenging to quote exact mental health data for Bulgaria because it does not have a unified, consistent policy for keeping statistics in this field. It is probably a heritage from the region's communist past when mental health has been treated separately from the general system of health care. It is peculiar, but even today, despite all implemented reforms aiming to abolish the outdated ill practices, psychiatric hospitals still have a different status from the rest of the medical facilities. Mental health reforms are in the pipeline.

Additional Information

Bulgaria will remain challenging to compete with the other EU States about salaries for skilled workers, as only about two per cent of the country's health budget marked for mental health.

10. Czech Republic

Brief history/background of Counselling

Counselling in the Czech Republic has always been strongly influenced by psychology, which has a long tradition (cf. Simons, Hutchison & Baštecká, 2012, p. 234). For example, such famous psychologists as Sigmund Freud (founder of psychoanalysis) and Max Wertheimer (founder of Gestalt Psychology) originally come from the Czech region (cf. Simons & Durcikova, 2013, p. 163f.).

After reviewing the literature in English and Czech, researchers* in this field claim that counselling was offered in the Czech Republic during most of the 20th century either as marriage counselling or vocational counselling (cf. Simons, Hutchison & Baštecká, 2012, p. 234). Later, academic counselling such as school and university counselling was added and has become common. However, professional psychological services are available. Counselling as a separate profession does not appear to have developed further in the country and is regarded as a psychology subfield.

Current Regulatory Status/Level of Recognition

Counselling in the Czech Republic is regulated by the Ministry of Labor and Social Affairs (http://www.mpsv.cz/cs/) and the Ministry of Education, Youth and Sports (http://www.msmt.cz) (cf. Simons & Durcikova, 2013, p. 164).

Regardless of the area of practice, most counsellors usually have a master's degree in psychology, unless they are former teachers who have taken additional courses to become school counsellors (cf. Simons & Durcikova 2013, pp. 163f.).

The majority of students graduate from universities in Prague, Brno or Olomouc (cf. Simons, Hutchison & Baštecká, 2012, p. 235). These universities offer bachelor's, master's and doctoral degrees in psychology, although, as already mentioned, only the master's degree entitles the holder to practice psychological counselling (cf. Simons & Durcikova, 2013, p. 169).

Challenges and Trends

In the Czech Republic, psychology has a long history, so there is also the potential for further growth of the country's counselling sector (cf. Simons & Durcikova, 2013, p. 164). Moreover, counselling is the second-largest department of the Czech Moravian Psychological Society (cf. ibid., p. 164). The number of counselling services in the Czech Republic always seems to continue to increase. However, laws and regulations still need to be passed to support the current movements (cf. Simons & Durcikova, 2013, p. 170). These include, for example, the provision of more services by counsellors and psychologists at schools, better coordination and establishment of psychological counselling centres at universities, and greater attention to the cultural differences of the population in counselling settings, taking into account the rising problem of alcoholism (cf. ibid., p. 170).

Furthermore, the example of non-Czech counsellors (for example, from the other European countries) can be used to show the Czech people that adding and expanding training programs can be beneficial (cf. Simons, Hutchison & Baštecká, 2012, p. 236). The counsellors*, where counselling already exists as an independent profession, can help establish the counselling profession in the Czech Republic (cf. ibid., p. 236). Also, they can help answer important questions such as whether there are fundamental differences between psychology and counselling. Which educational approaches best serve Czech society, what standards of competence should be established, and finally, what counselling practices are most useful for people living in the Czech Republic (cf. ibid., p. 236). Answering these questions would significantly advance the development of the profession.

Additional Information

For more information about the counselling profession in the country, interested readers are encouraged to read the following journal and website articles:

- Freibergová, Z., Fantová, V., Goulliová, K. & Menclová, L. (2003). Counselling Services at Czech Universities. Praha: National Training Fund (NTF).
- Simons, J. D. & Durcikova, A. (2013). The Czech Republic. In Thomas H. Hohenshil, Norman Amundson, & Spencer G. Niles (Hrsg.), Counselling around the world: an international handbook (S. 163–172). Alexandria: American Counselling Association.
- Simons, J. D., Hutchison, B. & Baštecká, Z. (2012). Counselling in the Czech Republic: History, Status, and Future. Journal of Counselling & Development, 90 (2), 233–237.

11. Denmark

Brief history/background of Counselling

The Scandinavian countries are often perceived as homogeneous in terms of their social welfare systems due to their geographical proximity and similar cultural and historical traditions (cf. Dixon & Hansen, 2010, p. 38). However, there are some differences. For example, compared to other Nordic countries, Denmark has tended to focus on applied psychotherapeutic approaches. Therefore, Danish counselling or psychology's development has been clinically based and application-oriented from the beginning (cf. ibid., p. 38).

Counselling or psychology have a relatively long history in Denmark and find their origin in the philosophical movement influenced by Harald Høffding (cf. Dixon & Hansen 2010, p. 38).

With the establishment of the psychophysical laboratory in Copenhagen in 1886, counselling / psychology first became an independent discipline. Since then, it has developed rapidly in Denmark, and more psychological associations have been founded. In 1993, counsellors and psychologists received official accreditation from the Ministry of Social Affairs. At the same time, a board was formed to examine counsellors/psychologists' qualifications (cf. Dixon & Hansen 2010, p. 39). Parallel to this, the Psychotherapeutic Association was founded in 1993 as an interest organization for professional psychotherapists (cf. ibid., p. 40). In Denmark, the standard medical term for professionals who provide mental health support is psychologist (cf. ibid., p. 40). In contrast, the term psychotherapist refers to a person who offers practical counselling (equivalent to the U.S. vocational counsellor) (cf. ibid., p. 40).

Current Regulatory Status/Level of Recognition

The Danish Psychotherapeutic Association is the only known Danish professional group promoting the counselling profession's development as a separate discipline from psychology (cf. Dixon & Hansen, 2010, p. 40).

There are no specific training programs or licensing and certification guidelines for psychotherapists in Denmark. And no licensing or certification requirements for psychotherapists who are not members of the Danish Psychotherapeutic Association (cf. ibid., p. 40). To become a member of the association, a person must have a bachelor's degree in psychology, social work, education, or nursing and have completed 250 hours of personal therapy, 150 hours of supervision, and 300 hours of theory (cf. ibid., p. 40).

Thus, in Denmark, there is no clearly delineated professional counselling profession. The absence of counselling associations can confirm this fact (cf. Zapolsky, 2020, p. 73). The terms "counselling" and "psychology" are used interchangeably, which blurs the boundaries of professional identity as counsellors*. At the same time, there are several counselling/psychology degree programs at the college level. However, there are no specific standardized criteria for the accreditation of counselling/psychology training programs (cf. Zapolsky, 2020, p. 73).

However, there is the so-called Danish Accreditation Institution in Denmark, an independent body that accredits institutions within the higher education system regardless of their professional specialization (cf. ibid., p. 72f.). The Danish Accreditation Institution (DAI) does not provide accreditation for specific programs but the 73 academic institutions. This institutional accreditation guarantees that institutions can produce quality assurance (QA) for all of their programs. Therefore, the development of specific standards of advising programs is up to the respective institutions (cf. Zapolsky, 2020, p. 72f.).

The following programs can be considered "counselling programs":

Master's programs in psychology offered at universities.

Professional Bachelor's programs for social workers (the translation of the Danish name/title "social worker" is literally "social counsellor") offered at "university colleges."

There are several private programs for psychotherapists offered at private institutions (cf. Zapolsky, 2020, p. 72).

Challenges and Trends

Psychological counselling and psychotherapy are closely related in Denmark.

More people are making use of counselling and psychological services. One reason for this could be the government's decision to channel more state aid into this area. This facilitates access to therapy and counteracts stigmatization (cf. Dixon & Hansen, 2010, p. 40). The development of psychological services is expanding, and the desire for international cooperation, in the sense of equal training standards and qualifications, is becoming louder and louder (cf. ibid., p. 40f.).

Also, counselling is offered in English with an increasing tendency, attributed to increased immigration (cf. ibid., p. 40f.).

Overall, Denmark has excellent living standards and therefore has good services to offer its citizens mental health (cf. Dixon & Hansen 2010, p. 40f.).

Additional Information

For more information about the counselling profession in the country, interested readers are encouraged to read the following journal and website articles:

- Dixon, A. L. & Hansen, N. H. (2010). Fortid, Nutid, Fremtid (Past, Present, Future): Professional Counselling in Denmark. Journal of Counselling & Development, 38–42.

- Thomsen, R. & Plant, P. (2013). Counselling in Denmark. In Thomas H. Hohenshil, Norman Amundson, & Spencer G. Niles, Counselling around the world: an international handbook (S. 173–181). Alexandria, VA: American Counselling Association.
- Zapolsky, N. (2020). A Meta-Synthesis of the American and the European Standards for the Accreditation of Counselling Training Programs. Chicago: Digital Commons@NLU.

12. Estonia

Brief history/ background of Counselling

There is not so much information about the history of counselling in Estonia.

This may be because the country does not have developed and established counselling structures. In contrast, psychology seems to have a long history in Estonia. For example, psychological schools focusing on clinical psychology or educational psychology have existed for a relatively long time. For this reason, these areas of work in terms of professional development, training (accredited programs at universities), and job opportunities (state funding) (cf. Kastepõld-Tõrs, 2020).

Current Regulation Status/ Level of Recognition

Psychological counselling in Estonia is not regulated by law.

Although psychologists are working as counsellors in various fields, the counselling profession has received little state support (cf. Kastepõld-Tõrs, 2020). The funds that are made available are usually very scarce and limited in time so that the counselling initiatives can hardly make a living from it. Furthermore, there is a lack of information on qualification standards, which is one reason why independent counselling associations have not yet existed in Estonia (cf. ibid.).

However, there are cases where the state subsidizes psychological counselling. For example, social insurance covers psychological counselling in victim assistance programs (victims of crime) and social rehabilitation (cf. Kastepõld-Tõrs, 2020). Social rehabilitation is intended for all persons with a disability and persons with partial or no ability to work who need assistance in their daily lives to cope with the limitations resulting from their disability or special needs.

Furthermore, the Estonian Unemployment Insurance Fund covers psychological counselling for the unemployed to assist them in finding a job (work rehabilitation). Moreover, the Ministry of Education covers psychological counselling in schools for pupils and students (cf. ibid.).

Challenges and Trends

Mental health enjoys increasing attention in Estonian society—many current problems such as depression and suicidality among the young discussed in public. More people recognize the need for psychological support in everyday life, which leads to a greater demand for psychosocial services, including psychological counselling (cf. ibid.). Nevertheless, there are still not enough specialists in this field. One of the biggest challenges is developing educational programs for counsellors (including lifelong education) (cf. ibid.).

Furthermore, a suitable qualification system should be implemented, and the counselling profession should be introduced in Estonia so that both employees and employers have specific guidelines to orient themselves.

Despite the increasing attention to mental health within the Estonian population, there is still a need to increase the counselling profession's reputation in society (cf. Kastepõld-Tõrs, 2020). It is possible that in the future, counsellors will also be allowed to offer their services under the state health insurance system (cf. ibid).

Additional Information

Unfortunately, there is no reading in English that would allow a deeper insight into Estonia's current state of the counselling profession.

13. Finland

Brief history/background of Counselling

Finland has a long history of good collaboration between the educational and employment sector regarding lifelong guidance, specifically career guidance.

Today, this is manifested by having a national strategy for lifelong guidance, good access to high-quality services and innovative pilots such as the One-Stop Guidance Centres for youth

Professional vocational guidance and counselling began in Finland in 1939 when a psychologist´s position was created in Helsinki's employment office. The pioneering career counsellor and counselling psychologist was Professor Niilo Mäki, who worked in the office from 1941 to 1946. In 1948 the International Labour Organization (ILO) Convention 88 on public employment services recommended that all nations provide free public employment services. During the '40s and '50s, 13 Finnish municipalities became involved invocational psychologists' career guidance and vacancies.

In the 1960s, career guidance as part of Finnish employment policies and practices strengthened further when written in the law. The labour administration developed a nationwide organisation of vocational guidance offices.

In the 1970s, vocational guidance offices and employment offices joined one employment service under the Employment Ministry. In Finland, during the late 1980s the labour administration was reorganised. Regional employment agencies changing to regional centres for trade and employment thereby diminishing, the role and position of vocational guidance in provincial administration. A new, efficient way to address individual customers' needs was developed in the employment offices by tiering services into self-help, group-based services, and intensive case-managed services, including individual counselling.

In 2007, the Ministry of Trade and Industry and the Ministry of Labour merged into the Finnish Ministry of Economic Affairs and Employment. The regional administration reorganised into 15 Centres for Economic Development, Transport and the Environment (ELY Centres). In 2009 the employment offices renamed similarly as 'Employment and Economic Development Offices (TE Offices)'.

Subsequently, vocational psychologists started working in a branch named 'vocational development services' in co-operation with educational advisors, vocational training advisors, rehabilitation advisors, and advisors for labour market training. In 2013, the vocational psychologists started to work within all the three service lines with the overall service model:

1. Employment and Business Services
2. Business Competence Development Services
3. Supported Employment Services

The national employment and economic offices were based on the goals of the national strategies on employment and entrepreneurship. The underlying principles in the reform were customer-orientedness, equal access, societal efficiency and productivity. Attention was given to core functions: the supply of skilled labour, immediate placement of job seekers. As an outcome of the reform, traditional vocational guidance came to an end as a stand-alone organisational service. Separate concepts of 'vocational guidance', 'educational advice' and 'vocational rehabilitation' were merged into one idea, 'vocational guidance and career planning' (cf. Toni & Vuorinen, 2020, p. 127f.).

Current Regulatory Status/ Level of Recognition

The Ministry of Education and Culture published the strategic objectives for lifelong guidance in 2011. The national cooperation group's task on lifelong guidance is to develop lifelong guidance in Finland from a strategic point of view. Guidance operators from different administrative sectors are represented in the group. The Ministry of Economic Affairs and Employment and the Ministry of Education and Culture take turns in chairing the cooperation group. The cooperation group publishes a topical overview of lifelong guidance.

In addition to the national cooperation group on lifelong guidance, the centres for economic development, transport and the environment (ELY centres) coordinate lifelong guidance at the regional level. Together with representatives of the world of work, they coordinate guidance and counselling services and ensure their availability. Also, they organise guidance-related continuing education in their area. There are 15 regional cooperation groups on lifelong guidance (cf. Finnish National Agency for Education, 2020b).

Challenges and Trends

Improving the Finnish knowledge and competence base is seen as a cornerstone for the nation's overall competitiveness in the global market and the European Union.

Consequently, the national and regional employment, economic and education policy must reflect the goals and facilitate proactive and rapid responses to change in working life and structural changes in the labour market. Ensuring a high level of competence and a sufficient workforce across sectors and regions calls for targeted strategies addressing the decreasing working-age population and diminishing younger age groups. Further, a pretty recent phenomenon is the increasing number of citizens who feature 2012: 40).

A big Trend in Finland is guidance and counselling in school. Every pupil is entitled to advice during school days. Guidance and counselling promote the successful completion of schoolwork, the studies' progress, productivity, and educational effectiveness. An essential task of guidance and counselling is to support student's growth and development in a way that enables them to promote their social maturity and capacity to study and to develop knowledge and skills required in life planning. Furthermore, guidance and counselling connect the school to society and the working life. Guidance and counselling promote fairness, equity, equality and participation, and prevent exclusion from education and working life.

Good guidance criteria are recommended to develop and ensure the quality of guidance in primary education, general upper secondary education, and VET. The aim is to promote high quality and diverse range of advice and ensure the availability of high-quality guidance for children and adolescents, regardless of their place of residence and circumstances. Furthermore, the criteria is used to ensure the equality, quality and availability of guidance services for pupils and students throughout Finland.

(cf. Finnish National Agency for Education, 2020a).

Guidance and counselling is a lifelong topic in Finland and also affect adults. Good guidance criteria is a recommendation that has been made to develop and ensure the quality of guidance in primary education, general upper secondary education and VET. The criteria aim to promote high quality and diverse range of guidance and ensure the availability of high-quality guidance for children and adolescents, regardless of their place of residence and circumstances. Furthermore, the criteria used to ensure the equality, quality and availability of guidance services for pupils and students throughout Finland (cf. Ministry of Education and Culture 2012: 31).

Additional Information

- Finnish National Agency for Education (2020). Guidance and Counselling in primary education. Online: https://www.oph.fi/en/education-and-qualifications/guidance-and-Counselling-basic -education
- Information, guidance and Counselling services. Online: https://www.oph.fi/en/services/information-guidance-and-Counselling-services
- Ministry of Education and Culture (2012). Guidance. Lifelong Guidance in Finland. Lönnberg Print & Promo. Online: https://cica.org.au/wp-content/uploads/25493_Lifelong_guidance_in_Finland.pdf
- Toni, A/ Vuorinen, R. (2020). LIFELONG GUIDANCE IN FINLAND. Key Policies and Practices. Online: https://brill.com/view/book/edcoll/9789004428096/BP000017.xml

14. France

Brief history/background of Counselling
Information and guidance centres (Centre d'Information e d'Orientation) were developed in France as early as the 1920s to inform pupils and students about the possibilities regarding studies and careers. The Ministry of Education manages the centres, and there are now over 600 centres with more than 4,700 counsellors (cf. Cohen-Scali, Guichard & Gaudron, 2009, p. 331).

Also, since the 1920s, psychoanalysis has played a significant role in France. Experts dealt with this subject in depth. Psychoanalysis reached the entire culture and society. Sigmund Freud's theories continue to play an important role, with approaches and methods evolving over the years to adapt to modern times. Despite the monopoly position of psychoanalysis, people are open to other procedures and practices (cf. Sonnenmoser, 2011).

Counselling is a new field in France. There is no good translation possibility into French for the word counselling. The verb 'Conseiller' (to counsel) rather refers to education and career counselling, which became established at the beginning of the 20th century. Accordingly, the 'counselling' field initially dealt with issues of general counselling and career development. In the 1980s, career counselling reformed. Counselling practices adapted to the new environment, and new methods developed. Over time, counselling services for students and young professionals expanded to include adults and organizations. Besides, new laws profoundly changed the practice of career guidance in the public sector (cf. Pouyaud & Guichard, 2013, p. 193f.).

Between 1970 and 1980, as the school system became more complex, the number of career counsellors doubled. Since 1981, school counsellors are officially called educational and vocational psychologists and employed by the state. Since the beginning of the 21st century, the number of these counsellors has decreased again. The number of career counsellors for adults has been in constant change since the 1970s (cf. ibid., p.195).

Since the 1990s, the need for counselling has increased. Globalization and the change in living conditions are among the reasons for this. This has led to both a significant increase in counselling services and a growing number of counsellors. (cf. ibid., p.194) covering all consulting fields. Since the 1990s, many companies' human resources departments have also increasingly offered consulting services to promote and support employees (cf. ibid., p. 196). Nevertheless, the profession of the counsellor is not regulated.

Current Regulatory Status/ Level of Recognition

In France, there is no legal regulation for counselling. There is no psychotherapist law in France, so the title psychotherapist and the training, access, and practice of this profession is not regulated by professional law. However, the title of psychologist and psychoanalyst and the associated activity is protected (cf. Sonnenmoser, 2011).

In state-run counselling and treatment centres, psychotherapy is free of charge. However, if the treatment occurs with a doctor or psychiatrist, the health insurance companies only cover part of the costs. The patient must pay the total price if they seek therapy from an independent psychologist/psychotherapist in private, non-medical practice. These therapies are neither recognized nor reimbursed by health insurance companies. The fee for the treatment depends on the patient's income. Private health insurance companies may cover part of the cost (cf. ibid.).

Only a small number of counsellors have received special training in counselling. Most of them have a master's degree in social sciences or psychology, complemented by a short training session in the respective institution where they work. Also, there are no courses in France that lead to a master's degree in counselling (cf. Cohen-Scali, Guichard & Gaudron, 2009, p. 330).

Challenges and Trends

There is an increasing need for counselling in all areas of life, but there is a lack of training and study programs that deal specifically with counselling. Counsellors do not form a homogeneous unit, and they do not consider themselves members of a real, specific profession, nor do they consider themselves part of the same professional group. In many cases, counselling professions are linked to other disciplines. In addition to traditional counsellors, such as counselling psychologists, marriage counsellors, and career counsellors, other professionals, such as nurses, teachers, and social workers, also offer counselling services. Therefore, the professional status, salaries, working conditions, and training of counsellors differ significantly from one another (cf. ibid. p. 330).

The spread of online counselling is increasing (cf. Pouyaud & Guichard, 2013, p. 197).

Another challenge is to develop scientific networks for counselling to create a body of knowledge, practices, and research to formalize counselling professions (cf. ibid., p. 200).

Due to the lack of legal regulation of psychotherapist and psychoanalyst professions, any person can pretend to be one and offer therapies without qualification and official registration. This has even led to sects and fundamentalist organizations offering counselling. Patients get too little information about the quality of the provided treatment. Through the development of a professional association, one could counteract these grievances (cf. Sonnenmoser, 2011).

Family- and systemic therapists can frequently receive qualified further training through special additional training funds. However, it is a problem that most of these therapists only work in child and adolescent psychiatric institutions and counselling centres. There is a shortage of such professionals in clinics for adults (cf. Cohen, 2002, p. 20).

Additional Information

Carl Rogers' work in the 1960's was translated into French. Since then, it has dramatically influenced counselling in France. The theoretical work of Holland and Super have also played an important role in practice since the 1970s (cf. Pouyaud & Guichard, 2013, p. 197).

Interested readers should read the following books and articles for a more in-depth discussion of the counselling profession:

- Cohen-Scali, V.; Guichard, J. & Gaudron J. (2009). Career Counselling in France: A Growing Practice Among Diverse Professional Groups. In: L. H. Gerstein, P. P. Heppner, S. Ægisdóttir, S-M. A. Leung, K. L. Norsworthy (eds) International Handbook of Cross-Cultural Counselling – Cultural Assumptions and Practices Worldwide. (329–336) Los Angeles: Sage Publications.
- Pouyaud, J. & Guichard, J. (2013). France. In T. H. Hohenshil, N. E. Amundson, S. G. Niles (Eds.) Counselling around the world. An international handbook (193–202). Alexandria: American Counselling Association.
- Van Broeck, N. & Lietaer, G. (2008). Psychology and Psychotherapy in Health Care: A Review of Legal Regulations in 17 European Countries. European Psychologist, Vol.13 (1), pp. 53–63.

15. Germany

Brief history/background of Counselling

The development of professional counselling is due to a change in society. From the 18th century to the 20th century, society changed from a feudal system to bourgeois society.

"In the course of industrialisation and progressive modernisation, the holistic life context of everyday life, working, educating, and gaining experience was broken up and outsourced to social institutions: working, educating, learning, as well as leisure life increasingly took place outside of the family in differentiated and largely independent social functional areas" (Schubert, Rohr & Zwicker-Pelzer, 2019, p. 2).

Due to this development, counselling by family, friends, and relatives became less critical since new requirements accompanied a change in lifestyles to which previous knowledge, as well as experience, can only be applied to a limited extent or not at all. At the beginning of the 20th century, institutionally run counselling facilities emerged as a substitute for the previous family counselling, which understood counselling as "education about living conditions" (ibid., p. 2). These services were made possible by helpful citizens, professionals, associations, professions, and political groups.

The curative education counselling centre founded in Hamburg was one of the first in Germany. As a result, educational and remedial education counselling centres were established in other places. At that time, terms such as "support, treatment, or nursing care" (Schubert, Rohr & Zwicker-Pelzer, 2019, p. 5) were used, as the term counselling was not yet widely used.

Due to a change in the labour market and women's right to work, an increased need for counselling arose. This resulted in career counselling before World War I, which made a "decisive contribution to a scientifically based counselling system" (ibid., p. 7).

With the end of the First World War, the range of counselling services also increased in education, pedagogy and sex education. For example, legal aid offices of the women's movement, information offices for women's professions, sexual counselling offices, and counselling offices for maternity protection were established (cf. Gröning, 2010, p. 43). These institutions provided advice, information, and recommendations for possible careers (e. g., the legal aid offices for women or the information office for women's professions). Likewise, sexual counselling centres provided information about the abortion ban and illegal abortion, offered assistance or, for example, distributed at the time banned contraceptives.

There were more than four hundred sexual counselling centres in the Weimar Republic, more than eighty legal protection centres of the women's movement, and about forty counselling centres for maternity protection and sexual reform (cf. ibid., p. 43).

Developments were initially halted in the guidance system when the National Socialists seized power. Vocational guidance became a state program designed to direct and influence the workforce. Only through the Child Guidance idea, carried from America to Germany from 1950, an "expansion of educational counselling ways of thinking and acting" (Schubert, Rohr & Zwicker-Pelzer, 2019, p. 9) has emerged. The Child Guidance Movement is a concept that includes both the "early detection, diagnosis, counselling and treatment of child behavioural and developmental disorders as well as counselling parents" (ibid., p. 5f). As a result, the children's environment and parents' attitudes and upbringing became increasingly crucial for the counselling process. From 1953 on, youth welfare offices needed to offer counselling services.

For the FRG, the 1960s and 1970s led to a "surge of scientific and methodological modernization" (ibid., p. 9). On the one hand, this can be attributed to economic and psychological developments. On the other hand, the "popularization of psychotherapeutic ideas in the context of the 1968 movement" (ibid., p. 9).

These years were a "phase of consolidation of counselling" (ibid.). Counselling followed, a professionalisation followed, significantly expanded: Marriage, family and life counselling, pregnancy conflict counselling, drug counselling, telephone counselling and, from the 1980s on, increasingly debt counselling services. Social services were obliged to offer counselling and binding standards formulated. A change in the education system led to more people graduating from higher education institutions. Accompanying this was a growing need for school career and academic counselling.

In the 1980s and 1990s, psychosocial counselling heavily influenced by psychotherapeutic procedures. "In many areas of psychosocial practice, the distinction between intensive psychosocial counselling processes and psychotherapeutic interventions has been all but abandoned since the early 1980s.

Additional psychotherapeutic training has long been part of the professional qualifications of counsellors." (Schubert, Rohr & Zwicker-Pelzer, 2019, p. 13). With the coming into force of the psychotherapists Act (PsychThG) of 1998, the possibility for counsellors with suitable additional training to work psychotherapeutically changed. This law led to a distinction between psychosocial counselling and psychotherapy.

Current Regulatory Status/Level of Recognition

"In Germany, counselling has been located as a continuation of bachelor's degree programs in the humanities in the sense of specialization" (ibid, p. 265). Master's programs in the field of counselling are considered consecutive and continuing. The only entry requirement is a bachelor's degree in the psychosocial field. "In continuing education contexts, the term "training to become a counsellor" is often used" (ibid, p. 264). However, apprenticeships are completed with a recognized professional or university degree and classified as formal learning. In continuing education institutes, learning is informal. Continuing education courses last several months, are oriented to a curriculum and structured according to modules, and are completed by certificates and not with a state-recognized certificate (cf. ibid., p. 264).

Since the state does not regulate counselling, there are no general, standardised continuing education programs that newcomers to the profession must complete to call themselves counsellors in Germany. Such specific courses exist only for school psychologists and school Counsellors. In contrast to psychologists and psychotherapists, the term "Counsellor" or "psychological advisor" is not protected by law. To become a psychologist, a master's degree in psychology is required. Also, to be allowed to practice as a psychotherapist, postgraduate education of 3-5 years must be completed (cf. Strasser, 2013, p. 209f). Therefore, those who work as counsellors may have significant differences in their specific knowledge and skills. However, professional associations, non-profit continuing education providers, and private continuing education institutions offer continuing education and training programs. These programs usually provide participants with basic theoretical knowledge as well as practical skills. However, participants must bear the costs themselves (cf. ibid., p. 210).

The German Society for Systemic Therapy, counselling and Family Therapy (DGSF) is one of Germany's largest systemic umbrella organizations with over 7000 members. Many other education institutes have their further systemic education certified by the DGSF to reduce training and additional education differences. This accreditation procedure serves as an assurance of the fundamental ethical attitudes and the professional quality of the further training. Through the institutes' description and presentation in the accreditation process, greater transparency for further education participants and the possibility of recognising differences and similarities between institutes arises. "The process of accreditation should foster mutual curiosity and interest, create the framework for support and cooperation, and promote development and innovation in the institutes" (DGSF 2020).

The example of the DGSF illustrates the quality and complexity of certified further education by institutional providers (different education institutions):

The training institute itself needs recognition.

The curriculum needs recognition and thus a clear orientation along with the standards and guidelines of the DGSF.

The Institute commits itself to active participation in quality assurance (quality circles, institute meetings, institute conferences).

The teachers in a continuing education program need a qualification as teachers (in the sense of a master-student relationship); pedagogical and adult education competencies do not need to be proven. However, by receiving their certification, teachers commit to their supervision and continuing education.

Participants present their institute certificate to the DGSF and apply for professional association recognition (in other professional associations, certification directly linked or tied to membership) (Schubert, Rohr & Zwicker-Pelzer 2019, p. 266).

Challenges and Trends

An examination of the current state of counselling reveals a great deal of ambivalence.

On the one hand, the counselling profession has developed into an established form of professional support, serving various groups of people with diverse problems and difficulties. On the other hand, it shows remarkable deficits in terms of professionalisation. Although the lack of professional regulations is considered constitutive for counselling, the need to establish a unified and systematic basis for the profession is recognized (cf. Strasser, 2013, p. 211).

"If counselling, especially psychosocial counselling, is to be established in society, three things are needed:

a) emancipation from therapy (schools) and explicit reference to lifestyles,

b) description of concrete competencies of the profession of counselling, and

c) elaboration of quality standards.

Psychosocial counselling must integrate into the health and education system, and employer-funded coaching must become an employee right like vacation and sick pay, as must team and case supervision" (Schubert, Rohr & Zwicker-Pelzer 2019, p. 272).

In all areas of counselling, the multicultural expansion will determine the future of German counselling. Opening up and adapting existing counselling services for minorities is a significant challenge for practitioners*. This applies not only to cultural diversity but also to variety in terms of age and gender. The counselling needs of older adults continue to neglect. There are only limited specific services for them, limited to a few problem areas (cf. Strasser, 2013, p. 211).

Additional Information
For a more in-depth examination of the counselling profession in Germany, interested readers are advised to read the following articles as well as books:

- Gröning, K. (2010). Geschichte der Beratung. In: Giesecke, W., Nittel, D., (Hrsg.), Pädagogische Beratung über die Lebensspanne–Handbuch, S. 42–49. Beltz Juventa.
- Nestmann, F., Engel, F., & Sickendiek, U. (2004). Das Handbuch der Beratung. Band 1: Disziplinen und Zugänge. Tübingen, Germany: dgvt.
- Schubert, F. C., Rohr, D., & Zwicker-Pelzer, R. (2019). Beratung: Grundlagen – Konzepte – Anwendungsfelder. Springer: Wiesbaden.
- Strasser, J. (2013). Counselling in Germany. In: Hohenshil, T. H., Amundson, N. E., & Niles, S. G. (Hrsg.). Counselling around the world: An international handbook, S. 203–2013. Alexandria, VA: American Counselling Association.

16. Great Britain

Brief history/background of Counselling
Counselling, psychology, and psychotherapy in the United Kingdom have initially been influenced by the idea of psychoanalysis by Sigmund Freud, which has been quite popular for a while. Psychotherapy has initially seen as a sub-discipline of medicine, with counselling emerging more as a separate discipline (cf. Joseph, Murphy & Holford, 2018, p. 388.). Eventually, however, counselling and psycho-

therapy have converged into one profession. There are still two distinct traditions in counselling and psychotherapy based on either mental illness treatment or an educational discourse (cf. ibid.).

In 1977, the British Association for Counselling (BAC) was founded. For the following two decades, counselling and psychotherapy have existed mainly as separate disciplines with separate professional organizations, namely the UK Council for Psychotherapies (UKCP) and the BAC, due to their different historical development (cf. ibid., p. 389).

Over time, however, the meaning of the term counselling has expanded to the point where the distinction from psychotherapy has become increasingly complex (cf. ibid., p. 389). This is because theoretical approaches that had previously mainly been exclusively associated with the term psychotherapy have now also become associated with the term counselling (cf. Joseph, Murphy & Holford, 2018, p. 389). Due to the similarity of the two terms and difficulty in distinguishing them, the BAC changed its name to the British Association for Counselling and Psychotherapy (BACP) in 2000 (cf. ibid., p. 389). The BACP is still the largest British organization representing counsellors and psychotherapists, although the differences and similarities between counselling and psychotherapy remain controversial (cf. ibid., p. 389).

Current Regulatory Status/Level of Recognition

The UK's counselling profession is currently not regulated by law, and the government has no intention to introduce legislation for counsellors and psychotherapists (cf. BACP, 2020).

Nevertheless, there are subsidies from the government, for example, in the area of school counselling. There is funding for school-based counselling in Wales. Scotland also provides 60 million pounds sterling for school-based counselling (cf. Kaur, 2020).

Challenges and Trends

According to Ms. Suky Kaur, the Head of Policy at BACP, (at the time of going to press), the coronavirus is one of the biggest current challenges facing counselling and counsellors in the United Kingdom. Professional therapists' role seems more critical than ever as the nation grapples with the psychological impact of changing work and family circumstances, financial insecurity, isolation, grief, societal breakdown, and the ongoing uncertainties caused by the Covid-19 outbreak (cf. Kaur, 2020).

To what extent and how long-term the crisis will affect the population's mental health is still unknown. However, the assumption is that the psychological therapy demand will increase significantly over a more extended period. Moreover, the Office of National Statistics analyses confirms that the crisis harms the population's psychological well-being.

Forty-nine per cent of respondents report having a "high" level of anxiety (cf. ibid.). Demographic analysis has also demonstrated that the virus has a more significant impact on more impoverished people, families, and BAME communities. These groups will need targeted psychological support in the coming months and years. Further, the physical distancing measures necessary for public health have exacerbated mental health problems (cf. ibid.). This has had unfortunate consequences for the bereaved, who have not been allowed to say goodbye to their loved ones or attend funerals. This may lead to an increase in complex grief reactions in the coming months.

There has also been a sharp increase in domestic violence – The number of calls to HelpLine has increased by seven hundred per cent in a single day – so there is an urgent need to expand the provision of specialist support for those affected (cf. Kaur, 2020).

The anxiety, uncertainty, and loss of routine of the crisis also profoundly impact children and their development. The most recent Department for Education summary report on school attendance in England since the start of the lockdown shows that less than 5% of vulnerable children currently attend school (cf. Kaur, 2020). Children from more impoverished families, who are more likely to have existing mental health problems or overcrowded live-in accommodation, are particularly vulnerable to the negative consequences of school closures and socially distancing restrictions (cf. ibid.).

Furthermore, the Corona crisis's broader economic impacts have also led to severe psychological distress, with increased job insecurity and personal debt. According to the estimates of insolvency experts, half a million British businesses are at risk of collapse. Many workers are asked to take pay cuts, work reduced hours or consider sabbaticals to help companies limit the number of redundancies. This is undoubtedly another factor contributing to the strain on mental health (cf. Kaur, 2020).

Quite a few counsellors and psychotherapists are already playing an essential role on the epidemic's front lines, providing support – sometimes voluntarily – to vulnerable people, including medical personnel and other key workers. However, several health care providers, private physicians, and charities have also experienced funding cuts and a decline in the number of sessions as social isolation measures have come into effect (cf. Kaur, 2020).

As the impact of the crisis grows, the demand for therapeutic support will continue to increase. So BACP's goal is to support the government in establishing a long-term plan in collaboration with professional associations and mental health service providers (cf. ibid.).

Subsequent to this, the distancing measures may make online therapy or online counselling a new future trend in the United Kingdom (cf. Kaur, 2020)

Additional Information
For more information about the counselling profession in the state, interested readers are encouraged to read the following journal and website articles:

- BACP (2020). Government update on statutory regulation of counsellors and Psychotherapists. Online: https://www.bacp.co.uk/news/news-from-bacp/2020/6-march-government-update-on-statutory-regulation-of-counsellors-and-Psychotherapists/
- Joseph, S., Murphy, D. & Holford, J. (2018). Counselling training in higher education in the United Kingdom: Challenges and opportunities for research. Counselling Psychotherapy research journal, 387–394.

17. Greece

Brief history/background of Counselling
In Greece, for a long time, there was no specialized service for counselling provided by a trained specialist. Greece is a collectivist culture where family, friendships and other social relationships are highly valued. Therefore, counselling was traditionally embedded in the complex support system of social relationships. Urban family life has

now moved from collectivist notions to individualistic ones. Traditional Greek culture remains more collectivist than most individualistic Western countries (cf. Malikiosi-Loizos & Ivey, 2012, p. 113).

Consequently, it is not surprising that parents, siblings, and close friends are still the people to whom Greeks turn to discuss their problems and find solutions. Nevertheless, more people living in larger cities are seeking professional counselling. It is a process that is very slowly spreading to more rural areas. There is a growing demand for psychological counselling, which leads to a greater need for experts in the field (cf. Malikiosi-Loizos & Ivey, 2012, p. 113).

In most Western societies, professional counselling has been developing steadily due to the countries' psycho-educational and economic changes. Such growth is not in the same way as Greece. The country's financial situation, based mainly on agriculture and tourism, nor the educational system provided favourable conditions for promoting the counselling movement. Therefore, its establishment and integration into the country's socio-political, educational system took some time (cf. ibid., p. 114).

The first emergence of guidance occurred in vocational guidance, which the Ministry of Labour and Education introduced in the 1950s. It was an attempt to address the problems resulting from the sudden and massive urbanisation that led to rapid economic changes and the labour market. However, efforts in the 1950s and 1960s to include career counselling in the curriculum were unsuccessful (cf. ibid., p. 114).

The definition of counselling as psychological assistance and support to help people cope with and overcome difficulties did not become popular in Greece until the 1980s. Two Greeks, Dimitropoulos and Malikiosi-Loizos, returned to Greece after studying counselling in the United States, spread their knowledge, and thus are considered pioneers of counselling and counselling psychology. They wrote the first textbooks, "Counselling and Counselling Psychology" (Dimitropoulos) and "Counselling Psychology" (Malikiosi-Loizos), which led to counselling psychology being considered a discipline in its own right in Greece. The first courses in counselling and counselling psychology offered in the late 1980s as part of the psychology and Education curriculum at the University of Athens (cf. Malikiosi-Loizos & Giovazolias, 2013, p. 216).

The Hellenic Society for Counselling was founded in 1985 and has been active in disseminating career counselling, school counselling, and counselling psychology ever since. The society now has more than 1,000 members and has published a scientific journal entitled Review of Counselling and Guidance since 1986 (cf. Malikiosi-Loizos & Ivey, 2012, p. 114).

Since 1991, a counselling centre has been in operation at the University of Athens to meet students' psychological needs. In 1995, the first 'Peer Counselling Center' was established in the Department of Early Childhood Education at the University of Athens, staffed by students who received basic counselling skills training. In addition to the peer counselling centre described earlier, most Greek universities have student counselling centres. However, funding is inadequate, and the professionals' ratio to students is unbalanced (cf. ibid., p. 115).

Current Regulatory Status/Level of Recognition

The lack of legal requirements motivates professionals from various fields to engage in Counselling activities for which they have not received adequate training. The absence of accreditation requirements has a threat to the development and recognition of Greece's Counselling field.

The first official degree programs in counselling and counselling psychology with theoretical and practical training started in 2009 (cf. Malikiosi-Loizos & Ivey, 2012, p. 115). Until that time, Counsellors* had studied abroad, mainly in the UK, the US, and Canada, or participated in private, non-officially recognized universities and organisations in Greece.

This reflects the limited government recognition given to counselling and counselling psychology, and they were not officially part of formal higher education until 2009. Society does not yet clearly delineate terms such as counselling and counselling psychology, which exacerbates recognition and acceptance issues (cf. Malikiosi-Loizos & Ivey, 2012, p. 116). Furthermore, counselling cannot separate from psychology and psychotherapy.

"What is confusing – and one could say even 'unethical' according to the standards in many other countries globally, both for professionals and the public in Greece, is that one only needs a bachelor's degree in psychology to gain state licensure. This means that such graduates do not have sufficient skills training and other components required to deal with mental health, and yet they get 'permission' to practise (Christodoulidi & Malikiosi-Loizos, 2019, p. 4).

There are now two officially recognized master's programs in the field of counselling / counselling psychology offered by Greek universities with a relatively similar curriculum. This includes approximately 10-12 theoretical courses, 2-3 seminars in counselling skills and processes, around 1000 hours of supervised practicum, and about 40 hours of individual therapy. These are two-three-year full-time programs that require a research-based master's thesis (cf. Malikiosi-Loizos & Giovazolias, 2013, p. 221).

Furthermore, there are also private and public continuing education institutions that offer counselling and psychotherapy programs. These courses complete with a certificate from the institution, which is not recognised by the state (cf. Malikiosi-Loizos & Giovazolias, 2013, p. 218).

Challenges and Trends

Although counselling and counselling psychology exist as professions, they lack a distinct identity. They are not recognised officially in Greece due to the lack of legal regulations and accreditation requirements. The number of counsellors working, teaching, and researching is steadily increasing, with many practicing counselling psychologists and counsellors having obtained their degrees abroad. Therefore, the fundamentally necessary step to strengthen Counsellors and counselling psychologists' professional position is to provide the profession with social and legal recognition (cf. Malikiosi-Loizos, Ivey 2012, p. 117). Therefore, it is necessary to offer systematically organized training that contributes to the development of counselling skills and techniques. "The focus in Greece should now be on training models and ethical guidelines and standards that should be modified to meet culturally specific needs, with the final objective to be relevant in a constantly changing world" (Malikiosi-Loizos & Ivey, 2012, p. 117).

In recent years, efforts to raise awareness of what counselling is and how it for years been practiced in other countries (cf. Christodoulidi & Malikiosi-Loizos, 2019, p. 13f). Counselling can help people deal with certain life events and give them more confidence. However, Greek society's overall income has dropped drastically, so difficulties are supporting such services financially. A reduction in counselling fees is necessary, but with disposable household budgets needing every Euro for basics, this would decrease counsellors' income* (cf. ibid.).

The rapid development of technology opens up new forms of counselling and psychological therapies. This leads to a change in counselling methods and creates the possibility to solve distance problems. In this context, some interesting initiatives have taken place. For example, online counselling offered to students at the University of Athens. Students can make contact through an anonymous online form or their email account. Surveys have shown that online counselling at the University of Athens is very popular among Greek students (cf. Malikiosi-Loizos & Giovazolias, 2013, p. 219). Looking to the future, predictions for the professions of counselling and counselling psychology are nevertheless favourable. This trend reflects the many applications for the two master's degree programs in Greece.

Additional Information

For a more in-depth examination of the counselling profession in Greece, interested readers parties should read the following articles as well as books:

- Christodoulidi, F. & Malikiosi-Loizos, M. (2019). Exploring the perceptions of Greek counsellors' and Counselling Psychologists' professional identity and training experience, through the lens of the first alumni graduates of a Greek state University. European Journal of Psychotherapy & Counselling.
- Malikiosi-Loizos, M., Giovazolias, T. (2013). Counselling in Greece. In: Hohenshil, T. H., Amundson, N. E., & Niles, S. G. (Hrsg.). Counselling around the world: An international handbook, S. 203–2013. Alexandria, VA: American Counselling Association.
- Malikiosi-Loizos, M., Ivey, A. E. (2012). Counselling in Greece. Journal of Counselling & Development, 90(1), 113–118.

18. Iceland

Brief history/background of Counselling

There is some literature describing the history of psychology in Iceland. Counselling as academic counselling or vocational counselling seems to have established in Iceland in the 20th century. Nothing can be found on Icelandic psychological counselling history possibly as it is considered a single entity.

Current Regulatory Status/Level of Recognition

Icelandic psychological counselling only recognises counselling as a speciality. Therefore, its training and practice philosophy is not included in the study programs and, accordingly, the state does not support it (cf. Ægisdóttir, Leach, Romano, Tomlinson-Clarke & Canel-Çınarbaş, 2019, p. 582).

School and university counselling, in particular, as well as career counselling, are widespread in Iceland. The Ministry of Education, Science and Culture regulate Academic counselling. Lifelong learning centres also provide career counselling and career guidance for students, but they are mostly subordinated to various trade unions and other public agencies (cf. EACEA National Policies Platform, 2018).

Under the Ministry of Welfare, the Directorate of Labour also provides career counselling and guidance for people of all ages as part of its labour market initiatives (cf. ibid.). The main level of each ministry controls public funding. The Ministry of Education, Science and Culture and the Ministry of Social Affairs are the two ministries most involved in career guidance and counselling services (cf. EACEA National Policies Platform, 2018).

Challenges and Trends

One of the biggest challenges for psychological counselling in Iceland is its acceptance as a distinct professional sector. It is also essential to define the difference between psychology and psychological counselling. At present, the two disciplines, psychological counselling and psychology, are difficult to distinguish from each other in Iceland (cf. Ægisdóttir, Leach, Romano, Tomlinson-Clarke & Canel-Çınarbaş, 2019, pp. 581ff.).

Additional Information
For more information about the counselling profession in the state, interested readers are encouraged to read the following journal and website articles:

- Ægisdóttir, S., Leach, M., Romano, J. Tomlinson-Clarke, S. & Canel-Çınarbaş, D. (2019). Sociopolitical, Cultural, and Historical Contexts That Influence Counselling Practice in Four Countries. The Counselling Psychologist, 47(4), 578–607.
- EACEA National Policies Platform (2018). Career guidance and Counselling. Online: https://eacea.ec.europa.eu/national-policies/en/content/youthwiki/34-career-guidance-and-Counselling-iceland

19. Ireland

Brief history/background of Counselling
In Ireland, people's thinking and behaviour were strongly influenced by the Catholic faith until the 1960s (cf. O'Morain, McAuliffe, Conroy, Johnson & Michel, 2012). This may explain why counselling until the 1970s and 1980s was unheard of by the public (cf. ibid.). This is because the church, among other things, rejected any intervention in family life and thus, counselling services, as they today, did not experience opportunities for development and evolution at that time (cf. ibid.). In the 1960s, counselling (psychiatric) services in Ireland were highly stigmatized and often took place in poor conditions and severely overcrowded hospitals (cf. O'Morain, McAuliffe, Conroy, Johnson & Michel, 2012). After the church's influence has declined, modern counselling has continually evolved and experienced rapid growth (cf. ibid.). The 1980s and 1990s marked the time with counselling no longer confined to specific fields or institutional control, it became established as a distinct profession in Ireland. The establishment of the Irish Association for Counselling and Psychotherapy (IACP) also took place at this time, in 1981, to be exact.

It is important to note a distinction between counselling and psychotherapy and psychology (cf. O'Morain, McAuliffe, Conroy, Johnson & Michel, 2012). For example, unlike counsellors, psychologists are allowed to bill some of their services through the statutory health insurance scheme (cf. ibid.). In Ireland, on the other hand, there is usually no distinction made between counselling and psychotherapy, as the same body that accredits counsellors is also responsible for the accreditation of many psychotherapists (cf. O'Morain, McAuliffe, Conroy, Johnson & Michel, 2012).

Current Regulatory Status/Level of Recognition

The Social Care Professionals Act of 2005 (cf. Government of Ireland, 2019) does not recognise counsellors and psychotherapists. The professional title is not yet legally protected in Ireland (cf. ibid.). There is no official license for counsellors*, but certification bodies try to offer qualified training. The training programs are quite diverse – efforts to standardise training and develop licensing requirements are under review. The two largest accrediting bodies are Irish Association for Counselling and Psychotherapy (IACP) and Irish Association of Humanistic and Integrative Psychotherapy (IAHIP). Further, counselling services are generally paid for by clients without reimbursement from health insurance companies.

Although the government pays for counselling for some special groups (e. g., people infected with hepatitis C through contaminated blood products), counselling is usually private. The cost must be borne entirely by the client (cf. O'Morain, McAuliffe, Conroy, Johnson & Michel, 2012).

Counsellor training in Ireland can be pretty varied and represents a mix of private and public, academic and non-academic, accredited and non-accredited training institutions (cf. O'Morain, McAuliffe, Conroy, Johnson & Michel, 2012). Training to become a counsellor is not necessarily linked to studying at a university.

Challenges and Trends

Most of the Irish population is very optimistic about the counselling profession, and more people dare to start therapy (cf. O'Morain, McAuliffe, Conroy, Johnson & Michel, 2012). But there are also a few problems. For example, in most cases, health insurance does not cover payments for counselling sessions, which makes access to counselling much more complex and problematic for people with low incomes. This aspect also poses a difficulty for counsellors, as they cannot afford to work full-time in private practice and therefore often only pursue their counselling activities on a part-time basis.

A change in the consulting cost situation soon is rather unlikely. There is no evidence that the government plan includes providing counselling services to those who cannot afford private counsellors* (cf. O'Morain, McAuliffe, Conroy, Johnson & Michel, 2012). For the profession to be legally regulated, several issues need to be clarified, such as the number of occupations to be held, as there is disagreement among professional associations regarding whether it should be one or two professions. Furthermore, it needs to decide which title should be protected and the qualification requirements for existing practitioners and future counsellors (cf. Government of Ireland, 2019).

However, there is now an indication that an official accreditation body for counsellors will indeed be established shortly (cf. Flynn, 2019). A registration committee, appointed by the Minister of Health consisting of thirteen members, is already working on this (cf. ibid.). This registration committee's main task is to protect the public by promoting high professional conduct, education, training and competence for counsellors and psychotherapists and advising the minister on the professional titles to be protected. In any case, this is another crucial step towards legal regulation concerning counselling and psychotherapy (cf. Flynn, 2019).

In summary, then, the counselling profession in Ireland is undergoing relatively rapid development, despite licensing restrictions and cost barriers.

Additional Information

For more information about the counselling profession in the state, interested readers are encouraged to read the following journal and website articles:

- Flynn, J. (2019). Minister for Health appoints Counsellors & Psychotherapists Board. Online: https://www.apcp.ie/latest-news-3/
- Government of Ireland (2019). Proposed regulation of Counsellors and Psychotherapists under the Health and Social Care Professionals Act 2005. Online: https://www.gov.ie/en/news/06a369-proposed-regulation-of-counsellors-and-Psychotherapists-under-the-he/

- O'Morain, P., McAuliffe, G. J., Conroy, K., Johnson, J. M. & Michel , R. E. (2012). Counselling in Ireland. Online: https://www.padraigomorain.com/history-of-Counselling-in-ireland/

20. Italy

Brief history/background of Counselling

Counselling and psychotherapy in Italy go back a long time and is difficult to limit to a few sentences. Born in 1889 in Triest, Dr Eduardo Weiss is the precursor to mental health counselling in Italy. He was a student of Freud. This time, however, was unfavourable for the development of the field of psychoanalysis. The influential Catholic Church and also the fascist regime regarded psychoanalysis as a threat to its authority.

Due to the profound social changes in the post-war period, the demand for psychiatric counselling became ever more vital. In 1970 psychology finally underwent an important scientific status, with the simultaneous start of the first two psychology degrees at the universities Padua and Rom.

However, academics were initially upset about mental health counselling, as they considered it too unscientific because it did not take place in the university curricula. It was a pliable ground for the spread of private schools in counselling. With law Nr. 5 In 1989, there were strict legal controls. However, these also made it possible for private schools to award the same degree as universities.

In Italy, the ability to interpret counselling as a discipline seeking to cooperate between clients rather than their passivity led to an extension of counselling interpretation. Nevertheless, reductionist and positivist approaches such as traditional psychoanalysis and psychiatry remain the leading forces in Italian counselling in mental health.

Current Regulatory Status/Level of Recognition

Counselling in Italy is not a regulated profession; the State does not dictate the minimum requirements for its operation. On 14 January 2013, the Italian Parliament passed Law 4, which offers individual professionals the opportunity to have a professional association issue a certificate of quality and professional qualification to the services, under art. 4 of L. 4/2013.

This new legislation has revolutionised the field of work by re-standardising reform partnerships, including those of counselling, and has enabled, as started by artwork. 7 of L. 4/2013, to protect clients and ensure the integrity of the professional services marketplace.

Professional associations can issue to their members, subject to the necessary checks and under the responsibility of their legal representative, a relative statement:

to the regular registration of the professional to the association.

the requirements for participation in the association

the quality and professional qualification standards that members are required to comply with in the exercise of professional activity to maintain membership in the association.

Or you have a professional liability insurance policy taken out by a trader.

The possession of a professional association certificate is not a prerequisite for the exercise of counselling activity: Membership in an association is not compulsory, unlike the requirements for regulated ordering professions.

But joining a trade association allows the members a professional framework, which guarantees its training and enables them to comply with a precise code of ethics, protecting the client.

Challenges and Trend

Italian research on counselling and psychotherapy is basically non-existent and highly dependent on North American contributions. Most scholars publish their works in Italian and rarely translate them into English. While the English-speaking world strongly influences the Italian academic context, the opposite is not happening. This prevents consultants who do not read Italian from learning from the quality work of Italian scholars.

21. Latvia

Brief history/background of Counselling

Counselling does not seem to have a long history in Latvia, as this profession or the job title "counsellor" does not exist at this time. In contrast, a discipline such as psychology can look back on a more extended and more traditional history.

Current Regulatory Status/ Level of Recognition

In Latvia, there is a distinction between the terms psychotherapist, psychiatrist and psychologist.

A psychotherapist is a specialist who can help solve people's problems. Including emotional and psychosomatic or physical health, with scientifically-based methods (cf. Rigas Stadina Universitate, 2020).

A psychologist is not a doctor and has no right to treat people, including prescribing medication. A psychologist's activity is not subject to the law on medical treatment, and a psychologist has no legal responsibility for the patient's health (cf. Rigas Stadina Universitate 2020). A psychiatrist can additionally treat the patient with medication (cf. ibid.).

Trained psychologists mainly offer psychological counselling (cf. Rigas Stadina Universitate, 2020). Above all, however, career counselling and school counselling seem to be well developed in Latvia. Thus, counselling in Latvia is in the education and labour sectors. Under the Ministry of Education and Science supervision, schools have the primary responsibility for providing career guidance to students. Under the Ministry of Welfare's control, Labour offices offer career guidance for the labour market (cf. Euroguidance.eu, 2020).

Higher education institutions are autonomous by law and can determine what services they provide to their students (cf. Euroguidance.eu, 2020). Many universities in Latvia offer psychological counselling to their students.

In the labour sector, the State Employment Agency (SEA) provides the full range of career counselling for job seekers, employees, and people undergoing training (cf. ibid.). It makes it easier for people to obtain information or psychological support to help them achieve their career goals (cf. ibid.).

The Ministry of Welfare and the Ministry of Education and Science are the prominent institutions overseeing Latvia's career guidance system and the guidance services offered in educational institutions and employment offices (cf. Euroguidance.eu, 2020).

The State Employment Agency is responsible for implementing career guidance policy by providing services in the labour sector. Its tasks include the development of guidance tools and methods and the training of guidance practitioners in their use, and monitoring the quality of the guidance services provided (cf. ibid.).

Under the Ministry of Education and Science, the State Agency for Educational Development is the main body developing recommendations and tools to improve schools' guidance, including online information on educational opportunities and the world of work, and career self-assessment tests (cf. Euroguidance.eu, 2020).

Challenges and Trends

Since the English-language literature analysis reveals little information about the state of counselling in Latvia, psychological counselling does not exist as an independent profession in the country. The development and establishment of the counselling profession's standards and regulation could be significant challenges.

Additional Information

For a more in-depth look at the counselling profession in the country, interested readers are encouraged to read the following journal and website articles:

- Euroguidance.eu (2020). Guidance System in Latvia. Online: https://www.euroguidance.eu/guidance-system-in-latvia
- Rigas Stadina Universitate (2020). A Psychotherapist, a psychiatrist and a Psychologist: Von Vilnius zur Kurischen Nehrung. Online: http://psihosomatika.lv/differences

22. Liechtenstein

Current Regulatory Status/Level of Recognition

In order to work as a psychological counselor in Liechtenstein, a degree in psychology is required (cf. Berufsverband der Psychologinnen und Psychologen Liechtenstein, 2020). What requirements apply to other areas of counselling was not clear from the literature. Liechtenstein law does not protect the professional title of a psychologist*. It gives them the right to provide psychological counselling, but not to provide treatment for mental disorders (cf. Professional Association of Psychologists of Liechtenstein, 2020).

The Health Act governs the practice of psychotherapy in Liechtenstein. It states that only persons who have obtained a license from the Office of Public Health may practice psychotherapy. Prerequisites for obtaining consent are a university degree in psychology (or medicine), specialized continuing education and several years of practical experience (cf. ibid.). Psychotherapy is part of primary care and covered by health insurance.

Challenges and Trends

Online and telephone counselling are in vogue. At the e-mail address help@helpmail.li, people seeking advice can ask questions answered by psychologically trained specialist staff. By dialling 143, there is a general, anonymous telephone counselling service available around the clock. Specifically for children, the telephone counselling service is available at 147. Especially in Corona times, the need for telephone or online counselling increases.

Additional Information

For a more in-depth examination of the counselling profession in Liechtenstein, interested readers should read the following articles as well as books:

- Berufsverband der Psychologinnen und Psychologen Liechtensteins (2020). Wissenswertes. Online: https://www.bpl.li/wissenswertes
- Berufsverband der Psychologinnen und Psychologen Liechtensteins (2020). Psychologie als Beruf. Online: https://www.bpl.li/psychologie-als-beruf

23. Lithuania

Brief history/background of Counselling

As in the other Baltic States, psychological counselling does not seem to be an independent profession in Lithuania, and no significant historical record can be found. On the other hand, psychology and psychotherapy and vocational and school counselling are present in Lithuania.

Current Regulatory Status/ Level of Recognition
The Ministry of Education and Science is responsible for vocational guidance policy related to providing quality vocational education, information and guidance services to pupils, students, adult learners, etc. (cf. EACEA National Policies Platform, 2020).

The Ministry of Education and Science establishes the procedure for providing vocational information and training in the education system. It is the aim that all pupils* and students* should have the opportunity to access career guidance services in their educational institution (cf. ibid.). These services assist in planning, developing, and assessing future careers (cf. ibid.).

Graduate psychologists usually provide psychological counselling.

There is no separate job title of "counsellor." Even the professional designation of "psychologist" is not clearly defined and protected by law (cf. PsychOpen, 2020).

Challenges and Trends
As a result of the Corona pandemic, which is placing an increasing psychological burden on the population, the Lithuanian government has drawn up and implemented a plan to support people (cf. Lietuvos nacionalinis radijas ir televizija, 2020).

This plan provides for the expansion of psychological counselling services and the hiring of more than two hundred psychologists (cf. ibid.). Also, hotlines strengthened for the emotional support of children, seniors and other groups during the Corona crisis (cf. Lietuvos nacionalinis radijas ir televizija, 2020). According to the prime minister, support also provided to non-governmental organizations that actively offered assistance during the coronavirus outbreak (cf. ibid.).

Despite the support for the country's residents*, the policy still needs to take additional steps to make psychological counselling more accessible to more people. Also, more detailed regulations and a legally protected professional title are still lacking.

Additional Information
For a more in-depth look at the counselling profession in the country, interested readers are encouraged to read the following journal and website articles:

- EACEA National Policies Platform (2020). Career Guidance and Counselling. Online: https://eacea.ec.europa.eu/national-policies/en/content/youthwiki/34-career-guidance-and-Counselling-lithuania
- Lietuvos nacionalinis radijas ir televizija (2020). Lithuania to hire 200 Psychologists to tackle Covid-19 effects on mental health. Online: https://www.lrt.lt/en/news-in-english/19/1179781/lithuania-to-hire-200-Psychologists-to-tackle-covid-19-effects-on-mental-health

24. Luxembourg

Current Regulatory Status/Level of Recognition

A person who has at least a master's degree in psychology can call himself a psychologist and work in counselling, coaching, training, and or diagnostics (cf. Association Luxembourgeoise de Étudiants en Psychologie, 2020). Apart from psychological counselling, there were no prerequisites for other counselling activities, which was not clear from the literature. A psychotherapist requires a degree in psychology or psychiatry and additional training. A course usually takes 3 to 4 years and is completed part-time. The profession of psychotherapist has only been protected by law since 2015 (cf. Association Luxembourgeoise de Étudiants en Psychologie, 2020).

Additional Information

For a more in-depth examination of the counselling profession in Luxembourg, interested readers are advised to read the following articles as well as books:

- Association Luxembourgeoise de Étudiants en Psychologie (2020). Online: https://alep.lu/student-area/qa-psychotherapie-zu-letzebuerg/qa-psychotherapie-zu-letzebuerg-de/
- BVPPT Berufsverband für Beratung, Pädagogik und Psychotherapie (2020). Online: https://bvppt.org/Counselling.html

25. Malta

Brief history/background of Counselling

The counselling profession emerged over 20 years ago when counsellors received a diploma in school counselling. At that time, school counsellors were concerned with students' psychosocial needs and their career choices. In 2008, the University of Malta offered the first master's course in counselling. Since then, the profession has become more regulated, and today counsellors must hold credentials to practice the profession. The majority of credentialed counsellors have a Master's degree, while the others were credentialed based on "grandfather rights", i. e. grandfathering. (cf. Zammit Genovese, 2020)

In 1999, a group of counsellors* began discussing the possibility of forming an association. They held the first meeting in January 2002 at the University of Malta, where they presented the constitution. MACP (Malta Association for the Counselling Profession) invested most of the annual National Conference and Training Weeks. The most crucial endeavour for MACP was the regulation of the profession. On February 24, 2015, the Counselling Bill's third reading finally came into force on March 3, 2015. The bill includes establishing practice standards that include supervision and CPD (Continuing Professional Development) hours. These standards must be met annually by counsellors* to continue practicing. (cf. Galea, 2020)

Current Regulatory Status/Level of Recognition

Counselling regulated by law since March 2015. (cf. ibid.)

The Maltese Act, Chapter 538 – Counselling Profession, deals with regulating the Counselling profession and all related matters.

The draft law can be found at.

Website: (https://legislation.mt/eli/cap/538/eng/pdf)

There is a register listing all authorized counsellors* with full authority and a record listing all certified counsellors* with temporary authority. The records are on the Ministry's website for the Family, Children's Rights and Social Solidarity.

Website: (https://family.gov.mt/ccp/Pages/default.aspx)

The Master in counselling program is offered at the University of Malta and lasts eight semesters. Applications are open to persons with a Category 2 Bachelor's degree in Humanities or Social Sciences, and any other field of study deemed relevant by the Board. Also, applicants* need practical experience of at least one year "in a formal human or psycho-social setting". (cf. The University of Malta – Master in Counselling, 2020) Finally, they must undergo a personal interview and personality test. There it will be determined if they are qualified for the profession.

Website: https://www.um.edu.mt/courses/overview/PMCOUPET0-2020-1-O

Challenges and Trends

The challenges and trends that survey participants consider essential are described below.

"Counsellors working in schools seem to be, sadly, phasing out. There seems to be a hidden agenda behind this. Counselling psychologists and play therapists are trying to find their way into the education system, which is good, but not at the expense of losing counsellors.

Counsellors never had opportunities in medical hospitals – only psychologists work there, unfortunately. It is saddening to see that there is still a considerable discrepancy between the different helping professions here in Malta. I work in a multi-disciplinary team, and the richness that comes out of these reflective conversations is superb. I feel blessed.

Another challenge that locally we encounter is supervision. There is no consensus with regards to whether counsellors can access supervision from, let's say psychologists or psychotherapists, or whether the qualified supervisor needs to necessarily be a qualified counsellor, even after one gets the warrant." (cf. Zammit Genovese, 2020)

"Even though it is a warranted profession, it is still not available in many sectors, e. g. health department/hospital. Psychology was awarded a warrant after counselling. However, there is still this social belief that psychology is superior for some reason or another. Any counselling jobs available are not well paid and not taken care of." (cf. Lehtonen, 2020)

"It needs to be respected more by psychologists and employers such as the government and welfare agencies." (cf. Zammit, 2020)

"Having been a 'cinderella'; profession for a long time & acquiring regulation long after that of psychology. Counselling still struggles to reach various entities.

The Covid era has opened a new window in online counselling, which was previously hardly practiced here because Malta is a small country, so distances are short. However, traffic jams are widespread.

Presently Malta has a population of about 440,000 with around 40,000 registered cars on an island measuring 316 km². Clients just calculated the extra time they needed to get to their session according to the traffic congestion at a particular time of day & the level of parking difficulty. Now, this issue might not be a stumbling block any more. Short courses on Online counselling help in this process." (cf. Galea, 2020)

Additional Information

"*The new chairperson at CCP will be building bridges with MACP to ensure the optimum for the counselling profession.*" (cf. ibid.).

26. Moldova

Brief history/background of Counselling

In 1995, four years after the declaration of independence of Moldova, the republic's healthcare was on the brink of a crisis. During the years of independence, the Republic of Moldova faced severe economic hardships that led to lower incomes and worsening financing of health care and social programs.

Psychological assistance should develop as a complex system of professional activities.

Since 2020 the Education Strategy Project proposes an objective for the development of counselling and guidance. It aims to provide essential support for higher education institutions to create and operate university centres for career guidance and counselling whose mission is to support citizens in the career design process and pursue career education. The Project also contains the Framework Regulation for the operation of the guidance centre and career counselling (career guidance methodology, its purposes, services provided, etc.). A series of annexes with examples of sheets and documents developed within the centres can help create and operate similar centres in universities in the Republic of Moldova (cf. Cerniţanu, 2017).

The current system of social assistance services is based on intervention and not really on prevention. Although several reforms have changed, they do not cover all disadvantaged people yet. There are not enough resources to build a robust counselling Service because there are problems in the (mental) health care that are more serious (cf. Chistruga-Sinchevici, 2013).

Current Regulatory Status/Level of Recognition

In most cases, counselling services are provided by non-governmental organizations. Medical services in the Republic of Moldova are offered based on the Compulsory Health Insurance System.

There is a Framework for counselling and guidance developed in the Education Strategy Project 2020, but counselling not regulated by the government (cf. Chistruga-Sinchevici, 2013).

The Framework mentions that, under the conditions of university autonomy, higher education institutions to develop their regulations on the creation and operation of guidance and counselling centres. Career counselling, approved by the senate, provided that they will not contain provisions in contradiction with this Regulation (cf. Cerniţanu, 2017).

Challenges and Trends

Unfortunately school psychologists are often unqualified and without sufficient theoretical and methodological knowledge in solving psychological issues, which they encounter in working with students, their parents and teachers. This situation can change for various reasons, both socio-economic and scientific.

Ideally, there should be a conceptual model of psychological assistance, which should be unified and become the basis for all psychological services. In this case, specialists in the field of psychology will be able to cooperate in exchanging experiences. In this context, it becomes relevant to improve curricula for training psychologists. Psychologists believe that traditional training in academic programs is not necessary and even not applicable in psychological practice.

Another challenge in Moldova is the organization of the psychological profession. There are no clear structures or frameworks in the domain, and the Mental Health Ministry's work, the Ministry of Education and Psychologists, is poorly organized.

The biggest issue in Moldova is that almost a quarter of the citizens do not know about psychological services.

In conclusion, under society's needs, it is essential to activate information on psychology and provide the necessary resources to promote psychological care development (cf. Kucher & Furdui n. y.).

There is no Trend when it comes to counselling in the Republic of Moldova. The biggest and only "trend" is to build more counselling services and organize the social structures.

Additional Information

- Cerniţanu, M. (2017). Serviciul de consiliere psihologică și ghidare în carieră din cadrul instituțiilor de învățământ superior din Moldova. Sănătate Publică, Economie şi Management în Medicină, 74(4), 26–30.
- Chistruga-Sinchevici, I. (2013). Politicile familiale din Republica Moldova în context european. In Creşterea economică în condiţiile globalizării (pp. 214–221).
- Kucher, A./ Furdui, E. (n. y.). Some Views on the Necessity of Psychological Care for Children with development problems in the republic of Moldova. Online: https://virtkafedra.ucoz.ua/el_gurnal/pages/vyp7/konf3/KucherP_Furduj.pdf
- McLehose, L. in McKee, M. (ed.) (2002). Health care systems in transition: Republic of Moldova. Copenhagen, European Observatory on Health Care Systems, 4(5).

27. Monaco

Challenges and Trends

The counselling Programme offered by the International School of Monaco is a good way for students to learn about various career options. Otherwise, the field of counselling and psychology is still not very present.

Additional Information

The sporadic sources of advice found for Monaco are:

- Rivera Wellbeeing; website: https://www.rivierawellbeing.com/
- Counselling Rivera; website: https://www.Counsellingriviera.com/

Monaco is a member of the "Small Countries Initiative." WHO established the initiative in 2013, and countries with a population of fewer than one million people can participate in the enterprise. The main goal is to promote a shared political commitment to develop good health practices in the local area. (cf. World Health Organization, 2020).

28. Netherlands

Brief history/background of Counselling

In the Netherlands, the first approaches to treating patients psychologically already existed at the end of the 19th century. General practitioners such as Frederik van Eeden and Albert Willem van Renterghem relied on conversations, hypnosis, directive approaches and cathartic methods, not just medical measures, and are thus considered the first psychotherapists in the Netherlands.

At the beginning of the 20th century, the treatment offered was limited to psychoanalysis and was practiced exclusively by psychiatrists in private practices. A small elite of well-heeled individuals was treated by them. This was criticised by other psychiatrists, who wanted to make psychotherapy accessible to all.

Therefore, the Nederlandse Vereniging voor Psychotherapie – in 1940, the NVP (Dutch Society of Psychotherapy) was established, the first Institute for Medical Psychotherapy (IMP) was founded (cf. Hutschemaekers & Van Dijk, 2013, p. 316). In addition to psychoanalysis, additional procedures were developed in the following years, which were primarily conducted daily.

After the Second World War, a process of differentiation between psychotherapists and psychiatrists began, as psychotherapy increasingly distanced itself from biomedical models of disorders (so-called anti-psychiatry movement) (cf. Hutschemaekers & Van Dijk, 2013, p. 316).

In 1961, five years before the NVP admitted psychologists*, "the Netherlands Institute for Practicing Psychologists (NIP)" introduced a formal distinction between psychological help (counselling) and psychotherapy. "Whereas Counselling was part of the university program, psychotherapy had to be learned in a specific professional schooling program. However, this distinction was never accepted among psychologists; accepting this viewpoint would imply the end of the unity of psychology" (Hutschemaekers & Van Dijk, 2013, p. 316). Counselling consequently became a fundamental component of psychotherapy.

"In the early 1970s, entrance to the profession widened further through opening membership of the NVP to academics from outside the medical and psychological disciplines. For instance, in 1973, social workers with advanced studies were also allowed into the NVP. Further, between 1970 and 1986, psychiatrists, doctors, psychologists, pedagogics, philosophers and even social workers could become psychotherapists.

The psychotherapist became the professional par excellence who used systematic psychological interventions and counselling in mental healthcare. Counselling was considered as a particular form of psychotherapy; those professionals who wanted to learn and use counselling had to become psychotherapists" (Hutschemaekers & Van Dijk, 2013, p. 317).

Current Regulatory Status/Level of Recognition

The profession of psychotherapist has been legally recognized since 1986. The entrance level, as well as the modality-training, is defined by governmental bodies" (EAP- Netherland, 2020). Beroepen regulates the training and the professional activity in de Individuele Gezondheidszorg (BIG). Only those who have trained according to the BIG requirements may call themselves psychotherapists. After completing the training (duration approximately four years), psychotherapists are listed in the BIG register.

A master's degree in medicine, clinical psychology, education, and health sciences gives access to professions in the health sector and the training program in health psychology and psychotherapy (cf. Hutschemaekers & Van Dijk, 2013, p. 318).

There are only five institutes in the Netherlands from which a degree entitles the holder to an entry in the BIG register. Besides, several other schools and institutes whose graduates are not included in the BIG record cannot use the psychotherapist's professional title. The demand for psychotherapeutic services is growing steadily. A wide range of schools and procedures exist, such as couple and family therapy, interpersonal therapy, client-centred therapy, problem-solving training, cognitive-behavioural therapy, short-term therapies and psychodynamic approaches (cf. Ibid., p. 218). The treatment is financed by statutory and private health insurance companies, but also by the clients themselves. Therapists must fulfil three requirements to be able to invoice services via health insurance:

Basic psychosocial knowledge (level 6) is required, is obligatory for health insurance companies.

Training by a facility recognized by the EAP.

Completion of CPD requirements every two years.

These ensure that professional work knowledge and skills are maintained and improved (cf. EAP Netherland, 2020).

If, on the other hand, a psychologist is consulted in outpatient primary care (PA Psychologist), treatment is free of charge for clients for up to eight sessions (and up to twelve if supplementary insurance is in place), as the state finances it. Psychological-psychotherapeutic treatment offered by the Dutch health care system on three levels:

The first level includes minor psychological and psychosomatic complaints that a psychologist can treat on an outpatient basis. PA Psychologists and general practitioners are responsible for this.

The treatment of moderately severe complaints and disorders belong to the second level. Treatment can take place on an outpatient or inpatient basis.

The third level includes severe mental and psychiatric disorders, the treatment of which, as an outpatient or inpatient, is reserved for specialists such as psychiatrists and psychotherapists (cf. Sonnenmoser, 2011).

Psychotherapists can treat patients of all levels, in contrast to PA Psychologists. These are the particular case that exists almost only in the Netherlands. PA Psychologists complete two years of additional training after graduating in psychology and become certified and enter a register. "They are allowed to diagnose and treat the entire spectrum of behavioural and mental disorders – but only the mild cases. Psychotherapists and psychiatrists are responsible for more severe cases. PA Psychologists are generalists, while psychotherapists and psychiatrists are specialists" (Sonnenmoser, 2011).

The profession of PA Psychologist has been around for more than 30 years.

"It was created after tough wrangling with professional associations, legislators, and the health care system to make psychological-psychotherapeutic primary care available to the general population quickly and free of charge. To make it easier to reach hard-to-reach patient groups, to facilitate contact with professional help, and to reduce inhibitions and prejudices." (Sonnenmoser, 2011).

This help relieves the burden on general practitioners, who were previously involved in the treatment of mild mental and psychosomatic disorders. On the other hand, psychotherapists and psychiatrists can concentrate more on severe cases. For problems such as nicotine addiction, pain without physical findings, anxiety, complicated grief or sleep disorders, PA Psychologists are the first port of call. They only accept patients from their district. If they belong to another, they refer them to colleagues. Thus reducing competition and promoting even distribution (cf. Sonnenmoser, 2011).

Challenges and Trends

Psychotherapy has seen tremendous growth, and psychotherapy has become one of the most important treatment options in mental health care in the Netherlands.

"It is also probable that the success of psychotherapy (an interdisciplinary profession of doctors and psychologists) opened the doors of the BIG law to non-strictly medical professions such as clinical and healthcare-psychologists. Formal settlement of these psychological disciplines reduced rivalries and disputes between professions, provided transparency in several professionals and what they do, and offered excellent opportunities for improvement of healthcare quality and professional schooling" (Hutschemaekers & Van Dijk, 2013, p. 322).

At the same time, however, the success of psychotherapy also has its downsides. Due to psychotherapy's interdisciplinary nature, it does not fully belong to either medicine or psychology and is not part of their academic schooling and research programs. Consequently, it grew distant from the academic world, where psychotherapy does not have its department or not recognized as a distinct academic profession. "With the rise of empirically supported therapies (EST) and their translation into evidence-based guidelines, the gap between the psychotherapists and the academic world became even more aggravated." (Ibid., p. 322).

With the complexity of the psychological professions comes a blending. However, if the various disciplines divided, this could lead to a more precise delineation between psychiatric and psychological help and psychotherapy and counselling (cf. Ibid., p. 322). In addition to interdisciplinary challenges, there may also be financial challenges for the client. Treatment fully reimbursed if the chosen psychotherapist is under contract with the client's health insurance and the three requirements are met (cf. ibid., p. 44 above). If there is no contract with the individual health insurance, only between 50% to 80% of the money reimbursed. The costs of psychotherapy by a psychotherapist who is not under contract can therefore be considerable (cf. Zorgwijzer – Overige vergoedingsvoorwaarden 2020).

Additional Information

For a more in-depth examination of the counselling profession in the Netherlands, interested readers are advised to read the following articles as well as books:

- Algemene Beroepsvereniging voor Counselling ABvC (2020). Online: https://www.abvc.nl
- EAP European Association of Psychotherapy – Netherland (2020). Online: https://www.europsyche.org/situation-of-Psychotherapy-in-various-countries/netherlands/
- Hutschemaekers, G. J. M., & Van Dijk, F. E. (2013). Psychotherapy and clinical Psychology in the Netherlands. In: Moodley, R., Gielen, U. P. & Wu, R. (Eds.). Handbook of Counselling and Psychotherapy in an international context, S. 315–325. Routledge.
- Idee psychologisch bureau – Therapie ed. / Over therapie (2020). Online: https://www.idee-pmc.nl/psychotherapie/therapie_over.html
- Sonnenmoser, M. (2011). Psychotherapie in Europa – Niederlande: Schnelle und niederschwellige Erstversorgung. Deutsches Ärzteblatt PP.

- Zorgwijzer – Overige vergoedingsvoorwaarden (2020). Online: https://www.zorgwijzer.nl/vergoeding/psychologie

29. Norway

Brief history/background of Counselling

Comparing the history of psychology in the Nordic countries, some similarities become visible due to the countries' close relations. The Nordic university psychologists inspired by German experimental psychology of the late 19th century.

After the war, applied psychology became increasingly important in the North. Psychologists became involved in psychotechniques, including aptitude testing, personnel selection, and career counselling. Over the years, there were many areas added. Clinical psychology, for example, became an essential factor. All Nordic countries were doing extensive research in psychophysiology, neuroscience, and mental disorders by the millennium turn. In Norway, the main focus was on psychological articles dealing with health treatment and prevention (cf. Pietikainen & Kragh, 2019).

Psychology and psychotherapy play a significant role in Norway. There is a large number of Psychologists.

The state grants them many privileges and responsibilities. (cf. Rønnestad, n. d.) However, the field of counselling does not seem to be a separate field. Workers in the professions of psychiatric nursing and social work in Norway perform counselling in addition to psychotherapy. In particular, this applies to institutions for children, adolescents and families (cf. ibid.).

Four universities in Norway offer professional training in psychology. These include the universities in Oslo, Bergen, Trondheim and Tromso. They each differ from one another in their psychological focus. The psychology department at the University of Oslo is the oldest in all of Norway (cf. ibid.).

Current Regulatory Status/Level of Recognition

In Norway, the law regulates the title of psychologist and the license to practice the profession. The training comprises a six-year course of study and one year of supervision. After this, graduates receive a psychology diploma, which is equivalent to a master's degree. With the certificate, it is possible to apply for recognition as a psychologist. After an examination by the Norwegian National Council of Health, the psychologists then receive a work license. (cf. Van Broeck & Lietaer, 2008, p. 57) The permit allows both the authorization to carry out treatments and bill psychotherapeutic services with the health insurance. (cf. Cohen, 2002, p.15).

Psychotherapy, on the other hand, is not regulated by law. Most psychotherapeutic training is by private training institutes, some of which are publicly funded. However, these institutions often require basic training in medicine, psychology, social work, or nursing. (cf. Rønnestad, n.d.) The delivery of psychotherapy takes place in both private and public institutions. The government and private funds finance these institutions. The majority of psychosocial services, including psychotherapy and counselling, are provided by outpatient clinics (cf. ibid.).

Challenges and Trends

The focus on treating mental illness in children and adolescents is now no longer on the long-term. Counselling and psychotherapeutic work, but on diagnostic procedures and shorter forms of psychotherapy and counselling. Furthermore, the market for non-traditional, alternative forms of treatment is increasing. Only a minority of psychologists and psychiatrists work outside the public health system. Patients have to pay for the costs of these treatments themselves. It is still uncertain what impact the 1999 Bologna reform will have on higher education in Norway. However, work is underway on a EuroPsy (European Certificate in Psychology) with standard professional education requirements in psychology. In 2004, the Norwegian Knowledge Center for Health Care was established. The centre is scientifically and professionally independent and summarizes and disseminates scientific knowledge relevant to the prevention and treatment of various physical and mental condition (cf. ibid.).

Additional Information

It is possible to obtain additional qualifications in private and public further education institutes. Further education is not linked to a specific professional group. There is a great interest, especially in family therapy and systemic therapy. Practice shows that primarily social pedagogues and social workers strive for these further education courses. However, graduates have no recognized privileges and rights after graduation. (cf. Cohen, 2002, p. 16).

Interested readers are recommended to read the following articles and books for a more in-depth discussion of the counselling profession:

- Pietikainen, P. & Kragh, J. V. (2019). Professionalization of Psychology in the Nordic Countries. Oxford Research Encyclopedia of Psychology. Oxford University Press. Online: https://oxfordre.com/Psychology/view/10.1093/acrefore/9780190236557.001.0001/acrefore-9780190236557-e-597
- Rønnestad, M. H. (o. D.). The Psychotherapeutic Professions in Norway. Online: http://citeseerx.ist.psu.edu/viewdoc/download?doi=10.1.1.499.5013&rep=rep1&type=pdf

30. Poland

Brief history/background of Counselling

Psychotherapists of various theoretical orientations practice most counselling services in Poland.

"Psychotherapist" is not protected, and the professionals are not registered. How many psychotherapists there are in Poland is unknown. The majority of psychotherapists with academic training are physicians (medicine), especially psychiatrists, while psychologists are in the minority.

There is intensive works in Poland in the law governing psychotherapy as a profession. The Ministry of Health is preparing the law in consultation with Polish psychotherapeutic associations. The law is to safeguard the patients' rights and regulate the qualifications of psychotherapists. The postgraduate training courses are to be run by the Psychotherapy Association, whose members must conform to ethics codes.

Since consistent legally prescribed training standards do not yet exist, at least the specialist psychotherapeutic societies ensure a certain quality assurance level.

They offer psychotherapy training, define the training content and award certificates that serve as proof of minimum standards. So far, each professional society follows its own rules and decides who is admitted to the training. The training content, requirements and duration are also highly heterogeneous.

Psychotherapy is covered not only by statutory health insurance but also private health insurance. Private practice psychotherapy is becoming more popular when patients have to pay, but they can choose their therapist and have no limitations on the number of sessions. But for Polish patients, it is difficult to find their way around the diversity and to distinguish serious from dubious providers.

Current Regulatory Status/Level of Recognition

Psychotherapists in Poland do not have protected legal status. In recent years, various draft laws, as well as legislative amendment, have been sought. However, the project has failed. Among other things, the aim is to become a pendant to the German psychotherapists Act.

Moreover, polish psychotherapists have currently no chambers but form associations specific to different approaches to psychotherapy. However, only three associations are recognized by the National Health Fund: The Association of Psychologists, the Association of Psychiatrists (representing Integrative Psychotherapy) and the Polish Association of Cognitive-Behavioral therapy.

Already organized courses involve four-year studies, involving 1200 hours of formal education, internship, clinical work under supervision, and own psychotherapy experience. The classes are open to any person with a humanistic or scientific degree.

The law allows a variety of recommended approaches to practise (not finally decided as yet). It is hoped to regulate that the most efficient psychotherapy methods are used, and evidence-based practice is required.

Challenges and Trends

It is difficult for polish patients to find their way around the diversity and distinguish serious from dubious providers.

The most important task for the future is to introduce the law governing psychotherapy. A reform of the regulation system should lead to:

the reduction of the presence of unprofessional therapists
replacing it with evidence-based approaches
it would improve access to recognized psychotherapy services and
it may result in reducing the high amount of drugs taken.

Psychotherapy is covered not only by statutory health insurance but also private health insurance. Private practice Psychotherapy is becoming more popular when patients have to pay, but they can choose their therapist and have no limitations on the number of sessions.

New, more proactive psychotherapy approaches are becoming popular and recognized, such as cognitive-behavioural therapy or motivational enhancement therapy. Such methods deal with a patient's weakness and build a patient's strengths, self-esteem, and self-efficacy.

31. Portugal

Brief history/background of Counselling

Counselling does not appear to be an independent profession in Portugal.

The career guidance, for example, dates back to the first decades of the 20th century. Counselling psychology services have also been implemented in schools and universities. The counselling services are organized mainly under the Ministry of Education and the Ministry of Employment, Solidarity and Social Affairs.

The majority of consultants in Portugal are qualified psychologists with a variable degree of specialisation.

Psychotherapy usually is not financed by the National System of Social Insurance unless prescribed by a psychiatrist. In general, private mental health insurance doesn't cover psychotherapy sessions. The public health care system includes a psychological service for diagnosis and consultation, available in most Health Centers. Some hospitals refer to mental health, although the number of clinical psychologists in the public service is quite limited.

Current Regulatory Status/Level of Recognition

Portugal has a compulsory regulated by law for the mental health professions (medical doctors, psychologists, nurses). Psychotherapy in this context is a specialization of those professions.

The Order of Portuguese Psychology is the national body responsible for the accreditation, training and regulation of psychologists in Portugal. Regulamento No. 258/2011 is a recommendation document that integrates ethical principles of the profession in psychology in every area and contexts of application.

Challenges and Trends

There is growing range of counselling. Every public school has counselling services for children aged 5–16 years at compulsory schooling. counselling is carried out by school psychologists.

32. Russia

Brief history/background of Counselling

In Russia, in the early 1980s psychological counselling was intensively developed with the emergence of the first social and psychological assistance services and psychological assistance telephone helplines. Before that, university psychology graduates were mainly engaged in client testing and research activities. Officially, they could not engage in psychotherapy (as, indeed, they cannot now), since according to the Russian Federation laws, only a specialist with higher medical education can be a psychotherapist.

The term "counselling psychology" appeared in the early 1990s, and in those same years, the profession of a consultant psychologist was actively developing. In the 1990s, several journal publications and books appeared that shaped the face of modern Russian counselling psychology. The experience of developing this branch of practical psychology and the great interest reflected the appearance in the 2000s of several unique books and teaching aids, creating psychological counselling and psychotherapy.

In recent years, the popularity of a new consulting area – coaching – has been actively growing in Russia, which is gaining the market of business services, and is also becoming in demand as personal assistance in solving life problems of clients (Life Coaching).

In recent years, various practice-oriented coaching schools are opening. Working according to the standards of the International Association of Coaches ICF (International Academy of Coaching, International Ericksonian University of Coaching), and according to the author's programs (Institute of Coaching A.D.Savkin, School of System-Integrative Coaching I. V. Rybkin, etc.).

Coaching as a different type of consulting was formed in the 80s of the last century at the intersection of psychology, philosophy, management and sports. At first, it was focused exclusively on the business environment, but gradually the coachs' services became in demand in other areas.

Currently, there are about five hundred types of coaching, which can be divided into two categories: coaching in business (coaching management, executive coaching, corporate, strategic, situational, project, innovative, career, motivational) and life coaching (coaching for adolescents, family coaching, leisure coaching, emotion management, etc.) (cf. Vinogradova, 2010, p. 200ff.).

Current Regulatory Status/ Level of Recognition

Although not regulated, counselling in the Russian Federation you need higher education in medicine to become a psychotherapist (cf. Vinogradova, 2010).

Challenges and Trends

Challenges: This direction is poorly studied, which leads to ambiguity and definition of the concept itself and the correlation of coaching with other anthropological practices. In this regard, studies devoted to the problem of comparing coaching and psychotherapy are becoming relevant.

Determining the boundaries and areas of intersection of these socio-anthropological practices will help better understand the professional competence and responsibility of a coach and psychotherapist and see ways of mutual enrichment with values and techniques. Also, psychologists with professional experience in psychotherapeutic practice often come to coaching. In their work, they inevitably come across questions about the boundaries of combining these areas' methods, about the practicality of their integration when working with a client, about the problem of attributing client requests to "coaching" or "psychotherapeutic".

On the one hand, there is an overwhelming number of universities across the country with psychology departments, including those with a specialization in "psychological counselling" (which means they train specialists in this profile). Still, on the other hand, it is not so simple to meet a knowledgeable professional not only with the necessary education but also with sufficient practical experience in the consulting services market. Characterised by the lack of a single curriculum and standard counselling, psychologists' academic training occurs in public universities. It is opposed by practical training in various non-state institutions and psychological centres, including many hours of individual and group psychotherapy.

In the last decade, such type of services as coaching has become increasingly popular. It sounds new, strange and raises many questions. Coaches – that is, coaching professionals – promise to change your life forever and only for the better, and in a reasonably short time.

Most of them (not all) insist that they have absolutely nothing to do with psychology and psychotherapy. The Counsellors in Russia tend to follow strict plans in their counselling-settings. Popular models are, for example, the four-state model and the six-step model by A. Blaser.

The four-step model of psychological counselling includes the following technical steps:

[A] establishment of rapport,

[B] "joining" the consultant to the client;

[C] leading the client towards the study and crystallization of the problem;

[D] therapeutic completion is the formation of the clients' motivation to solve the problem.

The Six-Step Model by A. Blaser contains:

[A] establishing rapport,

[B] drawing up a complaint,

[C] problem analysis,

[D] formulating the problem,

[E] working out the problem and

[F] completion, characterized by the "disconnection" of the client in the case of a positive solution to the problem, when the consultant makes it clear to the client that he must now be independent and do without the help of a specialist.

To become a Consolidate Counselling Community member, you have to accomplish training programs for 250 hours, have 25 hours of Supervision, have 25 hours of Group Therapy, and 25 hours of personal therapy.

The United Psychological Counselling Community is a member of the European Counselling Association.

They have the authority to accredit Russian specialists in the field of Psychological counselling according to world standards.

The members of the United Psychological Counselling Community are issued certificates of European-standard.

Specialists in the field of psychological counselling and the right to use this certificate to work in all countries of the European Community (cf. Russian Association for Psychological Counselling, 2020).

Additional Information

- Gestalt therapy center (2020). Coaching and Psychotherapy – what's the difference? Online: http://mpsy.ru/biblioteka/nashi-stati/kouching-i-psihoterapiya-%E2%80%93-v-chem-raznica.html
- Russian Association for Psychological Counselling (2020). There are several approaches to defining and structuring the space of psychological Counselling. Online: http://oapk.org/articles/122-modeli-struktury-psikhologicheskogo-konsultirovaniya
- Vinogradova E. L. (2010). Coaching and Psychotherapy: Possibilities of Intersection of Practices – Counselling Psychology and Psychotherapy. Online: https://psyjournals.ru/files/27896/mpj_ 2010_n1_Vinogradova.pdf

33. San Marino

Challenges and Trends

Currently, there are some people who deal with psychotherapy and counselling, but there is no legal regulation of the profession. Furthermore, universities do not offer training in this field, and other training institutes have not been found. The area is very opaque.

Additional Information

Some consulting services Theravive; website: https://www.theravive.com/cities/ca/Counselling-san-marino.aspx

Some psychologists and private counsellors San Marino is a member of the "Small Countries Initiative." WHO established the initiative in

2013, and countries with a population of fewer than one million people can participate. The main goal is to promote a joint political commitment to develop good health practices in the local area. (cf. World Health Organization, 2020)

34. Serbia

Brief history/background of Counselling

Counselling does not seem to be an independent profession in Serbia. There is no historical background.

On the other hand, the need for counselling is all the more urgent as about a third of the population suffers from mental health problems due to the economic crisis, which has led to unemployment and rising poverty.

With 7.2 million inhabitants, Serbia has only 350 certified psychotherapists and 900 psychiatrists. The Association of Psychotherapeutic Societies in Serbia quantifies the need for psychotherapists at 6000-8000. About 1500 experts are currently being trained and will soon have the conditions included in the system.

35. Spain

Brief history/background of Counselling

In Spain, the field of counselling is not independent. Psychology, on the other hand, has a long history. It was taught at universities in Spain as a branch of philosophy until the 20th century. The cities of Madrid and Barcelona played a significant role. Here, psychology was studied both inside and outside the universities and established itself as applied science. The two cities differed in their psychological focus. While Madrid was primarily concerned with pedagogy and philosophy, Barcelona was more experimental in natural science. (cf. Erb, 2005, p. 63ff.).

Founded in 1918, the Institute for Vocational Guidance in Barcelona. Here, young people examined psychologically, socially and medically and assigned to an occupational group accordingly. (cf. ibid., p. 103).

Over time, psychotherapy was shaped by many influences.

1920s, psychoanalysis, phenomenological psychology and psychiatry

1950s, the person-centered approach

1970s, and Gestalt therapy

1980s and cognitive therapy

2000s. (cf. Marín-Martín & Prieto, 2015, p. 211) Many different directions of psychology, chairs, institutes, journals, professional associations, and societies developed. (cf. Erb, 2005, p. 255)

In 1991 psychotherapy was recognized as a service in clinics and psychiatric institutions. (cf. Cohen, 2002, p. 19).

Current Regulatory Status/Level of Recognition

In Spain, there is no psychotherapist law, so psychotherapy is not regulated (cf. ibid., p. 18). However, the law does protect the title of psychologist and clinical psychologist. A council in the Ministry of Health does grant identification and the authorization to practice the profession. Psychologists and physicians' official panels are responsible for accrediting training programs and organizing certified examinations for psychologists who specialize in clinical psychology. Furthermore, the councils take care of the accreditation of hospitals and centres that accept trainees (cf. Van Broeck & Lietaer, 2008 p. 57f.)

Recognition after successful completion of studies and four years of clinical work under supervision as a psychologist (Cohen). Psychologists registered in the professional association can continue their education in private seminars, workshops or summer schools. (cf. Marín-Martín & Prieto, 2015, p. 211)

Psychotherapy can only bill to private health insurance companies in rare cases. Statutory health insurers generally do not pay for psychotherapy. (cf. Cohen, 2002, p. 19).

Challenges and Trends

There is no numerus clausus for psychology studies in Spain, and the chances to enter the labour market are relatively low. The rate of unemployed psychologists is therefore very high. There are comparatively many self-employed psychologists in Spain since citizens usually pay for psychotherapy themselves (cf. ibid., p. 18f.).

After thorough research and review of the literature, no indications of further challenges or trends could be found.

Additional Information

Interested readers are advised to read the following articles and books for a more in-depth discussion of the counselling profession:

- Erb, A. (2005). On the history of Psychology in and between Spain and Germany from the late 19th century to the mid-20th century: aspects of German-Spanish scientific relations. Online: https://refubium.fu-berlin.de/handle/fub188/12896
- Marín-Martín, C. & Prieto, J. M. (2015). Counselling and Psychotherapy in Spain: Andres's Story. In: R. Moodley; M. Lengyell; R. Wu & U. P. Gielen. International Counselling. Case Studies Handbook. (S. 211–218) Alexandria: American Counselling Association.
- Van Broeck, N. & Lietaer, G. (2008). Psychology and Psychotherapy in Health Care: A Review of Legal Regulations in 17 European Countries. European Psychologist, Vol.13 (1), S. 53–63.

36. Sweden

Brief history/background of Counselling

The field of psychology has existed in Sweden for over 100 years. The word psychology has often been used in this country as a generic term for psychological treatment orientations, clientele, and treatment duration.

There is no Swedish translation for counselling psychology, counselling and counsellors, which is why counselling is not considered an established psychological field. (cf. Nilsson & Lindgren, 2009, p. 322).

Similarly, as in many other European countries, mental health treatments in Sweden were influenced by psychoanalysis. From the middle of the 20th century, different treatment orientations, such as cognitive therapy and behavioural therapy, began to gain acceptance (cf. ibid.).

Until World War II, psychology in Sweden was the academic responsibility of the faculties of philosophy. In 1943, the first psychotechnical institute established at the 'Högskola of Stockholm'

(Stockholm University Institute). Towards the end of the 1950s, more formal training for psychologists was introduced at the universities.

Currently, this training consists of a five-year degree program focusing on applied psychology offered at a total of eight universities in Sweden (Gothenburg, Linköping, Lund, Stockholm, Umea, Uppsala and Örebro).

The program concludes with a Master of Science in psychology. However, admission is highly competitive as the program is one of Sweden's most popular (cf. ibid., p. 322f.).

In recent years, psychology programs and all other university programs have to meet the Bologna Reform standards. In Sweden, the main focus has been on adapting and amending the degree levels, the grading system, and the admission procedure (cf. ibid., p. 323).

Current Regulatory Status/Level of Recognition

Counselling is not regulated by law because it is not an established speciality. In 1985, the Psychotherapists Act introduced in Sweden. It states that only those who can prove that they have undergone appropriate further psychotherapy training can obtain psychotherapy recognition. (cf. Cohen, 2002, p. 12)

Despite the Psychotherapists Act, there is a confusing situation concerning training offers and providers of spychotherapy. The quality and seriousness is not checked to any depth. Universities and professional societies, however, follow European and worldwide training standards and offer five-year training. (cf. Sonnenmoser, 2011)

As a rule, this psychotherapeutic training divides into three stages.

First, basic training of about three years must be completed. After completing the training, one receives a bachelor's degree. With this degree, one can practice psychotherapeutic interventions under supervision.

The second stage, training in psychotherapy, takes place

In the Third stage, psychotherapists qualified to be able to work as supervisors. (cf. Van Broeck & Lietaer, 2008, p. 58).

In 1995 a national law was passed in which the right to treatment was guaranteed. This law gives society a right to health care, including psychotherapy, enacted to enforce equal treatment in health care in all parts of Sweden. As a result, the regional governments were required to comply with this guarantee of treatment. There is one restriction for psychotherapy. It is only guaranteed and subsidized if it is considered medically necessary. (cf. Nilsson & Lindgren, 2009, p. 325).

The "Swedish National Board of Health and Welfare" authorizes psychologists to work as licensed psychologists. The license is issued only after a five-year course of study in psychology (master's degree), supplemented by one year of supervised training. Furthermore, the Swedish National Board of Health and Welfare sets guidelines on licensing for title and practice as a psychotherapist and accreditations for training institutions. (cf. Van Broeck & Lietaer, 2008, p. 58).

Challenges and Trends

There are continuing education programs in psychotherapy offered primarily at universities but also at some accredited training institutions. The programs offer psychologists in-depth training in psychoanalytic, psychodynamic, behavioural or cognitive group or family therapy. Swedish psychologists take advantage of these programs and continue their education to a greater extent than any other professional group in their country. (cf. Nilsson & Lindgren, 2009, p. 323).

Currently, psychologists complete five years of academic training in applied psychology, followed by one year of supervised internship. Of note is the desire to advance training and develop a specialization in the field. This desire may be a reflection of responsible and dedicated professionals who want to expand their skills and meet the diverse psychological needs of the Swedish population. However, it may also be an indication that students find the training too general and do not adequately prepare them to work with specific people and problems (cf. ibid., p. 325).

Furthermore, it should be pointed out that not only the primary health care system employs a low number of psychologists. The same problem arises in the school system. In Sweden, the number of school psychologists is lower than in many other countries in Western Europe. The low number of psychologists in primary health care as well as in the school system can ultimately contribute to a lack of awareness of the profession and to the feeling that psychological services can only be used by the seriously mentally ill (cf. ibid.).

In Sweden, mentally ill patients are initially treated with medication. Primary care does not include therapy. Only in exceptional cases is it used as a supplement to medication. However, especially in the areas of anxiety disorders and depression, treatment is a very good, if not the better, alternative. (Cf. Sonnenmoser, 2011). Studies from 2004 showed that over two-thirds of respondents would prefer therapy to medication. Furthermore, 60% felt that individuals with mental health problems do not receive the treatment they would want from available subsidized mental health services. (cf. Nilsson & Lindgren, 2009, p. 325)

Many patients have to pay co-payments for their psychological treatments, if not pay for them entirely. For example, a therapy carried out by a psychologist in her private practice costs between 600 and 1000 kronor and is usually not subsidized. Swedes with a medium-income often cannot afford such a treatment in the long run.

So, the question arises what do people in Sweden do when they feel the need to talk to a psychologist due to depression or a crisis (cf. ibid.).

There is an overall problem with the availability of affordable treatment options, as most psychologists are self-employed and work in private practices (cf. Sonnenmoser, 2011). The Swedish health care system does not seem to meet the treatment needs of people with milder forms of mental illness. Here, the country could learn a lot from the field of counselling psychology. By developing such a psychological speciality, the availability of psychological resources would increase (cf. Nilsson & Lindgren, 2009, p. 326).

In summary, there is still much need for action. The need for psychotherapeutic interventions is steadily increasing in Sweden. The number of existing psychotherapists, trainers, institutions, supervisors is not sufficient. The counselling area is not yet sufficiently covered. However, the awareness of the need for psychological health care in therapy is growing, and the Swedish Psychological Association seems determined to develop these specialities further (cf. ibid.).

Additional Information

Interested readers are advised to read the following books and articles for a more in-depth discussion of the counselling profession:

- Nilsson, J. E. & Lindgren, T. (2009). Applied Psychology in Sweden: A Brief Report on Its Role, Ambitions, and Limitations. In: L. H. Gerstein, P. P. Heppner, S. Ægisdóttir, S-M. A. Leung, K. L. Norsworthy (Hrsg.) International Handbook of Cross-

Cultural Counselling – Cultural Assumptions and Practices Worldwide. (321–328) Los Angeles: Sage Publications.
- Sonnenmoser, M. (2011). Psychotherapie in Europa – Schweden: Psychotherapie wird kaum genutzt. Deutsches Ärzteblatt PP.
- Van Broeck, N. & Lietaer, G. (2008). Psychology and Psychotherapy in Health Care: A Review of Legal Regulations in 17 European Countries. European Psychologist, Vol. 13 (1) (53–63).

37. Switzerland

Brief history/background of Counselling
Counselling in Switzerland, as in many other European countries, developed mainly from the work of the clergy, social workers, nurses, and Christian associations as they provided pastoral care in the community.

There are several examples of internationally known Swiss contributors to the field of mental health, including the transactional analyst Leonhard Schlegel and the psychologist Carl Gustav Jung. Their contributions provide a foundation on which Swiss counsellor education programs continue to be based today (cf. Thomas & Henning, 2013, p. 264).

In supporting the development of counselling throughout Europe, the European Association for Counselling (EAC) was founded in 1991. In 2005, the Associazione Nazionale di Counselling (ANSCo) was formed, which was a member of the EAC. This was considered a "reference association" (ibid., p. 265) for counselling and served counsellors as a platform for support. In May 2006, the Swiss Society for Counselling (SGfB) was founded. This organization emerged from a network of eleven counselling-related associations and institutions. The aim is to strengthen the counselling profession's identity, ensure quality, and further develop basic scientific and professional principles (cf. Thomas & Henning, 2013, p. 265). In June 2012, the ANSCo dissolved, and its members were able to transfer their membership to the SGfB (cf. Thomas & Henning, 2013, p. 266).

Current Regulatory Status/Level of Recognition

Since 2013, the professions of psychology and psychotherapy have been protected. Terms such as psychological, psychological counselling or the term therapy did not receive protection. People without a master's degree in psychology can continue to advertise with it (cf. Fueter, 2013).

Due to the quadrilingual character of Switzerland (four national languages: German, French, Italian, Romansh), the education, training and professional practice of counsellors* are divided between regional and linguistic interests. The counselling practice in Switzerland's different regions enriched by France, Germany, and Italy and more complex.

"The result is indistinct relationships between accrediting organizations concerning the management and validation of the counselling profession. The absence of literature and the limited collaboration between the various counselling associations and credentialing agencies in Switzerland is confused by the cantonal manner. This has meant that until recently peoples' moral, existential, legal, and psychological dilemmas continued to be dealt with in a cantonal rather than the federal manner, a factor that lends itself to fragmentation" (Thomas & Henning, 2013, p. 264).

Nevertheless, as counselling is becoming a highly demanded form of intervention, Swiss counsellors face the challenges that come with the profession. Nonetheless, it still takes time until questions of definition, training, and accreditation can be answered concretely (Thomas & Henning 2013, p. 263).

Counselling has been expanded and enriched since the beginning of the 21st century by qualified counsellors who have completed training in a wide variety of therapeutic approaches.

Practising counsellors include psychologists, psychiatrists, and psychoanalysts, some of whom have also completed specialized training as counsellors. Psychologists are allowed to provide psychological counselling even if they do not have an additional qualification for psychotherapy (cf. ibid.).

Counselling programs show too few uniform criteria in obligatory training standards, consistent terminology, legislation and awarding of certificates. This heterogeneous field of professional counselling "has much self-growth and realization yet to undergo in Switzerland"

(Thomas & Henning, 2013, p. 265). As a result, counselling in Switzerland took many different forms and carried out by a diverse group of people, both professionals and laypeople – with varying degrees of preparation and training (cf. ibid., p. 265).

Challenges and Trends

"Swiss counselling programs will evolve and expand as the profession seeks to meet the demands of individuals seeking mental health services, as training opportunities develop, as the quantity and quality of research grow, and an awareness of the profession spreads" (Thomas & Henning, 2013, p. 270).

Although Switzerland's counselling profession has begun to develop its associations and ethical stances, it still struggles for recognition in Switzerland and Europe. Frustration fueled by the realization that the translation of the word counselling has different meanings, becoming a challenge in a country with four national languages (ibid., p. 270).

Since June 2012, the Swiss Association for Counselling (SGfB) has attempted to cover regional and linguistic interests. This association aims to develop further and ensure the quality of psychosocial counselling in the country. "With the validation of the federal examination, counselling may be fully legitimized as a separate profession within the mental health community" (Thomas & Henning, 2013, p. 270).

Increasingly, Switzerland offers online counselling. The public is delivered an anonymous, voluntary counselling session in a protected chat room via a secure website. The aim here is to convey understanding, empathy and impartiality while preserving anonymity and confidentiality (cf. Thomas & Henning, 2013, p. 268).

Additional Information

For a more in-depth examination of the counselling profession in Switzerland, interested readers are advised to read the following articles as well as books:

- Fueter, O. (2013). «Psychologische Hilfe» bleibt Graubereich – SRF. Online: https://www.srf.ch/sendungen/kassensturz-espresso/themen/gesundheit/mehr-schutz-vor-falschen-psychologen

- Schweizerische Gesellschaft für Beratung, Portrait (2020). Online: https://www.sgfb.ch/de/ueber-die-sgfb
- Schweizerische Gesellschaft für Beratung, Psychosoziale Beratung (2020). Online: https://www.sgfb.ch/images/Dokumente_2018_Signatur/1.06_D_Psychosoziale_Beratung. pdf
- Thomas, R., Henning, S. (2013). Counselling in Switzerland. In: Hohenshil, T. H., Amundson, N. E., & Niles, S. G. (Hrsg.). Counselling around the world: An international handbook, S. 203–213. Alexandria, VA: American Counselling Association.

38. Turkey

Brief history/background of Counselling

Counselling has a relatively short history in Turkey. The current Turkish counselling movement and its programs influenced mainly by American counselling programs, models, and philosophy, all of which introduced in the 1950s when exchange programs implemented them as part of the Marshall Program for post-WWII development. Started in the 1950's Turkish counselling has been influenced by movements and advances in United States counselling. Doğan (2000) divided the history of counselling in Turkey into five periods:

(1) taking initial steps (1950–1956);
(2) formative years (1957–1969);
(3) establishing counselling services in schools (1970–1981);
(4) establishing undergraduate programs in counselling (1982–1995); and
(5) assigning counsellors to schools
(1996–present) [Owen/Güneri 2015].

In Turkey, guidance services are carried out in various contexts by the Ministry of National Education (MONE). Turkish Employment Agency (İŞKUR) is an affiliated institution of the Ministry of Family, Labour and Social Services (MFLSS), universities, private sector, trade unions, and employer associations. MONE and İŞKUR provide most of the current services.

To become a guidance practitioner, one should have a bachelor's degree in psychological guidance and counselling. Students enter these programmes on entry to the university. Besides, to be a job and vocational counsellor, one should have a bachelor's degree diploma and vocational qualification certificate.

Current Regulatory Status/Level of Recognition
There are some guidelines for the services in guidance and counselling. The Turkish Association for Psychological Counselling and Guidance has published these guidelines. For the time being, there is no national ethical guideline in Turkey.

Challenges and Trends
Counselling is still vague and confused with other disciplines such as psychology, social work, and even psychiatry. Although the history of counselling in Turkey is long enough to have established a tradition, it lacks textbooks and sufficient literature to use in both undergraduate and graduate programs. There is still much dependence upon American literature and research in this field. "Counsellor" is an occupational title that is new and sometimes confusing to those who do not know or agree that counselling is a necessary "third force" in school, after the administration and teachers. There are no formally recognized certification requirements as a professional counsellor; neither are there procedures for official accreditation of undergraduate and graduate training programs in counselling [Dogan 2000].

A few books are written locally about school counselling in Turkey. In other words, there is a severe lack of indigenous textbooks and literature 206 Counsellor Education in Turkey for undergraduate and graduate counselling education programs. The counselling field still depends heavily on American literature and research findings. The absence of indigenous literature has reduced the quality of the education programs. Moreover, there is a lack of standardized counselling tools, such as interest, aptitude, intelligence, and personality tests. Organized occupational information is also unavailable. These hindered the work of counsellors and decreased the quality of counselling [Yüksel 2003].

The most significant trend in the counselling field is career guidance. Most counsellors in Turkey work in schools and universities to empower the students.

The concrete results of 50 years of counselling developments establish guidance and research centres in each province. The establishment of counselling services in some elementary and secondary schools, undergraduate and graduate counsellors' education programs in universities, "guidance" as an elective course included in the teaching knowledge certification program.

Some in-service counselling training programs arranged by the Ministry of National Education establish counselling units as divisions of the medical-social, health, culture and sport activities departments in universities.

The association publishes the Psychological counselling and Guidance Association, the national psychological and guidance congresses held by the association every two years, the Journal of Psychological Counselling and Guidance, ethical standards, and some tests, textbooks in counselling [Dogan 2000].

Additional Information

- Dogan, S. (2000). The historical development of Counselling in Turkey. International Journal for the Advancement of Counselling, 22(1), 57–67.
- Euroguidance (2020). National Guidance System. Guidance System in Turkey. Online: https://www.euroguidance.eu/guidance-system-in-turkey
- Owen, F. K. & Güneri, O. Y. (2015). Counselling in Turkey. Counselling around the world: An international handbook, 293–302.
- Yüksel, G. (2003). The development of counsellor education in Turkey: Current status and future challenges. Asian Journal of Counselling, 10(2), 193–214.

39. Ukraine

Brief history/background of Counselling

There has been done a considerable amount of work in Ukraine in recent years to introduce a system of alternatives. The initial programme of work initiated by the Ukraine Social Investment Fund in the early part of the decade was followed by a range of recent very positive reforms which have taken place since the Orange Revolution.

Much of the recent policy reform has focused on providing family type placements and establishing a social services system for children and families.

However, the training established incorrectly across the system of state social services. As a result, there is a wide variation in counsellors' skills and capacity across the country (cf. Lushyn, 2020).

Counselling is often combined with psychotherapy and is part of Ukraine's health care facilities. Counselling on its own is mainly given in career counselling or in family centres, which provide a range of services to support vulnerable families.

Practical psychology and counselling, in particular, started to develop after the breakdown of the USSR. In 1991 the first school psychology service was founded all over Ukraine.

Many of the universities opened counsellor's preparation courses. By the end of 1990, there were 24000 practical school psychologists, although a third of them having counselling competence but still very little practice. Following the Russian War, many were re-educated and started a military career or cooperation with the military.

Since the country has gone through multiple critical situations like the fall of the USSR, Chernobyl catastrophe, Afghan War, etc., counselling was centred on the issues of transition to new personal and communal identities. Facilitation modalities are gaining popularity. "New norm" elaboration and assistance are a trend (cf. Luyshyn, 2020).

Current Regulatory Status/ Level of Recognition

The government does not regulate counselling. It is a new field in Ukraine, and the standards are not very clear. Counsellors must not have diplomas or a certain degree to call themselves a counsellor. Only if you perform psychological counselling, you must have a degree (cf. Lushyn, 2020).

Challenges and Trends

Unfortunately, in Ukraine, the idea of a counselling service is relatively novel, and hence it is still at an early stage that requires development and improvement. A significant break of the counselling service development is that it uses primarily verbal, declarative methods, without providing any possibility to try themselves in various activities.

Many cities and regions are not provided with current staffing requirements; the career's counselling services are poorly qualified specialists. Career guidance services need to be professionalised, and their identity strengthened as they currently tend to be marginalised in favour of personal counselling (cf. Pilgui & Gaj, 2016, p. 83f.)

One of the biggest trends in counselling is the career and counselling services in Ukrainian schools. In a situation where there are options for someone to choose, one is likely to face the problem of choice. This has been a severe problem for most people found in secondary schools between 10 and 17.

Henceforth this period will be dubbed 'adolescence'. Due to this period's demanding nature in people's lives, many ends up being unable to make the appropriate choices. The resulting emotional and vocational misalignment causes several problems, including dissatisfaction in work, frustration, conflicts, and life failure. To prevent people from suffering caused by these problems, counselling is a widely spread service in Ukrainian schools (cf. Pilgu & Gaj, 2016).

Counselling in Ukraine denotes a more therapeutic and personalized intervention when therapy and counselling are separated from many other countries. In Ukraine, the term more commonly used is guidance, assisting humans in critical life courses.

Counselling contains different aspects, such as psychological, educational and medical aspects. The psychological and educational part helps clients realise themselves as active participants in social and cultural activities when the medical factor determines the physical fitness of a client.

Another trend nowadays is positive psychology (Lushyn, 2020), the scientific study of what goes right in life, from birth to death and stops in between. It is a newly-christened approach within psychology that takes seriously as a subject matter those things that make life most worth living. Everyone's life has peaks and valleys, and positive psychology does not deny the valleys. It assumes that life entails more than we are not frittering life away (Peterson, 2006, p. 3ff)

References

Ægisdóttir, S., Leach, M., Romano, J. Tomlinson-Clarke, S. & Canel-Çınarbaş, D.(2019). Sociopolitical, Cultural, and Historical Contexts That Influence Counselling Practice in Four Countries. The Counselling Psychologist, 47(4), 578–607.

Association Luxembourgeoise de Étudiants en Psychologie (2020). Abgerufen von https://alep.lu/student-area/qa-psychotherapie-zu-letzebuerg/qa-psycho therapie-zu-letzebuerg-de/ [aufgerufen am 05.09.20].

"AYG" Centre for Psychological Services (2020): Services. https://hogeban.am/our-services/ [07.09.2020].

BACP (2020). Government update on statutory regulation of counsellors and psychotherapists. Von BACP: https://www.bacp.co.uk/news/news-from-bacp/2020/6-march-government-update-on-statutory-regulation-of-counsellors-and-psychotherapists/ [abgerufen am 16.07.2020].

Berufsverband der Psychologinnen und Psychologen Liechtensteins (2020). Psychologie als Beruf. Abgerufen von https://www.bpl.li/psychologie-als-beruf [aufgerufen am 03.09.20].

Berufsverband Österreichischer PsychologInnen (2020) Geschichte des Berufsverbandes. Abgerufen von: https://www.boep.or.at/berufsverband/ueber-den-boep/geschichte [abgerufen am 09.10.2020].

Bundesgesetzblatt (1998).260. Verordnung: Standes- und Ausübungsregeln für das Gewerbe der Lebens- und Sozialberatung. Abgerufen von: https://www.ris.bka.gv.at/Dokumente/BgblPdf/1998_260_2/1998_260_2.pdf [abgerufen am 09.10.2020].

Bundesgesetzblatt (2003). 140. Verordnung: Lebens-und Sozialberatungs-Verordnung. Abgerufen von: https://www.ris.bka.gv.at/Dokumente/BgblPdf/2003_140_2/2003_140_2.pdf [abgerufen am 09.10.2020].

Cerniţanu, M. (2017): Serviciul de consiliere psihologică și ghidare în carieră din cadrul instituțiilor de învățământ superior din Moldova. Sănătate Publică, Economie şi Management în Medicină, 74(4), 26–30. https://ibn.idsi.md/sites/default/files/imag_file/26-30_1.pdf [07/09/2020].

Christodoulidi, F. & Malikiosi-Loizos, M. (2019). Exploring the perceptions of Greek counsellors' and Counselling psychologists' professional identity and training experience, through the lens of the first alumni graduates of a Greek state University. European Journal of Psychotherapy & Counselling, 1–17.

Chistruga-Sinchevici, I. (2013): Politicile familiale din Republica Moldova în context european. In Creşterea economică în condiţiile globalizării (pp. 214–221).

Dixon, A. L. & Hansen, N. H. (2010). Fortid, Nutid, Fremtid (Past, Present, Future): Professional Counselling in Denmark. Journal of Counselling & Development, 38–42.

Cohen, M. L. (2002) Zur Situation systemischer Therapie in Europa. Zeitschrift für Systemische Therapie, 20 (2), 88–100.

Cohen-Scali, V.; Guichard, J. & Gaudron J. (2009) Career Counselling in France: A Growing Practice Among Diverse Professional Groups. In: L. H. Gerstein, P.P. Heppner, S. Ægisdóttir, S-M. A. Leung, K. L. Norsworthy (Hrsg.) International Handbook of Cross-Cultural Counselling –Cultural Assumptions and Practices Worldwide. (S. 329–336) Los Angeles: Sage Publications.

Dogan, S. (2000): The historical development of Counselling in Turkey. International Journal for the Advancement of Counselling, 22(1), 57–67.

Domoratsky, V.A. (2017). Teaching short-term methods of psychotherapy in a practice-oriented master's program "Psychological Counselling and psychocorrection".

EACEA National Policies Platform (2018). Career Counselling and Counselling. Von EACEA National Policies Platform: https://eacea.ec.europa.eu/national-policies/en/content/youthwiki/34-career-Counselling-and-Counselling-iceland [abgerufen am 01.09.2020].

EACEA National Policies Platform (2020). Career Counselling and Counselling. Von EACEA National Policies Platform: https://eacea.ec.europa.eu/national-policies/en/content/youthwiki/34-career-Counselling-and-Counselling-lithuania [abgerufen am 17.07.2020].

EAP European Association of Psychotherapy –Netherland (2020). Abgerufen von https://www.europsyche.org/situation-of-psychotherapy-in-various-countries/netherlands/ [aufgerufen am 17.08.20]

Erb, A. (2005). Zur Geschichte der Psychologie in und zwischen Spanien und Deutschland vom ausgehenden 19. Jahrhundert bis zur Mitte des 20. Jahrhunderts: Aspekte der deutsch-spanischen Wissenschaftsbeziehungen. Abgerufen von: https://refubium.fu-berlin.de/handle/fub188/12896 [abgerufen am 09.10.2020].

EuroCounselling.eu (2020). Counselling System in Iceland. Von EuroCounselling.eu: https://www.euroCounselling.eu/Counselling-system-in iceland#:~:text=Counselling%20practitioners%20must%20have%20a,university%20in%20Iceland%20or%20abroad. [abgerufen am 01.09.2020].

Finnish National Agency for Education(2020a): Counselling and Counselling in basic education. https://www.oph.fi/en/education-and-qualifications/Counselling-and-Counselling-basic-education [03.09.2020].

Finnish National Agency for Education(2020b): Information, Counselling and Counselling services. https://www.oph.fi/en/services/information-Counselling-and-Counselling-services [03.09.2020].

Flynn, J. (2019). Minister for Health appoints Counsellors & Psychotherapists Board. Von Association of Professional Counsellors & Psychotherapists in Ireland: https://www.apcp.ie/latest-news-3/ [abgerufen am 01.09.2020].

Galea, C. (2020) Antworten zu Malta aus dem Online-Fragebogen.

Government of Ireland (2019). Proposed regulation of Counsellors and Psychotherapists under the Health and Social Care Professionals Act 2005. Von gov.ie: https://www.gov.ie/en/news/06a369-proposed-regulation-of-counsellors-and-psychotherapists-under-the-he/ [abgerufen am 28.08.2020].

Gröning, K. (2010). Geschichte der Beratung. In: Giesecke, W., Nittel, D., (Hrsg.), Pädagogische Beratung über die Lebensspanne–Handbuch, S. 42–49.
Gugitscher, K. (2016). Bildungs- und Berufsberatung in Österreich historisch betrachtet. Vom Fürsorgewesen über individualisierte Bildungsberatung zur lebensbegleitenden Beratung und Kompetenzvermittlung. Magazin erwachsenenbildung.at, 29, 1–14.
Hofer, G. (2010). Bildungsberatung in der Arbeiterkammer Oberösterreich. AK-Angebote und Entwicklungsaspekte für die Beratung in Österreich. Magazin erwachsenenbildung.at, 9, 1–6.
Hutschemaekers, G. J. M., & Van Dijk, F. E. (2013). Psychotherapy and clinicalpsychology in the Netherlands. In: Moodley, R., Gielen, U. P., & Wu, R. (Eds.). Handbook of Counselling and psychotherapy in an international context, S. 315–325.
Iarussi, M. (2020): Integrating Motivational Interviewing and Cognitive Behavior Therapy in Clinical Practice. New York: Routledge.
International University of Sarajevo (2020). Psychology. Abgerufen von: https://psy.ius.edu.ba/ [abgerufen am 09.10.2020].
Joseph, S., Murphy, D.& Holford, J. (2018). Counselling training in higher education in the United Kingdom: Challenges and opportunities for research. Counselling psychotherapy research journal,387–394.
Karimova, M. (2020): Antworten des Onlinefragebogens. Aserbaidschan.
Kastepõld-Tõrs, K. (2020). Antworten zu Estland aus dem Online-Fragebogen.
Kaur, S.(2020). Antworten zum Vereinigten Königreich aus dem Online-Fragebogen.
Kucher, A./ Furdui, E. (n. y.): Some Views on the Necessity of Psychological Care for Children with development problems in the republic of Moldova. https://virtkafedra.ucoz.ua/el_gurnal/pages/vyp7/konf3/KucherP_Furduj.pdf [07/09/2020].
Lehtonen, K. Z. (2020) Antworten zu Malta aus dem Online Fragebogen Legislation.
Lietuvos nacionalinis radijas ir televizija (2020). Lithuania to hire 200 psychologists to tackle Covid-19 effects on mental health. Von Lietuvos nacionalinis radijas ir televizija: https://www.lrt.lt/en/news-in-english/19/1179781/lithuania-to-hire-200-psychologists-to-tackle-covid-19-effects-on-mental-health [abgerufen am 17.10.2020].
Lushyn, P. (2020): Antworten des Onlinefragebogens. Ukraine.
Malta–Counselling Profession Act (2020) Abgerufen von: https://legislation.mt/eli/cap/538/eng/pdf [abgerufen am 14.10.2020].
Malikiosi-Loizos, M., Giovazolias, T. (2013). Counselling in Greece. In: Hohenshil, T. H., Amundson, N. E., & Niles, S. G. (Hrsg.) Counselling around the world. An International Handbook. VA: American Counselling Association.
Malikiosi-Loizos, M., Ivey, A. E. (2012). Counselling in Greece. Journal of Counselling & Development,90(1), 113–118.

Marín-Martín, C. & Prieto, J. M. (2015) Counselling and Psychotherapy in Spain: Andres's Story. In: R. Moodley; M. Lengyell; R. Wu & U. P. Gielen. International Counselling. Case Studies Handbook. (S. 211–218) Alexandria: American Counselling Association.

Ministry of Education and Culture (2012): Counselling. Lifelong Counselling in Finland.Lönnberg Print &Promo. https://cica.org.au/wp-content/uploads/25493_Lifelong_Counselling_in_Finland.pdf [03.09.2020].

Ministry of Justice of the Republic of Azerbaijan (2020): About psychological help. http://www.e-qanun.az/framework/41280 [04.09.2020].

Motschnig, R. /Nykl, L. (2014): Person-Centred Communication: Theory, Skills and Practice. Maidenhead: McGraw-Hill Education.

Nilsson, J. E. & Lindgren, T. (2009). Applied Psychology in Sweden: A Brief Report on Its Role, Ambitions, and Limitations In: L. H. Gerstein, P. P. Heppner, S. Ægisdóttir, S-M. A. Leung, K. L. Norsworthy (Hrsg.) International Handbook of Cross-Cultural Counselling –Cultural Assumptions and Practices Worldwide. (S.321–328) Los Angeles: Sage Publications.

Olifirovich, N. I., & Kopteva, S. I. (2008): Counselling psychology in Belarus: problems and development prospects. Psychol. zhurn, (4), 97–101. https://core.ac.uk/reader/74331194 [04.07.2020].

O'Morain, P., McAuliffe, G. J., Conroy, K., Johnson, J. M.& Michel, R. E. (2012). Counselling in Ireland. Von padraigomorain.com: https://www.padraigomorain.com/history-of-Counselling-in-ireland/ [abgerufen am 25.08.2020].

Peterson, C. (2006): A primer in positive psychology. Oxford university press.

Pietikainen, P.& Kragh, J. V. (2019). Professionalization of Psychology in the Nordic Countries. Oxford Research Encyclopedia of Psychology. Oxford University Press. Abgerufen von: https://oxfordre.com/psychology/view/10.1093/acrefore/9780190236557.001.0001/acrefore-9780190236557-e-597 [abgerufen am 09.10.2020].

Pilgui, N., & Gaj, A. (2016): Career's and Counselling services in Ukraine schools. http://repository.kpi.kharkov.ua/bitstream/KhPI-Press/25589/1/Elita_2016_45_2_Pilgui_Career%60s.pdf [14.07.2020].

Pouyaud, J. & Guichard, J. (2013) France. In: T. H. Hohenshil, N. E. Amundson, S. G. Niles (Hrsg.) Counselling around the world. An international Handbook (S.193–202). Alexandria: American Counselling Association.

PsychOpen (2020). Clinical Psychology in Lithuania: Current Developments in Training and Legislation. Von PsychOpen: https://cpe.psychopen.eu/index.php/cpe/article/view/2835/2835.html [abgerufen am 17.10.2020].

Rigas Stadina Universitate (2020). A psychotherapist, a psychiatrist and a psychologist: Von Vilnius zur Kurischen Nehrung. Von Rigas Stadina Universitate: http://psihosomatika.lv/differences [abgerufen am 17.10.2020].

Rønnestad, M. H. (o. D.) The Psychotherapeutic Professions in Norway. Abgerufen von: http://citeseerx.ist.psu.edu/viewdoc/download?doi=10.1.1.499.5013& rep=rep1&type=pdf [abgerufen am 09.10.2020].

Russian Association for Psychological Counselling (2020): There are several approaches to defining and structuring the space of psychological Counselling. http://oapk.org/articles/122-modeli-struktury-psikhologicheskogo-konsultirovaniya [21.07.2020].
Scacchi, J. (2004). Bosnien-Herzegowina. Behandlungsmöglichkeiten für schwer traumatisierte Personen. Abgerufen von: https://www.ecoi.net/en/file/local/1196034/1006_1187252082_bosnien-behandlung-bei-traumatisierung.pdf [abgerufen am 09.10.2020].
Schubert, F. C., Rohr, D., & Zwicker-Pelzer, R. (2019). Beratung: Grundlagen – Konzepte –Anwendungsfelder. Springer: Wiesbaden.
Simons, J. D. & Durcikova, A. (2013). The Czech Republic. In Thomas H. Hohenshil, NormanAmundson, & Spencer G. Niles (Hrsg.) Counselling around the world: an international handbook (S. 163–172). Alexandria: American Counselling Association.
Simons, J. D., Hutchison, B. & Baštecká, Z. (2012). Counselling in the Czech Republic: History, Status, and Future. Journal of Counselling & Development,90 (2), 233–237.
Sonnenmoser, M. (2011) Psychotherapie in Europa –Frankreich: Hochburg der Psychoanalyse. Deutsches Ärzteblatt PP.
Sonnenmoser, M. (2011). Psychotherapie in Europa –Schweden: Psychotherapie wird kaum genutzt. Deutsches Ärzteblatt PP.
Strasser, J. (2013). Counselling in Germany. In: Hohenshil, T. H., Amundson, N. E. & Niles, S. G. (Hrsg.). Counselling around the world: An international handbook, S. 203–213. Alexandria, VA: AmericanCounsellingAssociation.
Thomas, R., Henning, S. (2013). Counselling in Switzerland. In: Hohenshil, T. H., Amundson, N. E., & Niles, S. G. (Hrsg.). Counselling around the world: An international handbook, S. 203-213. Alexandria, VA: American Counselling Association.
Toni, A/ Vuorinen, R.(2020): LIFELONG COUNSELLING IN FINLAND. Key Policies and Practices. https://brill.com/view/book/edcoll/9789004428096/BP000017.xml [03.09.2020].
University of Malta; Master in Counselling (2020) Abgerufen von: https://www.um.edu.mt/courses/overview/PMCOUPET0-2020-1-O [abgerufen am 14.10.2020]
Van Broeck, N. & Lietaer, G. (2008). Psychology and Psychotherapy in Health Care: A Review of Legal Regulations in 17 European Countries. European Psychologist, Vol.13 (1), S.53–63
Van Broeck, N., Stinckens, N. & Lietaer, G. (2013). Counselling and Psychotherapy in Belgium. In: Moodley, R., Gielen, U. P., & Wu, R. (Eds.). Handbook of Counselling and psychotherapy in an international context, S. 261–270. Routledge.
Vinogradova E. L. (2010): Coaching and Psychotherapy: Possibilities of Intersection of Practices – Counselling Psychology and Psychotherapy. https://psyjournals.ru/files/27896/mpj_2010_n1_Vinogradova.pdf [21.07.2020]

Weltgesundheitsorganisation (2020) Abgerufen von: https://www.euro.who.int/de/media-centre/sections/press-releases/2014/eight-small-countries-in-europe-join-forces-to-improve-health [abgerufen am 14.10.2020]
Zammit Genovese, M. (2020). Antworten zu Malta aus dem Online-Fragebogen.
Zammit, J. (2020). Antworten zu Malta aus dem Online-Fragebogen.
Zapolsky, N. (2020). A Meta-Synthesis of the American and the European Standards for the Accreditation of Counselling Training Programs.Chicago: Digital Commons@NLU.
Zorgwijzer – Overige vergoedingsvoorwaarden (2020). Abgerufen von https://www.zorgwijzer.nl/vergoeding/psychologie [aufgerufen am 18.08.20]

5 Europeanwide Associations

Within the Mapping Research Group at the University of Cologne we built a subgroup concerning the research of European-wide Associations. During the process, we quickly realised that some of the Associations differ between counselling and psychotherapy, and others do not. This is related to 'culture' – similar to the countries (see chapter 4).

5.1 Counselling and psychotherapy

When discussing counselling and psychotherapy in a context, it is essential to delimit them and point out existing similarities and differences. The discussion about the two disciplines' delimitation has taken up a great deal of space for many years and has not yet been concluded (cf. Nestmann, Engel & Sickendiek, 2004, p. 33). In the world's countries, there are different views on the interplay of the two fields.

Overall, there are three developmental strands of counselling that are still relevant in society today. Psychotherapeutic improvement of counselling, permits a psychotherapeutic basis through an aggregate of medical, psychological and philosophical ideas (cf. Schubert, Rohr & Zwicker-Pelzer, 2019, p. 3). In the eighteenth and twentieth centuries, the social change ended in a psychological-pedagogical strand of development. It is characterised by the fact that counselling wasn't provided by the family or neighbourhood but by state institutionalised institutions. Increasing demand for counselling centres developed mainly after the two world wars, when many people had to find a new way in life (cf. ibid., p. 5 ff.). Different educational development strands of counselling emerged with time, such as academic, sexual and vocational counselling (cf. Gröning, 2015, p. 19).

Also, there is the developmental strand of systemic counselling, which evolved in the 20th century from the ideas of various protagonists of psychotherapy in different places at the same time (cf. Schwing, 2016, p. 15). More and more psychotherapists began to see crises no longer as personal problems of the individual but to expand the context and include the families' perspective in their work. Leading to the development of family therapy, from which systemic therapy emerged a few years later. The family is a subsystem, and this and other subsystems are the basis for the individual construction of reality. One can speak of systemic counselling when this approach is not applied in a psychotherapeutic framework (cf. Von Schlippe & Schweitzer, 2007, p. 17).

To distinguish the two disciplines from each other, they can be differentiated as follows. Psychotherapy is described as a "healing discourse" given a clearly defined framework by the psychotherapists Act. By determining a diagnosis, various indicators, concrete procedures and a relationship between doctor and patient, treatment-oriented towards disorders with a definable disease value. On the other hand, counselling can be an "open, integrative discourse of help" in which lifeworld-oriented support given in decision-making and coping issues (cf. Nestmann, Engel & Sickendiek, 2004, p. 36 ff.). Psychology can be seen as the basis of counselling because it provides many essential models and research results fundamental for the counselling activity. Thus counselling and psychotherapy are strongly interrelated with smooth transitions from one to the other (cf. Dietrich, 1983, p. 12).

To provide an even deeper insight into counselling, unique forms of counselling are presented below.

Coaching

There is modern coaching, whose origins traced back to a USA's sports coaches activities. In the 1980s, the trend found its way to Europe and was initially applied here at the management level of companies (cf. Schubert, Rohr & Zwickler-Pelzer, 2019, p. 236 f.). The German Federal Association Coaching e.v. (2019, p. 18) defines coaching as "the professional counselling, guidance and support of persons with management and control functions and of experts in companies or organisations as well as of freelancers. In both individual and multi-person coaching, the organisational context is always taken into account. Although coaching involves many psychological concepts, the two professions can be distinguished from each other. Coaching serves as an offer for psychologically healthy people who want to deal with conflicts in their professional life. Psychotherapy on the other hand, is an offer for mentally ill people who may only be cared for by trained psychotherapists. (cf. Thomas, 2020, p. 6)

To distinguish coaching from general counselling, however, it is useful to look at the sub-areas' target group. For example, counselling is aimed at an inclusive target group and coaching primarily at specialists and managers from the business context (cf. ibid., p. 7).

Supervision

Another form of counselling is supervision. The German Society for Supervision describes it as the "scientifically based, practice-oriented and ethically bound concept for the person- and Organisation-related counselling in the world of work" (Deutsche Gesellschaft für Supervision und Coaching, 2020). Supervision is thus aimed at many different professions to reflect on and optimise work results and organisational networks jointly. Depending on the occasion and the target group, there are other forms, such as individual supervision, group supervision and team supervision (cf. Sporré, 2020, p. 1 ff.). Some use the term supervision and coaching as synonyms (cf. ibid., p. 6), while others differentiate the terms. Here, the term coaching is mainly tied to a business context. On the other hand, they are using supervision in many areas, such as psychosocial and health care.

5.2 Our Research

The aim of our research is to identify the existing associations of psychotherapy and counselling in the European area and collect specific data.

Data analysis

In the context of this research, we used a hybrid model. Thus, the basis of the data collection is the quantitative content analysis with SPSS. To make the answers comparable via SPSS, they are analysed qualitatively and coded into variables to guarantee a numerical representation of the solutions, we carried out extensive online and literature research. To supplement the missing data

Target group

It was essential to identify and contact European counselling associations by email. Professional associations that are represented in various European countries and are specialised in the profession. The list of the European Wide Accrediting Organisations (European Association for Psychotherapy, 2020) and in-depth online research served as a basis. We found twenty-nine different associations through this research, a selection is presented in chapter 6.3.

Data collection

The chosen data collection method is the fully structured and standardised survey based on an online questionnaire via LimeSurvey. This is a method in which targeted, systematic verbal and numerical self-reports are collected from respondents. The advantage of the online questionnaire is, on the one hand, the comparability of the data. On the other hand, the temporal and spatial independence the limitation of interviewer effects and the effects of social desirability (cf. Wagner-Schelewsky & Hering, 2019, p. 787).

Analysis procedure

The data collected via the online questionnaire is analysed using various analytical procedures. In this study, we used the statistical programme SPSS. This programme makes it possible to calculate multiple statistical values, such as absolute and relative frequencies and position measures, from a data set. (cf. Tachtsoglou & König, 2017, p. 78)

Furthermore, three selected open questions are analysed qualitatively according to Mayring. Here, the relevant information is summarised and divided into inductive categories by abstracting the content step by step (cf. Mayring, 2015, p. 69). First, we paraphrased the sentences to be analysed, then generalised, and finally reduced. The reduced contents are coded into numerical variables in SPSS to make them comparable with each other.

After presenting methodological principles, the following chapter presents some of the study's results. Here, the information from the quantitative and qualitative analysis and the internet and literature research is presented in summary form.

5.3 Presentation of selected associations

In this book we present only a selection of our results. The list of all different European associations of psychotherapy and counselling will be published at the EAC website (https://eac.eu.com). First, the associations and the associated therapeutic approach of the respective association are shown. Then the organisational structures and working methods are offered to make the individual associations comparable with each other.

The associations are presented based on the literature research and the quantitative and qualitative analysis procedures. These are shown in the following section sorted by categories of counselling and psychotherapy.

5.3.1 Association of National Organisations for Supervision in Europe (ANSE)

1. Contact information

President	Agnes Turner	ANSE®
Email	office@anse.eu	
Website	http://www.anse.eu	

2. Presentation of the form of therapy and Counselling

The Association of National Organisations for Supervision in Europe (ANSE) is a European umbrella organisation for supervision. As described in 2.2.2, supervision is a form of counselling in which the work process is reflected on. This is used in various fields, such as psychosocial and health care (cf. Sporré, 2020, p. 1 ff.).

3. Objective

The association aims to promote professional information exchange, disseminate high-quality supervision and coaching, and further develop research and teaching of leadership (cf. Association of National Organisations for Supervision in Europe, 2019a).

4. Membership

ANSE offers four different types of membership. First, full membership for national associations of supervision that meet the standards of ANSE. Secondly, associate membership for associations that aspire to work together but do not meet the necessary criteria. The third option is the supporting membership for individuals who wish to support ANSE financially. As a final membership type, ANSE offers honorary membership for all those individuals who have made an extraordinary contribution to the advancement of supervision or coaching. An association must first submit an application to obtain membership, which the association's board must approve (cf. Association of National Organisations for Supervision in Europe, 2019a).

5. Funding

As a non-profit association, ANSE is financed by membership fees, donations and subsidies (cf. Association of National Organisations for Supervision in Europe, 2019a).

6. Publication

Since 2017, the association has published an online newsletter called The Journal at least twice a year. Current topics in supervision and coaching are made available here, thus promoting professional dialogue (cf. Association of National Organisations for Supervision in Europe, 2019b).

7. Conferences and congresses

ANSE organises a General Assembly at least every two years, at which all members can participate. Associations with full or associate membership can provide two representatives per meeting (cf. Association of National Organisations for Supervision in Europe, 2019a).

8. Differentiation of Counselling and psychotherapy

The association has not released a statement in this context.

5.3.2 European Association for Supervision and Coaching (EASC)

1. Contact information

President	Susanne Rieger	EASC European Association for Supervision and Coaching
Email	Office@easc.onlie.eu	
Website	https://www.easc-online.eu	

2. Presentation of the form of therapy and Counselling

The European Association for Supervision and Coaching (EASC) is a European association for supervision and coaching. As described in 2.2.1 and 2.2.2, supervision is a person- and work-related counselling to reflect on specific work processes. Coaching is mainly counselling for leaders and managers.

3. Objective

The association aims to build a European network and offer training with high quality standards (cf. Rieger, 2020).

4. Membership

EASC is active throughout Europe and has about 700 members from twelve European countries. A coach/supervisor must have completed training that meets the quality standards (cf. Rieger, 2020).

5. Funding

The association is financed by membership fees (cf. Rieger, 2020).

6. Publication

EASC does not issue any publications (cf. Rieger, 2020).

7. Conferences and congresses

The association currently organises monthly virtual meetings for members and interested professionals. Also, meetings are held annually in different locations in Europe (cf. Rieger, 2020).

8. Differentiation of Counselling and psychotherapy

EASC distinguishes between coaching, supervision, mentoring supervision and training (cf. Rieger, 2020).

5.3.3 Marte Meo

1. Contact information

President	Maria Aarts	marte-meo® international
Email	aartsmaria@martemeo.com	
Website	www.martemeo.com	

2. Presentation of the form of therapy and Counselling

Furthermore, there is the Marte Meo method. In this counselling method, they are using video material to promote the development of the client. Thus, the target group receives care, for example, infants, children with and without disabilities, and adults with disabilities. On the other hand, there is the complementary target group of parents, educators, teachers and many more (cf. Bünder et al., 2013, p. 17). Interestingly, this method is based on different ways, such as developmental psychology, learning theories, and systems theory (cf. ibid., p. 25 f.).

3. Objective

The association pursues the fundamental goal of training professionals and providing them with information on an ongoing basis. Here, constructive interaction is to be promoted by activating and developing skills. Furthermore, it is essential to learn to use one's strengths and to integrate them into the counselling process. This should improve people's everyday lives and quality of life (cf. Aarts, 2020).

4. Membership

Marte Meo International is internationally active and has about 70,000 members in 53 countries. To become a member of this association, the person must complete a Marte Meo training (cf. Aarts, 2020).

5. Funding

The association finances itself through training courses, supervision offers, presentations, books and other publications (cf. Aarts, 2020).

6. Publication

Marte Meo International regularly publishes books on the Marte Meo method (cf. Aarts, 2020).

7. Conferences and congresses

The association regularly organises events to which members and interested professionals from other organisations are invited. The target groups include early childhood associations, child mental health associations and child and youth protection associations (cf. Aarts, 2020).

8. Differentiation of Counselling and psychotherapy

The association differentiates between counselling and psychotherapy (cf. Aarts, 2020).

5.3.4 European Network for Person-Centred and Experiential Psychotherapy and Counselling (PCE Europe)

1. Contact information

President	Leonore Langner
E-mail	info@pce-europe.org, chair@ pe-europe.org
Website	http://www.pce-europe.org

2. Presentation of the form of therapy and Counselling

The European Network for Person-Centred and Experiential Psychotherapy and Counselling (PCE Europe) is an association focusing on person-centred and experiential psychotherapy and counselling. According to Carl Rogers, person-centred therapy focuses on interpersonal relationships and human lifeworlds. In the course of treatment, the therapist should help the client to develop their self-awareness. Important components here are the basic attitudes of therapists and methods that promote experience, which should enable clients to achieve greater self-acceptance and flexibility in their behaviour (cf. Kriz, 2014, p. 207 f.). PCE Europe is member of EAC.

3. Objective

The association aims to promote personal development and the humanisation of interpersonal and social relationships. To achieve this, the association wants to spread the person-centred and experiential approaches in individual, social and cultural life and strengthen the fields of counselling and psychotherapy (cf. Langner, 2020).

4. Membership

PCE-Europe is active in 16 European countries and has 30 member organisations, with up to a thousand individual members. To be accepted as a PCE-Europe member, an application must be completed via the website. This should prove that the applying organisation supports the principles of person-centred and experience-based approaches. So far, individual membership is not possible, but this is still being considered (cf. Langner, 2020).

5. Funding

Membership fees and small revenues finance the association from issuing the PCE-Europe certificates (cf. Langner, 2020).

6. Publication

PCE-Europe does not publish any publications or newsletters (cf. Langner, 2020).

7. Conferences and congresses

The association organises a symposium twice a year where members and experts meet. A general assembly is also held twice a year, where the supervisors of the member associations meet. Also, a regulars' table is prepared four times a year, which serves the exchange between colleagues. The symposium and general assembly used to occur in alternating locations in Europe, but now all forms of meetings occur via Zoom (cf. Langner, 2020).

8. Differentiation of Counselling and psychotherapy

The association does not differentiate between counselling and psychotherapy and thinks that the difference has narrowed in recent years (cf. Langner, 2020).

5.3.5 European Association for Gestalt Therapy (EAGT)

1. Contact information

President	Beatrix Wimmer
Email	info@eagt.org
Website	https://www.eagt.org/joomla/index.php

2. Presentation of the form of therapy and Counselling

According to Fritz and Laura Perls, the European Association for Gestalt Therapy (EAGT) is a European association for Gestalt therapy. This approach functions primarily as a way of life, with attention and engagement with the living world. New experiences, among other things, must be made by trying out behaviour and movements. To achieve a holistic gestalt, attention must be drawn to as many areas as possible (cf. Kriz, 2014, p. 218 f.).

3. Objective

The association aims to connect different associations of Gestalt therapy and professional individuals. Also, the scientific exchange of Gestalt therapy and the dissemination of approaches and standards are to be promoted. Through the association, public relations work, health, and professional initiatives are to be supported, and cooperation with other institutions made possible (cf. European Association for Gestalt Therapy, o. J. a).

4. Membership

EAGT distinguishes between six different types of membership. First, full membership for professional European associations and institutes of Gestalt therapy and trained individuals. Second, partner membership for individuals in training or already retired and organisations that do not yet meet the standards of EAGT. Third subscriber membership for individuals or organisations who wish to support EAGT financially. Fourth, Cooperative Membership for associations that want to network with EAGT. Fifth, honorary membership for distinguished individuals or associations and lastly, joint membership for distinguished National Organisations for Gestalt Therapy (NOGT). To obtain one of the above memberships, an application must be submitted to the Executive Committee (cf. European Association for Gestalt Therapy, o.J.a).

5. Funding

EAGT is a non-profit organisation financed by membership fees (cf. European Association for Gestalt Therapy, o.J.a).

6. Publication

The association publishes a newsletter twice a year in which the topics discussed by the various committees are presented (cf. European Association for Gestalt Therapy, o.J.b).

7. Conferences and congresses

EAGT has so far organised five congresses at which the new research aspects of Gestalt therapy are discussed and exchange between therapists is made possible (cf. European Association for Gestalt Therapy, o. J. a).

8. Differentiation of Counselling and psychotherapy

The federation has not released a statement in this context.

5.3.6 European Association for Transactional Analysis (EATA)

1. Contact information

President	Peter Rudolph
Email	office@eatanews.org; president@eatanews.org
Website	https: / / eatanews.org

2. Presentation of the form of therapy and Counselling

According to Eric Berne, the European Association for Transactional Analysis (EATA) is a European association for transactional analysis. This approach is used to maximise the perception of interpersonal action. Various therapeutic interventions are used here, such as structural, play or script analysis, in which different ego states are examined (cf. Kriz, 2014, p. 108 f.).

3. Objective

The association pursues three main goals. The first objective is to promote knowledge and research on transactional analysis issues. Furthermore, EATA wants to support Europe-wide cooperation in the field of transactional analysis. The third objective is to enable EATA members to network with each other and thus create a network between regional, national and international associations (cf. European Association for Transactional Analysis, o.J.a).

4. Membership

EATA has 44 member associations with more than 7,500 individual members and is thus represented in 29 European countries. To become a member of EATA, associations must submit an application and adhere to the standards and regulations of EATA (cf. European Association for Transactional Analysis, o.J.a).

5. Funding

Membership fees finance the association, donations and other income from activities (cf. European Association for Transactional Analysis, 2012, p. 1).

6. Publication

The association publishes the "EATA Newsletter" about three times a year. Information about the association and news about research are published (cf. European Association for Transactional Analysis, o. J. b).

7. Conferences and congresses

EATA organises three different conferences. First, there are the EATA Conferences where participants are supposed to get new information about transactional analysis. Secondly, the World Conference, where EATA organises a conference and the International Transactional Analysis Association (ITAA). Thirdly, the Theory Development and Research Conference aim to share new ideas in transactional analysis and support exchange between colleagues. The three conferences occur every three years (cf. European Association for Transactional Analysis, o. J. c).

8. Differentiation of Counselling and psychotherapy

The federation has not released a statement in this context.

5.4 Presentation of the quantitative results

This chapter presents the data collected through the online questionnaire. For this purpose, various statistical values calculated from the data set with the help of SPSS. This information serves to provide a better overview and comparability of the data.

In total, 13 out of 29 European counselling and psychotherapy associations participated in the online questionnaire via LimeSurvey.

It shows that more than 84% of the associations pursue networking, i. e. networking with each other. 69% of the associations strive to improve the training and further education of their association constantly. No less important for the associations (69%) is disseminating the individual counselling and psychotherapy approaches. It is interesting to note that only 38.5% of the associations stated that they wanted to support human health through their work (see Fig. 3).

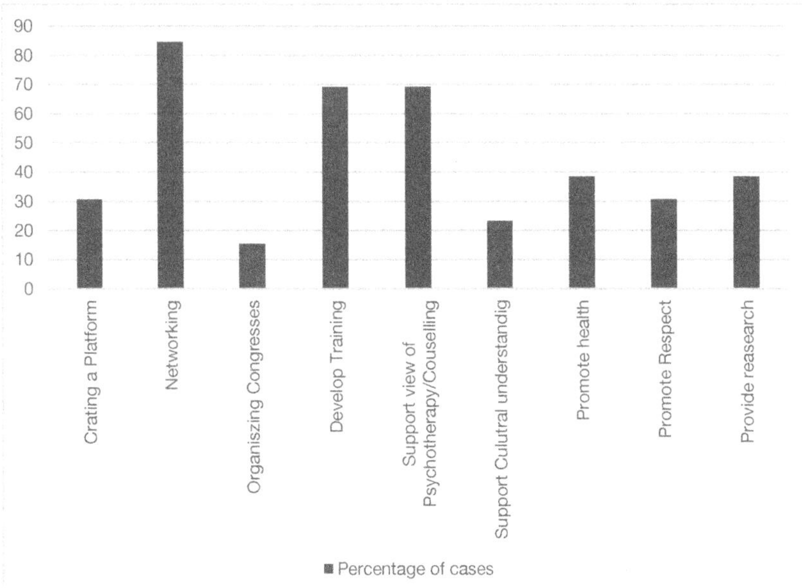

Figure 3: Goals of the associations (own figure according to SPSS)

To be able to pursue the respective goals, an association needs specific financial resources. 92.3% of associations state they charge membership fees in addition to income from conferences in 38% of the cases and income from training or further education in 30.8% of the cases.

Question – how can an association or an individual obtain membership in the respective association. Due to the different structures of the associations, very different answers were given. Some associations function more as a European umbrella organisation for national associations and others as associations that connect individuals. Accordingly, additional requirements apply to the application. Nevertheless, there is a high level of agreement (53.8%) that a certain quality standard, such as education or training in the respective field, must be met to apply.

Due to the structural differences, the number of members also varies widely. These vary between ten and seventy thousand members, whereby the national member associations were listed as the umbrella organisations. On the other hand, the European area's individual members were enumerated for individual members' associations. Besides, the associations are distributed differently within Europe, so that these associations are represented in nine to fifty-three countries. On the one hand, this underlines different associations, and on the other hand, some associations are also active outside the European Union. In further research, it would be interesting to determine how the individual clubs cooperate with international clubs or function.

Also, it was surveyed how often the associations organise congresses or joint meetings. The results show that every association observed a meeting at least once a year. 53.8 % of the associations state that interested professionals are also allowed to attend their events (see Appendix 7). 76.9 % of the associations state that they hold their congresses in changing locations in Europe. Due to Corona, some events were postponed or held as online meetings.

Furthermore, it was asked whether the associations publish newsletters or magazines. Eight of the thirteen associations interviewed answered in the affirmative. 50% of them say they publish a newsletter twice a year, and the remaining 50% publish their newsletter three to four times a year.

In the context of this work, it seems crucial to ask whether the associations distinguish between counselling and psychotherapy. Two associations did not make a statement on this, and another two associations answered the question in the negative, and nine associations stated that they distinguish between counselling and psychotherapy.

Finally, 92.3% of the associations stated that they would like to network with other European counselling or psychotherapy associations. This indicates a high interest in exchange and reflects networking's primary objective, which most associations thus pursue.

The following chapter will now discuss the results and the resulting future tasks.

5.5 Future vision

This subgroup of the Cologne "World mapping of the Counselling Profession Project" aims to map the different European associations of Counselling and psychotherapy. In the course of the processing, the distinction between the two professions became particularly relevant. The survey shows as many as 30% of associations do not distinguish or have no consensus on the topic. The difference between associations results on one hand from the different national regulations within Europe and, on the other hand, from the intense controversy in this discourse.

To obtain a precise framing and differentiate the two professions, public and intensive discourse was conducted between professionals and academia. The aim must be to guarantee better support for clients and patients in crises to promote mental health. More than 92% of the associations are interested in contact with other European associations. The EAC will put that networking on their agenda.

This interest must be used to revive this discourse and to benefit from each other. This discourse could take place, for example, on an interactive website, where attention is drawn to upcoming congresses and discussed topics.

In this context, the professions' barriers could be broken down in guest lectures at the annual congresses or through Europe-wide interdisciplinary workshops to benefit all sides. Regularly published newsletters could also be helpful for this discourse. Guest contributions from different European associations could open up an exciting and essential speech here. The broad knowledge that the individual approaches bring with them can draw attention to both differences and commonalities.

Apart from the interdisciplinary discourse, the need for further research becomes apparent here. To what extent the professions overlap or complement each other, with the critical aim of alleviating the feeling of competition between disciplines. The common goal of human health and well-being should be the top priority for all here and enable new opportunities for cooperation.

The professions' different training paths should be researched more intensively, which constantly form the basis of the discourse. But also the practice, as well as the implementation of counselling and psychotherapy, should be explored more deeply.

This could help to document the transformation of the professions and thus to identify further similarities and differences.

Due to the great interest in professionals' European exchange, an interactive list of the various European associations should be included and the interactive world map. This could also enable cooperation between the associations as needed. The EAC will be one player in this field.

References

Aarts, M. (2020) Responses to Marte Meo International from the online questionnaire.

Association of National Organisations for Supervision in Europe (2019a). Statutes. Retrieved from: https://anse.eu/about-anse/statutes [last found 26.01.2021].

Association of National Organisations for Supervision in Europe (2019b). Statutes. Retrieved from: https://anse.eu/publications/anse-journal [last found 26.01.2021].

German Federal Association Coaching e. V. (2019). Guidelines and recommendations for the development of coaching as a profession. Osnabrück: Deutscher Bundesverband Coaching e. V.

German Society for Supervision and Coaching (2020). Retrieved from: https://www.dgsv.de/services/praktische-hinweise/basiswissen/ [last found 26.01.2021].

Dietrich, G. (1983). General Counselling Psychology. An introduction to the psychological theory and practice of Counselling. Göttingen: Verlag für Psychologie.

European Association for Gestalt Therapy (o. j. a). Statutes. Retrieved from: https://www.eagt.org/joomla/index.php/2016-02-25-13-29-31/statutes [last found 26.01.2021].

European Association for Gestalt Therapy (o. j. b). Newsletter. Retrieved from: https://www.eagt.org/joomla/index.php/2016-02-25-22-21-51/ [last found 26.01.2021].

European Association for Transactional Analysis (2012). Statutes of EATA. Abgerufen von: https://eatanews.org/wp-content/uploads/2019/04/EATA_statutes_councilreg.pdf [zuletzt gefunden 26.01.2021].

European Association for Transactional Analysis (n. d. a). About EATA. Retrieved from: https://eatanews.org/about-eata [last found 26.01.2021].

European Association for Transactional Analysis (o. J. b). TA Resources. Abgerufen von: https://eatanews.org/ta-resources [zuletzt gefunden 26.01.2021].

European Association for Transactional Analysis (o. J. c). TA Conferences. Abgerufen von: https://eatanews.org/conferences/ [zuletzt gefunden 26.01.2021].

European Family Therapy Association (2020a). Statutes of the European Family Therapy Association. Abgerufen von: https://www.europeanfamilytherapy.eu/statutes-of-efta/ [zuletzt gefunden 26.01.2021].

Gröning, K. (2015). Lines of development of educational Counselling. On the history of educational, vocational and sexual Counselling in Germany. Gießen: Psychosozial-Verlag.
Kriz, J. (2014). Basic concepts of psychotherapy. Weinheim, Basel: Beltz Verlag.
Langner, L. (2020). Responses to European Network for Person-centred and Experiental Psychotherapy and Counselling (PCE Europe) from the online questionnaire.
Lumma, K. (1999). Counselling – Theory and practice of Counselling pedagogy. Humanistic Psychology, 22nd year, special issue 1/99. Eschweiler: IHP-Bücherdienst.
Mayring, P. (2015). Qualitative Content Analysis. Fundamentals and techniques. Weinheim, Basel: Beltz.
Nestmann, F.; Engel, F.; Sickendiek, U. (eds.) (2004). The Handbook of Counselling. Volume 1, disciplines and approaches. Tübingen: dgvt.
Rieger, S. (2020). Responses to European Association for Supervision and Coaching (EASC) from the online questionnaire.
Schubert, F.-C.; Rohr, D.; Zwicker-Pelzer, R. (2019). Counselling. Foundations-concepts- fields of application. Wiesbaden: Springer VS.
Schwing, R.; Tryszer, A. (2016). Systemic Counselling and family therapy. Short, concise, suitable for everyday use. Göttingen: Vandenhoeck & Ruprecht.
Sporré, O. (2020). Supervision for mediators. Quality assurance through Counselling and support. Osnabrück: Springer VS.
Tachtsoglou, S., König, J. (2017). Statistics for educational scientists (1st ed.). Wiesbaden: VS Verlag für Sozialwissenschaften.
Von Schlippe, A.; Schweitzer, J. (2007). Textbook of systemic therapy and Counselling. Göttingen: Vandenhoeck & Ruprecht.
Wagner-Schelewsky, P.; Hering, L. (2019). Online survey. In: Baur N., Blasius J. (eds) Handbuch Methoden der empirischen Sozialforschung. Wiesbaden: Springer VS.

6 A Comparison between the European and the American Standards of Counselling Training Programs

I owe this chapter to the intensive collaboration with Natalia Zapolsky. Natalia contacted me in my role as President of EAC in September 2019. At that time, she was writing her dissertation "A Meta-Synthesis of the American and the European Standards for the Accreditation of Counselling Training Programs" (Zapolsky, 2020) and I was just beginning to research the European standards. In this respect, we benefited enormously from each other in the following months and worked together very well. I thank Natalia for allowing me to share some of her insights here.

As I mentioned in this book, Natalia also sees a change in the counselling profession in the course of globalization. Due to globalization it is necessary to research both the worldwide community and the professional counselling society. In order to build an effective global counselling society, it is important to count and consider the specific features and needs of each local community, so that unified global standards for counselling training can be developed. "Marriages between people from different nations, global businesses and interactions, and other types of affairs require the worldwide community seeking counsellors with global perspective and worldview. This new realm represents an opportunity to form a new generation of cross-national professionals" (Zapolsky, 2020, 1).

The meta-synthesis research by Natalia Zapolsky provides clear understanding of the current local specifics of counselling development in the U.S. and in different European countries. The qualitative comparison of this meta-synthesis can be used for the discussion of how the worldwide professional counselling community can be effectively consolidated in the future.

The outcome of this study can become a solid foundation for the further discussion of the effective ways of globalizing counselling. The purpose of this study is, to explore how the European standards for the accreditation of counselling training programs compare to CACREP (Council for the Accreditation of Counselling and Related Educational Programs) standards and to each other. This study seeks unified global accrediting standards for counselling training programs, to grow interaction among health professionals.

6.1 The Process of Counselling Globalization

There is a growing interest in the issues of globalization. The issue of counselling globalization is particularly limited in the field of higher education counselling training. At the same time, there are several researchers who began raising questions to initiate the professional discussion. They provided insights regarding the role of culture in the globalization process. They discussed the challenges that psychiatrists encounter while applying psychiatric theory, research, and practice in diverse cultural and social contexts. The authors shared their observations and noted that most of the cross-cultural studies simplify the cultural aspect by framing the discussion within geographical borders (see chapter 10). Kirmayer and Swartz (2014) stated that the concept of culture is much wider than a geographic location. They explained the most popular approaches to culture that have been used in the United States for the last decades and expressed their opinion regarding the relevance of those approaches to the current global mental health. The authors confronted the idea that "cultural differences are disappearing with globalization, " and they discussed the complex processes that inevitably appear while "cultural hybridization" stimulates the creation of new forms of culture (p. 43).

Researchers should switch their focus from "replication of studies in samples that represent local diversity" to an active search of the effective and conceptual models that will help the global professionals explore how culture influences psychopathology and healing.

6.2 Internalizing the Counselling Training Programs

The process of globalization requires reconsideration of counselling theoretical approaches and methodologies when applied to the global community.

While internalizing the counselling profession, the worldwide community should be involved in the discussion in order to create a methodology that could address the needs of all cultures around the globe. Scholars and researchers acknowledge that the new realm requires a new type of a mental health professional. In order to grow such specialists, the reformation of counselling training programs is required.

One of the significant obstacles hindering the development towards counselling globalization is the difficulty gaining accessibility to an international sample and to persuading individuals to participate in "a non-native research". Stated that future research is needed to explore the validity and applicability of U.S.-based or European-based multicultural counselling competencies in the settings of international counselling work. Natalias' proposed qualitative meta-synthesis research contributes to those counselling professionals' request. Freeman's (2011) dissertation also addressed the issues of globalization in counselling, with a specific focus on how Japanese counsellors adapt the training they received in counselling and psychology graduate programs in the United States into their counselling practices in Japan. The findings of that study revealed that the applicability of the U.S.-based methodologies is limited in different cultural settings, and the researcher suggested further exploration regarding effective strategies for counselling internationalization.

6.3 Obstacles for Globalization

Despite the fact that globalization is an inevitable process dictated by the reality of global progress and integration, there are also factors that hinder the progression of counselling internationalization. The histories of oppression and creation of homogenous systems of knowledge force many nations to protect their identities and uniqueness by avoiding any interactions that may be considered as colonization or domination.

Smith (2017) assumed the nations that experienced different types of oppression in their past have a tendency to resist any outside influences because of their fear that hegemonic power can be transformed to a less visible yet still dangerous form.

Problems of counselling globalization can be two-sided. On the one hand, the U.S. professionals, as carriers of the dominant methodology, hinder the process of internationalization by demonstrating professional superiority relative to other countries and by having a tendency to believe one's own behaviors are typical of others. On the other hand, non-U.S. professionals can be resistant to accept any of the counselling U.S. approaches (even if culturally appropriate) due to fear and suspicion of colonization.

The author listed three major reasons for the necessity of the internationalization of higher education: "interest in international security; maintenance of economic competitiveness; and fostering of human understanding across nations" (Qiang, 2003, p. 251). Qiang demonstrated that the internationalization of higher education can bring numerous benefits to a country as a whole, by enhancing the country's position and role as nation in the world scene, as well as at institutional and personal levels.

6.4 American 'Council for the Accreditation of Counselling and Related Educational Programs' (CACREP)

King (2017) indicated that the CACREP is more respected and recognized in the professional community by providing numerous examples when such organizations as the American Counselling Association (ACA), the National Board for Certified Counsellors (NBCC), the Council on Rehabilitation Education (CORE), the American Mental Health Counsellors Association (AMHCA), and the American Association of State Counselling Boards (AASCB) recognized the privilege of CACREP over MPCAC due to its credibility.

King (2017) emphasizes that CACREP has "an established history as the "flagship" accrediting body indicating to professional and regulatory authorities, as well as the public, quality education, training, and preparation of graduates for state licensure or national certification in the practice of master's level counselling services" (p. 1). As an accrediting body, CACREP is dedicated to developing and controlling standards and procedures for high quality training in the counselling profession. CACREP standards are developed on the culture and the educational system in the U.S., so it is not possible to apply them on non-U.S. programs due to cultural inappropriateness. The CACREP Board keeps searching for a solution. The result of that exploration was the development of IRCEP (the International Registry for Counsellor Education Programs) that approached accreditation standards and processes for international community in a culturally appropriate manner. Thus, IRCEP is becoming the CACREP's global representative that, possibly, can develop a powerful voice in the nearest future.

The data garnered from this study could help CACREP, IRCEP, EAC, IAC, and the global professional community to more clearly and effectively understand the unique features and needs of each European culture and to consider those distinctive cultural aspects in further development of the international accrediting standards for counselling training programs around the world.

6.5 European Accreditation Systems

As mentioned several times in this book there were some challenges while conducting the European segment of the literature review for Natalia, too. There were only limited informational resources available and the language barriers and the diverse terminologies from country to country complicated the search from the European databases as well. It was a great advantage that some researchers in the research group at University of Cologne speak different European languages.

The major factor for elimination decisions was that no counselling was developed in a reviewed country and, as a result, there is no an accrediting institution. While reviewing the available information concerning counselling development as a profession in European countries, an observation was made that many countries lack recognition of counselling as a distinct area of practice. In many countries counselling is distinguished as a separate profession, but it is still considered as an integral part of psychotherapy (as in the UK, Ireland, Switzerland, and Malta). This factor revealed the terminology confusion of utilizing the words "counselling" and "psychotherapy" in the United States and different European countries (see chapter 5). For many years now, no universal definition of "professional counselling" has been accepted.

It is a fact that counselling as a distinct profession is still developing in most European countries (see chapter 4). That state of evolvement inevitably reflects the current status of the accrediting training system as well. The most common issue of the European counsellors is that they are competing for the professional niche that is already occupied by other Mental Health professionals (Mariotti, 2018; Remley et al., 2010). This is the case in nations such as Germany, France, and Romania and many others (Cates, 2002; Martin, 1997; Rott & Wickel, 1996; Watanabe-Muraoka, 1997; Wehrly, 1987).

Thus, the European counsellors have, for quite some time now, two options: 1) clinical counselling must compete with psychology, psychiatry, and other helping professions for its place within that system; or 2) counselling may only serve a role within other mental health systems rather than as an independent profession (Stockton, Garbelman, Kaladow & Terry, 2008). The review of literature regarding the current issues of counselling globalization displays that the international professional counsellors have recognized the necessity of developing a professional identity on a global scale (Hoskins & Thompson, 2009).

The major goal of the world-wide counselling community is to develop recognition of the counselling profession around the globe with a clear understanding of who those professionals are by default. Hoskins and Thompson (2009) emphasized that "The development of an international counselling identity involves three key components: collaboration, research, and training" (p. 2). At the same time, the literature review revealed several challenges that the international counselling society currently experiences: unequal developmental stages of counselling in different countries; the absence of unified standards for counselling training programs; and, the complexity of development of the global code of ethics (Gerstein, Heppner, Ægisdo'ttir et al., 2009).

Unequal Developmental Stages of Counselling in European Countries

Counselling in the United States is more developed as a profession than it is in many other parts of the world (Gerstein, Heppner, Ægisdo'ttir et al., 2009). Over the past century, the individuals making up the US counselling society were able to move the perspective of their profession from being an ill-defined, difficult to distinguish from other helping professions, to being one with a defined and distinguishable professional identity (Gerstein, Heppner, Ægisdo'ttir et al., 2009; Neukrug, 2012).

Some countries, such as United Kingdom, Ireland, Malta, and Switzerland have already developed graduate counselling programs and control their quality with accreditation bodies. Other countries, such as France, Italy, Romania, Greece, and Germany have no autonomous counselling discipline in higher education institutions and have some training programs that operate outside the university structure (Moodley, Gielen, & Wu, 2013; Maassen & Musselin, 2009).

Also, there are no accreditation bodies to control the quality of this training.

The Absence of Unified Standards for Counselling Training Programs

Another issue revealed through the literature review was the absence of the unified standards for counselling training programs around the world (Woo, Henfield, & Choi, 2014; Gerstein, Heppner, Ægisdóttir et al., 2009; Moodley et al., 2013; Gerstein, Heppner, Stockton, et al., 2009). That situation creates obstacles to establishing a united global network of professional training around the world and to providing competent counselling services for the global community.

The European Association for Counselling has already initiated the first steps to uniting counselling professionals in Europe (see chapter 2). The countries where counsellors were unable to find support on the national level began using the EAC platform and the set of standards as a guidance for their professional development (Hohenshil, Amundson, & Niles, 2013). The EAC Strategy and Plan 2014-2020 declared that one of the goals of the association was to set up the accreditation process for training courses and training organizations (EAC, 2019) and to "develop criteria for the accreditation of training programs" (EAC, 2015, p. 5; see chapter 2).

6.6 The Complexity of Development of the Global Code of Ethics

The global training programs should be developed on the set of standards that, in turn, should be grounded on a professional code of ethics. A very sensitive question arises here: Based on which philosophy and worldview assumptions should this code be developed? Is the direction to be the Western one based on its leadership in the counselling professional development? Or is the Non-Western one the solution, due to its numerical advantage and prevalence?

Gerstein, Heppner, Stockton, et al. (2009) explained that worldwide community often considers counselling globalization as hegemony of U.S. methodology and Western civilization in general. The current research is full of different terminology such as "McDonalization", "Westernization" with quite a negative connotation behind those terms (Gerstein, Heppner, Stockton, et al., 2009; Gerstein, Heppner, Ægisdóttir et al., 2009; Patel, Minas, Cohen, & Prince, 2014).

discussed the two-sided problem of counselling globalization, when the U.S. professionals demonstrate professional superiority relative to other countries and when the non-U.S. professionals resist accepting any of the U.S. counselling approaches due to fear of colonization. Those two perspectives and attitudes should be carefully taken into account while the global counselling profession and the code of ethics are in the development process.

To find and enact compromise is essential for the growing international community. Also, this is an ongoing process of formation of a new global culture. This qualitative meta- synthesis is intended to contribute to this process by initiating the first step to recognizing and to acknowledging the existent differences between the U.S. and the European accrediting standards for counselling training programs that inevitably reflect the cultural differences in their foundations.

6.7 Conclusion

This study was intended to contribute to the process of counselling globalization by exploring the commonalities and differences between the European and the CACREP accrediting standards for counselling training programs.

The outcomes of this meta-synthesis are intended to underpin the formation of the prospective unified standards for global counselling training. The conducted study was undertaken for the purpose of contributing to the process of counselling globalization. Globalization of the worldwide community and the professional counselling society requires the development of unified global standards for training quality assurance and for competent counselling services throughout the world. To prepare for this important transition, the exploration and definition of specific needs and requirements of each national community, for the purpose of considering those aspects and reflecting them in the prospective unified global standards for counselling training programs, would be beneficial. This meta-synthesis, analyzing and comparing the American and the European standards for the accreditation of counselling training programs, was conducted to contribute to that exploration process, to be carried out by scholars and researchers around the globe.

The evaluation of the European accreditation schemes revealed that the BACP and the IACP sets of standards can currently be considered as the most developed accrediting models in Europe.

At present, counselling is more developed as a profession in the United States than it is in many other parts of the world (Gerstein, Heppner, Ægisdóttir et al., 2009).

The key of that success was the development of nationally recognized graduate level counselling training. The training standards provided by the Counsel for Accreditation of Counselling and Related Educational Programs (CACREP) significantly enhanced the reputation of counselling as a profession (Stanard, 2013).

One of the noticeable differences of the CACREP standards from the European ones is the detailed extension of standard regulations with regards to each counselling specialty area (clinical mental health counselling; school counselling; college counselling and students affairs; career counselling; addiction counselling; marriage, couple, and family counselling; and clinical rehabilitation counselling).

References

European Association for Counselling (EAC). (2015). Training standards, accreditation, and ethical charter booklet. Retrieved from http://eac.eu.com/

European Association for Counselling (EAC). (2019). European counsellor training organization. Retrieved from https://eac.eu.com/membership-applications/training-organisation/

Freeman, S. D. M. (2011). The transcultural adaptation of western Counselling in Japan: A grounded theory. Dissertation Abstracts International Section A: Humanities and Social.

Gerstein, L. H., Heppner, P. P., Ægisdóttir, S., Leung, S.-M. A., & Norsworthy, K. L. (2009). International handbook of cross-cultural Counselling: Cultural assumptions and practices worldwide. (L. H. Gerstein, P. P. Heppner, S. Ægisdóttir, S.-M. A. Leung, & K. L. Norsworthy, Eds.). Thousand Oaks, CA: Sage Publications, Inc.

Gerstein, L. H., Heppner, P. P., Ægisdóttir, S., Leung, S.-M. A., Norsworthy, K. L. (2009). Cross-cultural Counselling: History, challenges, and rationale (pp. 3-32). In L. H. Gerstein, P. P. Heppner, S. Egisdottrir, S. A. Leung, & K. L. Norsworthy (Eds.), International Handbook of Cross-Cultural Counselling: Cultural Assumptions and Practices Worldwide. Los Angeles, CA: Sage.

Gerstein, L. H., Heppner, P. P., Stockton, R., Leong, F. T. L., Ægisdóttir, S. (2009). The Counselling profession in- and outside the United States (pp. 53–67). In L. H. Gerstein, P. P. Heppner, S. Egisdottrir, S. A. Leung, & K. L. Norsworthy (Eds.), International Handbook of Cross-Cultural Counselling: Cultural Assumptions and Practices Worldwide. Los Angeles, CA: Sage.

Hohenshil, T. H., Amundson, N. E., & Niles, S. G. (Eds.). (2013). Counselling around the world:An international handbook. American Counselling Association.
King, J. H. (2017). Understanding the differences between CACREP and MPCAC. Retrieved on June 18th, 2019 from https://www.mellivoragroup.com/data/documents/Understandingthe-Differences-Between-CACREP-and-MPCAC_White-Paper.pdf
Maassen, P., & Musselin, C. (2009). European integration and the Europeanisation of higher education. In A. Amaral, G. Neave, C. Musselin, & P. Maassen (Eds.), European integration and the governance of higher education and research (pp. 3–14). Dordrecht: Springer.
Mariotti, D. (2017). Towards a New Profession: Counselor Professional Identity in Italy: A Delphi Study. Norfolk: Old Dominion University.
Moodley, R., Gielen, U. P., & Wu, R. (2013). Handbook of Counselling and psychotherapy in an international context. New York, NY: Routledge.
Neukrug, E. (2012). The world of the counselor: An introduction to the Counselling profession, (4th ed.). Belmont, CA: Brooks/Cole, Cengage Learning.
Patel, V., Minas, H., Cohen, A., & Prince, M. J. (2014). Global mental health: Principles and practice. New York, NY: Oxford University Press.
Qiang, Z. (2003). Internationalization of Higher Education: Towards a Conceptual Framework. Policy Futures in Education, 1(2), 248–270.
Remley, T., Bacchini, E., & Krieg, P. (2010). Counselling in Italy: current status of Counselling in Italy. Journal of Counselling & Development, 88, 28–33.
Smith, P. H. (2017). Transnational faculty work in counselor education: A Delphi study. Dissertation Abstracts International: Section B: The Sciences and Engineering. ProQuest Information & Learning.
Stanard, R. P. (2013). International registry of counsellor education programs: CACREP's contribution to the development of Counselling as a global profession. Journal of Counselling & Development, 91(1), 55–60.
Stockton, R., Garbelman, Kaladow, J. K., & Terry, L. J. (2008). The international development of Counselling as a profession. In W. K. Schweiger, D. A. Henderson, & T. W. Clawson, Programs of counselor training outside of the United States. Counselor preparation (pp. 77–97). New York: Routledge.
Woo, H., Henfield, M. S., & Choi, N. (2014). Developing a unified professional identity in Counselling: A review of the literature. Journal of Counselor Leadership and Advocacy, 1(1), 1–15.
Zapolsky, N. (2020). A Meta-Synthesis of the American and the European Standards for the Accreditation of Counselling Training Programs. Chicago: Digital Commons@NLU.

7 Teaching Counselling

7.1 Context of Training in Counselling

In European countries, it varies whether counselling is taught at universities or private institutes (e. g. Continuing Professional Development) – or both.

First and foremost, this depends on whether counselling is enshrined in law. A general comparison will be made, starting with non-university counselling training.

Sometimes, professional action pathways no longer seem suitable for the future, and people want to expand their competencies. Because they perhaps wish to reorientate themselves and exploit the diversity of the fields of work in the social area more thoroughly. In the meantime, however, the unclear occupational fields for Bachelor's and Master's graduates – as well as the entry requirements for newcomers to the profession – are increasingly responsible for the registration for further training (but then without 'professional and without counselling experience').

In any case, it is essential to clearly define the terms used in addition to the reason for participation in CET. The word 'training' is often misused in CET contexts. However, training is everything that contributes to a vocational, state-recognised qualification. Training on the background of the European Qualifications Framework (EQF) is "formal" learning; this differentiates it from "semi-formal" learning, which in most countries usually takes place in further education provided by national associations. It concludes with certificates, not with a BA/MA degree etc.

In principle, additional training courses lasting several months are modularised and oriented towards a curriculum. This distinguishes them from further training courses, which are e. g. lectures, conferences, one-day seminars, and workshops lasting one day or several days, but not months. These can be 'completed' with certificates of participation but not with credentials.

Counsellor training has changed through the years, even if it has not yet reached the world of continuing education institutes everywhere. The EQF is our reference point as a dimension and in some countries implementing the EQF in a national Qualifications Frameworks (see chapter 7.3).

Lifelong learning (LLL) had been part of the overall education plan since 1970 and thus was also adopted by EQF. At that time, educational science realized more clearly than ever before that the phases of life after school, college and university are also and still relevant to learning. Many studies relevant to education at that time proved how vital learning could be in the adult phase.

Continuing education is gaining an increasingly important place and space in today's world – and thus in the time of the EQF and the European labour marketing perspective. Vocational qualification in the increasingly specialised world of work is gaining importance. Complexity and flexibility currently characterise the working world and demand flexible and permanently new competencies from people. Social professionals do not feel fit enough for the profession after their studies. Despite the BA/MA (Bologna Process), unfortunately, nothing has changed in this regard. This observation is mainly independent of age. The "risky" world of work – as described by Haubl and Voß (2011) seems to have reached and taken hold of all ages.

For people aged 40 and older, the question of how they can remain healthy, motivated and self-developing in their profession and the working world during their entire working life, or how they can change and fulfil their tasks as they keep changing. On the other hand, the focus is also on a successful career start for the young generation sociologically referred to as Generation Y. On the one hand the short study period and on the other hand the increased and complex demands of the working world increase the personal feeling of insufficiency. They almost "inevitably" want to continue learning. In most cases, these young participants in further education do not even ask their employers about cost-sharing or even cost absorption and/or credit for working hours, even though the chosen further education is motivated by professional reasons.

In the field of Counselling and therapy, we distinguish:
Training offers are for those with a formal qualification – the technician, the educator, etc; training in a career that builds: the licensed child and youth psychotherapist after studying psychology, educational science or medicine, etc. The examinations are state-controlled and take place in public "settings" according to the respective training specifications.

Further education in Counselling: Teaching & learning Counselling

They need to design teaching-learning processes at different ages of students and in other settings. Continuing education in counselling usually corresponds to adult education/further education and special university didactics if it is a degree programme.

Based on our personal experiences in higher education teaching (and scholarship about it), we would like to outline the same, as we believe it can have (positive) implications for the cross-institutional teaching of counselling.

Huber (1995) distinguishes between "working approaches" of institutionalised adult education, which are either part of science research, (initial and continuing) education research or social science, interdisciplinarily oriented educational science and of which five are relevant for the context of "initial and continuing education in counselling":

1. Curricular or didactic approach: The goals and contents of continuing education are considered insufficiently well-founded and lead to orientation, motivation and learning problems—curriculum research solutions sought at all levels.
2. Employment-oriented approach: Emphasise occupational relevance of continuing education strongly, and employability comes to the fore.
3. Socialisation theory approach: How can participants and teachers develop within continuing education? Essential topics are identity and habitus
4. Instructional technology approach: research and development of efficient teaching provision based on empirical classroom research.
5. The science-theoretical and science-didactic approach: The problem of further education is a crisis of science itself, expanding and fanning out individual empirical sciences.

The central questions are: What is good teaching? And how can good teaching be promoted? In the broad discussion, the concept of a change in adult education's teaching-learning culture is increasingly gaining acceptance (Huber, 2009; Schneider, Szczyrba, Welbers &

Wildt, 2009; Tremp, 2009). The so-called "shift from teaching to learning" (Wildt, 2004) refers to a paradigm shift away from the teacher and input-centred teaching towards teaching that focuses on the process of learning and the associated output. Since the 1990s, the concept of competence orientation in education at universities and the Bologna Process and the spread of consecutive study programmes and the modularised Bachelor's and Master's degrees. This will be examined in more detail in the following section, as it is of central importance.

Competence orientation in teaching

In 2000, the European Council announced that the EU should become the most competitive and dynamic knowledge-based economy in the world by 2010. This goal, formulated as part of the so-called Lisbon Agenda, was the starting point for an arguably unprecedented European intergovernmental reform effort in the education sector, which later became known as the Bologna Process. The Bologna Process aimed to create a single European higher education system by developing a general framework for modernising and reforming European higher education (cf. Paetz, Ceylan, Fiehn, Schworm & Harteis (2011). This should promote students and academic staff's international mobility and the employability of university graduates in particular. These structural framework conditions represented deep cuts in existing German higher education. The realisation of these framework conditions also required a far-reaching change in the didactic and content-related organisation of teaching, learning and examination processes (cf. Wildt, 2007). This is what is now coming to the front of further education in counselling.

From the teaching objective to the learning outcome

In competence-oriented adult education, the focus is on active, self-directed and self-responsible learning. This objective requires a departure from the traditional understanding of teaching. The emphasis placed on the teacher and their content. No matter what the teacher considers relevant or vital to the learning process and the student's competencies and how these can be verified in performances at the end of the learning process as a learning outcome.

This view is based on constructivist thinking, according to which knowledge does not exist in an objective, transportable form but requires, above all, an individual cognitive performance. The learner's active construction of knowledge is the goal of the teaching-learning process and thus requires learner-centredness. The learning environment is to be designed based on the needs of the learners. The teacher acts in the role of a learning guide or is more often referred to in higher education didactic literature – as a learning advisor. The teacher's role is no longer that of a 'know-it-all' but of a 'multi-know-it-all' (cf. constructivist didactics in Reich, 2012, p. 118). This contradicts the widespread master-pupil relationship that is 'still' practised in many systemic training courses.

At present, in further education at private institutes, additional education is usually assessed as 'passed' after attendance and completed counselling practice, and a certificate is issued; there is no 'fail' in colloquia at almost any institute. At universities, assessment is not based on attendance but exclusively on knowledge – and academic debate in oral and written examinations. There are usually only passed further education courses (which are, however, differentiated based on grades).

Competence orientation, in turn, implies or leads to a new kind of 'graduation' or verification of what has been 'achieved'. Let us once again use the insights from recent higher education didactics:

Constructive Alignment

Constructive alignment (cf. Biggs and Tang, 2011) means a fit between objective, method and examination (see figure 4). For example, if I conduct case analyses in my seminar, I can also require case analyses in the test. However, if the students have never performed a case analysis, I should not be surprised if the examination results are desolate. Examinations and examination formats can test different forms of competencies. However, not all forms of examinations are suitable for all competencies. An exam, for example, can (if at all) only cover a social competence in a roundabout way.

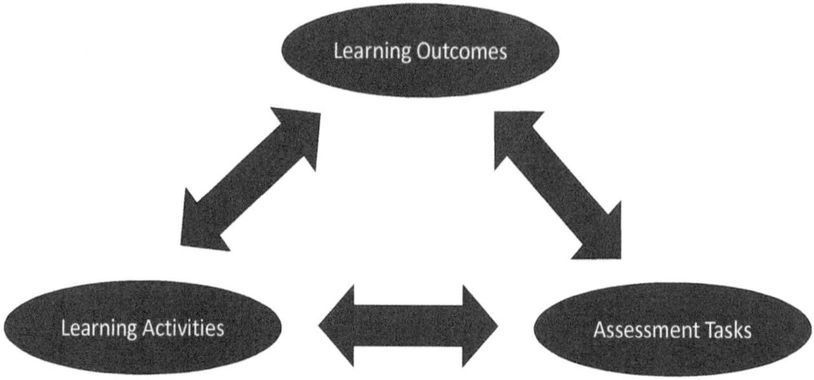

Figure 4: Constructive alignment (cf. Biggs and Tang, 2011)

In preparing the course, the teacher must be clear about their intended learning outcomes. Based on which learning objective areas they choose, and illustrate these in more detail via taxonomy levels (e. g. related to cognitive learning objectives taking Bloom (1971) into account). Then the teacher must choose the appropriate activity for the students to achieve the learning outcomes and finally compile a form of examination that corresponds to this, which in its weighting adequately takes into account the topics actually dealt with and enabling the students to be able to demonstrate the competences learned in realistic settings. Only then can one speak of a valid and competence-oriented examination in terms of content.

The constant adaptation of teaching and examination to Constructive Alignment and Learning Outcomes alone means a massive cut in proven teaching and examination procedures for many continuing education providers.

In the final examinations of continuing education, the participants should demonstrate their acquisition of competencies across the entire continuing education. The final examinations challenge is that teachers have to agree that content is addressed in the individual parts.

There are clear KMK framework guidelines (2003, 2005) for higher education institutions that stipulate that study programmes' qualification goals and individual modules formulated as competencies. The forms of teaching contributed to the achievement of competences and examined in final module examinations. For competence-oriented tests to support effective competence acquisition, the examination tasks and requirements must be closely oriented to the intended learning outcomes (cf. Biggs and Tang, 2011). Meaning, in the best case, those competencies demonstrated in the final module examination and that could equally be acquired and trained as partial competencies in the module manuals' courses have already been determined in the module manuals' formulation.

If, for example, the learning outcomes aimed at acquiring skills for solving complex subject-related problems, corresponding problem-solving requirements and scenarios (for example, in project work or problem-based learning settings) should appear in the examinations and noted as examination achievements in the module handbooks. How little this requirement has been implemented consistently at higher education institutions is shown by an expert report on competence orientation in teaching and learning, which Schaper prepared et al. (2012) for the HRK. They criticise that many higher education institutions continue to adhere to traditional examination formats and that the examinations disconnect from the learning outcomes formulated in the module handbooks. They conclude that for the conception of competence-oriented examination procedures, "less knowledge-producing examination formats should be chosen and designed, but rather formats that demand the application of knowledge, its implementation in action contexts as well as the assessment and reflection of realistic problems" (ibid., p. 62f.). They see examination tasks or formats as particularly suitable for this. Which make the problem- or action-oriented demands and require complex cognitive performances. These tests correspond in each case to the competence requirements of the targeted learning outcomes (for example, carrying out experiments, working on 'complete' action contexts in case examinations, construction tasks, carrying out complex cases and projects depending on the respective field of study). Live counselling – ideally with a reflecting team of the participants (cf. Andersen, 1996; Schindler, Kricke & Rohr, 2013) or video counselling with subsequent, supervision-like, and theoretical reflections be complementary for further systemic education.

In this book, we can only touch on university experiences of competence orientation; they <- WHO? meant to make two things clear: first, that this development – which is also a development towards standardisation – is 'unstoppable' in the field of training in counselling, and secondly, that this development is critically and reflectively accompanied. The learning-outcome and thus competence orientation ultimately implies a clear understanding of objectifiable, 'good counselling', which in turn contradicts a systemic-playful attitude.

Diversity

As described in the introduction, the groups of participants in training groups are increasingly 'diverse'. Gardenswartz and Rowe (2010) represent human diversity in organisations in their model "Four Layers of Diversity" (ibid., p. 30f.; see Figure 5). In this model, distinguishing characteristics can be differentiated based on the dimensions of personality characteristics, demographic aspects, external demographic aspects and organisational aspects. This model makes it possible to take a look at the complexity and multidimensionality of diversity without falling into the old pattern of attributions in the sense of concluding person-related characteristics to behaviour-related aspects.

However, let's consider diversity as a didactic starting point, in the sense of a holistic view (cf. von Thomas, 1996). Diversity is an umbrella term for differences and similarities that exist between people and used constructively. The teacher's diversity competence then refers to the ability to perceive participants in further education as individuals, far from attributions. To respond to them in interaction and communication appreciatively and respectfully, to develop openness towards their approaches and approaches to the topic and to design these didactically and take them into account in planning in an anticipatory manner. This also leads away from a master-pupil relationship!

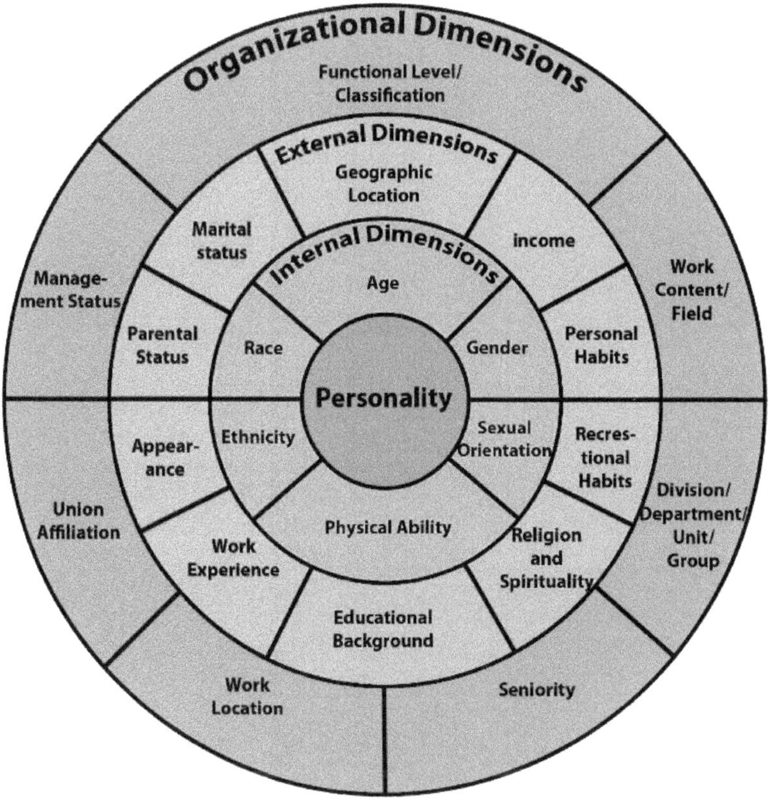

Figure 5: "Four Layers of Diversity" (Gardenswartz & Rowe, 2010)

	Tertiary Education	Quaternary Education
Format	Study program	Vocational further education
Access requirements	Higher education entrance qualification	Completed university degree Or: Vocational experience Or: No specific access requirement in some cases
Duration	3 years (BA), 2 years (MA)	Varies; approx. 2–3 years according to the definition of reputable umbrella organisations
Framework	Higher education legislation, academic accreditation	Understanding of Counselling and further education of individual associations and umbrella organisations And / or: Understanding of Counselling and further education of the respective institution
Acquired qualification	BA or MA	Certification by umbrella organisations Certification by the further education institution
Timing	Commonly after graduating from school	Commonly after graduating from university or after (longer) vocational practice

To consciously deal with these so-called lines of difference that we draw in everyday life (mostly unconsciously) and that guide our behaviour, it is necessary to become aware of one's ideas of normality in relation to 'the participants' and to reflect on them critically: What does a 'normal participant' look like for me? What do I expect (unasked, so to speak) from 'my' participants'? What habitual patterns do I assume in advance? Which behaviours do I see as 'normal', which as 'non-normal', etc.?

Peer Learning

The aspects mentioned above all lead to the fact that continuing education should be an individual process and that teachers continuing education should be individualised. The teacher's role is no longer that of a 'know-it-all' but of a 'multi-know-it-all' and learning guide – or learning advisor (cf. constructivist didactics by Reich, 2012, p. 118).

Learning takes place in informal or formalised peer learning processes (cf. Deutsch & Rohr, 2021), e. g. in peer groups of a continuing systemic education group (see above).

Peer learning can't replace experts' teaching but is, in our understanding, a helpful supplement. However, as a supplement and reinforcement, it is a promising approach whose effectiveness and efficiency have already proven in other contexts. Mellany, Rees and Tripp provide a summary of 13 randomised studies. According to these studies, peers are 85.7% more successful than teachers in knowledge transfer and attitude change (Mellany, Rees & Tripp, 2000). In 63.6% of the studies relating to behaviour change, peer educators were also more effective in counselling activities (cf. also Rohr et al., 2016)).

All communication and interaction processes should always be guided by the basic idea of empowerment, i. e. the idea that "professional helpers do not have to act or care 'for' their addressees, but that it is their task to professionally support and consult those affected in dealing with their affairs. This requires a changed professional attitude" (Theunissen, 1997, p. 1).

Conclusion

Of course, we could only touch on the fundamental issues of high-quality professional development. From education and educational science, we wanted to adjust the spotlight and invite professional discourse.

Continuing education has a long history with us and always needs invigorating discourses and explanations on basics can be learned in which way.

Systemic learning relies on the learners' full autonomy, the high sensitivity of the teachers and their didactic core competencies.

Analogue learning instead of digital teaching, own practice instead of the knowledge of...: all these are striking basics for successfully acquiring competencies.

The worlds of formal learning and semi-formal learning are slowly converging, and a pedagogically sound language and rationale for further education are gaining more and more format. In this context of understanding, the rather traditional learning process in continuing systemic education is newly able to connect to national and international developments. The new results can newly inspire it.

References

Andersen, T. (Hrsg.) (1996). Das Reflektierende Team. Dialoge und Dialoge über Dialoge. Dortmund: Moderndes Lernen.

Biggs, J., Tang, C. (2011). Teaching for Quality Learning at University. What the student does. Maidenhead: Open University Press and Society for Research into Higher Education.

Bloom, B. (1971). Taxonomy of Educational Objectives. The Classification of Education Goals, Handbook I: Cognitive Domain. New York: McGraw-Hill.

Deutsch, C., Rohr, D. (2021). Lehr- und Praxisbuch für Peer Learning – Peer-Projekte initiieren, begleiten und beraten. Weinheim: Beltz.

Gardenswartz, L., Rowe A. (2010). Diverse Teams At work. Capitalizing on the Power of Diversity. Chicago: Irwin Professional Publishing.

Haubl, R., Voß, G. G. (2011). Riskante Arbeitswelten im Spiegel von Supervision. Göttingen: Vandenhoeck & Ruprecht.

Hohenshil, T. H., Amundson, N. E., & Niles, S. G. (Eds.). (2013). Counselling around the world:An international handbook. American Counselling Association.

Huber, L. (1995). Hochschuldidaktik als Theorie der Bildung und Ausbildung. In D. Lenzen (Hrsg.), Enzyklopädie Erziehungswissenschaft. Ausbildung und Sozialisation in der Hochschule, Band 10 (S. 114–138). Stuttgart: Klett.

Huber, L. (2009). Lernkultur – Wieso »Kultur«? Eine Glosse. In R. Schneider, B. Szczyrba, U. Welbers & J. Wild (Hrsg.): Wandel der Lehr- und Lernkulturen. Bielefeld: W. Bertelsmann Verl. S. 14–20 (Blickpunkt Hochschuldidaktik; 120).

Mellany, A. R., Rees, J. B., Tripp, J. H. (2000). Peer-led and adult-led school health education. A critical review of available comparative research. Health Education Research, 15, 533-545.

Paetz, N. V., Ceylan, F., Fiehn, J., Schworm, S., Harteis, C. (2011). Kompetenz in der Hochschuldidaktik. Ergebnisse einer Delphi-Studie über die Zukunft der Hochschullehre. Wiesbaden: Springer VS.

Reich, K. (2012). Konstruktivistische Didaktik: Lehr- und Studienbuch mit Methodenpool. Weinheim: Beltz.

Schaper, N., Reis, O., Wildt, J. (2012). Fachgutachten zur Kompetenzorientierung in Studium und Lehre. Ausgearbeitet für die HRK, Projekt nexus, Konzepte und gute Praxis für Studium und Lehre, verfügbar unter: http://www.hrk-nexus.de/fileadmin/redaktion/hrk-nexus/07-Downloads/07-02-Publikationen/fachgutachten_kompetenzorientierung.pdf

Schindler, I., Kricke, M., Rohr, D. (2013). Nach der Praxis Mehr-Sehen: Die Methode des Reflecting Teams. In D. Rohr, A. Hummelsheim, M. Kricke, B. Amrhein (Hrsg.), Reflexionsmethoden in der Praktikumsbegleitung (S. 99–109). Münster: Waxmann.

Schneider, R., Szczyrba, B., Welbers, U., Wildt, J. (Hrsg.) (2009). Wandel der Lehr- und Lernkulturen. Bielefeld: Bertelsmann.

Theunissen, G. (1997). Familie – Behinderung – Ablösung. Heilpädagogik, 2, 1–9.
Thomas, R. R. (1996). A Diversity Framework. In M. C. Chemers, S. Oskamp, M. A. Constanz (Hrsg.), Diversity in Organisations. New Perspektives for a Workplace (S. 245–263). Thousand Oaks: Sage.
Tremp, P. (2009). Hochschuldidaktische Forschungen – Orientierende Referenzpunkte für didaktische Professionalität und Studienreform. In R. Schneider, B. Szczyrba, U. Welbers, J. Wildt (Hrsg.), Wandel der Lehr- und Lernkulturen (S. 206–219). Bielefeld: Bertelsmann.
Wildt, J. (2004). »The Shift from Teaching to Learning« – Thesen zum Wandel der Lernkultur in modularisierten Studienstrukturen. In H. Ehlert, U. Welbers (Hrsg.), Qualitätssicherung und Studienreform. Strategie- und Programmentwicklung für Fachbereiche und Hochschulen im Rahmen von Zielvereinbarungen am Beispiel der Heinrich-Heine-Universität Düsseldorf (S. Kontext von Beratungs-Weiterbildung, S. 233).
Wildt, J. (2007). Anschlussfähigkeit und professionelle Identität der Hochschuldidaktik – ein Blick zurück nach vorn auf dem Weg vom Lehren zum Lernen in der Hochschulbildung (Thesen). In K. Reiber, R. Richter (Hrsg.), Entwicklungslinien der Hochschuldidaktik. Ein Blick zurück nach vorn: Beiträge zur Tübinger Tagung vom 29.11 bis 01.12.2006 (S. 187–201). Berlin: Logos.

7.2 Professionalisation – "Don't play what's there. Play what's not there" (Miles Davis)[3]

In the discourse on counselling, a persistent thematisation of the goodness and quality of counselling practice can be observed, which Ehmer and Busse aptly formulate with the question "Do we know what we are doing when we provide counselling" (cf. Busse & Ehmer, 2010, p. 7). Despite or precisely because of all professionalisation efforts, efforts to shed light on the "black box of counselling" (Galdynski & Kühl, 2009) seem to be more critical than ever.

One might be inclined to assume a professional identity deficit. A desire for self-assurance, or a call for legitimising points of reference for professionals working in the field of counselling. However, the presumed vagueness and uncertainties in counselling say nothing

[3] We have used quotes from Miles Davis as headings for the sections of this text. For us, these sometimes contain something very pertinent, sometimes something very contrary to what we see as the playfulness of the counselling process. In any case, they have given us food for thought

about the actual quality of counselling in practice. The problematisation of counselling quality instead points to questions asked and answered by sure sides with specific intentions and interests.

In our view, assigning one answer can to a political-institutional strand of discourse. Professional societies and associations have a legitimate interest in identifying their profession's quality. To exclude dilettantism and charlatanism, separate the "good into the pot and the bad into the jar". In this selection process, the field of counselling is currently following a classic professionalisation path. Through standardisation, formalisation and norming of quality criteria and training formats (cf. e. g. DGfB, 2010).

Another relevant answer comes from the theoretical-scientific discourse on counselling, which is without doubt closely interrelated with the first discourse strand. On the one hand, an adaptation of the currently hegemonic educational discourse focusing on competency models and outcome orientation can be observed (cf. Zwicker-Pelzer, 2010; Schiersmann & Weber, 2013). tacit knowledge to explain the expertise of counselling experts and subsequent considerations on how the "silence of the experts" (Neuweg, 2015) can be brought up and made available for teaching/learning processes (cf. e. g. Böhle, 2010; Gold, 2014).

With the metaphor of play, we would like to explore another way of describing counselling expertise in our contribution. We want to explore which meaningful connections arise for the teaching of counselling. This ties in with the search movement to teach and learn counselling in diverse ways. We started with the project of inviting thirty counselling teachers to report anecdotally and personally on their teaching experiences (cf. Rohr, Hummelsheim & Höcker, 2016).

"I'll play it first and tell you what it is later." (Miles Davis)

Arist von Schlippe has described the complexity of (systemic) counselling as an intersection of "craft, art, science and profession" (von Schlippe, 2008). One could then ask whether experiential knowledge transferring to counselling requires a master's apprenticeship, whether into systematic book knowledge or developing structured didactics for teaching counselling. But if the "salt in the soup" of counselling processes is found in a playful-human togetherness. Which runs through the above categories as it were (von Schlippe, 2008, p. 462ff), would it not then be appropriate to ask how, above all, play in counselling can be learned and taught? To pursue this question further, we would like to tie in with the Dreyfus and Dreyfus' model of expertise encounter in the professionalisation debate.

Expertise research has dealt in detail with and upgraded so-called experiential knowledge, application knowledge or action knowledge. In particular, experts found, i. e. people who consistently show outstanding performance in a field, differ from beginners in the amount of explicit specialised knowledge, but even more so in the use of incorporated or implicit expertise (cf. Gruber & Ziegler, 1996). Thus, experts quickly appear as "intellectual magicians" (ibid., p. 7) whose tricks remain closed and intangible. In this respect, the stage model developed by Dreyfus and Dreyfus (1987) can consider demystifying, which illuminates the application of different knowledge organisation, decision criteria and action premises within the path from novice to expert. In this way, "mastery" is not declared an expression of genius but fundamentally learnable. The model in a nutshell:

1. **Novice learners** use abstract, context-free rules explicit in theories, models and receptive procedures to analyse the current situation and plan and execute actions.
2. **Advanced beginners** increasingly act in a way that adapts the situation based on concrete experience. Non-objectifiable, context-bound aspects of conditions are recognised but still processed within the corset of action-guiding rules.
3. **Competent people** have developed routines of action through increasing experience, which enable them to perceive situations as a set of elements. Enabling competent people to recognise, select and prioritise relevant factors that seem to achieve the goal. Finally, qualified people can break rules that do not lead to a goal.
4. **Experienced people** choose their courses of action based on situational experience. Situations are now perceived holistically in analogy to conditions already experienced. The intuitive ability to use patterns instead of breaking conditions down into individual components develops.
5. **Experts** act intuitively solely based on their experience. Decisions made can hardly be justified in an understandable way to others, let alone articulated in the form of explicit knowledge. One's intuition questioned in the case of new,

> non-comparable situations. However, this is not done as rational-analytical problem solving but through situational-holistic comparison to modifying one's intuition.

The model of stage progression makes it clear that in the development to become an expert, there is no accumulation and differentiation of declarative knowledge, but rather a qualitative reorganisation of thinking and acting from "rule-guided 'know-that' to experience-based 'know-how'" (Dreyfus & Dreyfus, 1987, p. 41). The modalities of decision-making processes change from the analytical to the planning to the intuitive problem-solving mode.

So would Miles Davis not have been able to say afterwards how what he played came about? Neuweg (2004, p. 297) assumes that large parts of expert knowledge can is neither verbalised nor formalised. For even if experts articulate the rules of their intuitive action, according to Neuweg it is an "ex-post rationalisation" since a knowledge base is updated or even constructed that was not at all effective in the experimental process (ibid., p. 83). Kaiser also does not believe in the possibility of transferring implicit into explicit expert knowledge. However, he believes that it is possible, for example, to make the experiential knowledge of experts accessible to learners by telling memories in the form of experienced situations or stories. Since the access here is not via explicit rule knowledge, but via the level of situational similarities (cf. Kaiser, 2006).

Either way, for us, the question arises at this point whether it is at all desirable for counsellors to reach an intuitive mode, because, especially for process counselling – in contrast to specialist, expert or knowledge counselling – it seems to be counterproductive at first to reach the status of expert. Here, the maxim is to recognise the clients as experts for their knowledge structures and reality construction and their own problem-solving and refuse their knowledge offers, and solution proposals since counsellors cannot be the "better knowing" experts. If it makes sense to speak of "Counselling expertise" at all, one might think, then paradoxically ex negativo as the expertise of not knowing. Therefore, we would first like to examine what the expertise of counsellors might consist of, what knowledge is linked to it, and to what extent a playful approach to the paradox described above allows access to the "salt in the soup" of counselling processes.

"The note is only 20 percent. The attitude of the motherfucker who plays it is 80 percent." (Miles Davis)

They base Systemic thinking and action on the constitutive opacity of inner maps. They recognise the self-organisation and inherent logic of systems. The resulting impossibility of instructing non-trivial machines (von Foerster). Counsellors and clients inevitably remain black boxes for each other. Suppose people construct their reality based on their subjective world of meaning and experience. In that case, it does not seem very helpful to give advice or suggest solutions in counselling. Counsellors cannot always have objective knowledge at their disposal from which they can produce answers for the client's problems. It, therefore, makes sense to recognise clients as "experts" (Hargens, 2016) for their life-world and to trust that they will generate suitable solutions for themselves and their contexts.

The systemic perspective accordingly takes into account the uniqueness and complexity of any social interaction. It recognises that counselling processes do not follow a manual but are "different every time" (Neumann-Wirsig, 2011), that the counsellor-client system is challenged to "start all over again, as it were" (Hargens, 2011, p. 11). From this insight, the attitude of not knowing, sometimes also referred to in Zen Buddhism terminology as "beginner's mind" (Suzuki, 2001), has developed as a counsellor's fundamental attitude. This attitude springs a curiosity for clients' stories, narratives and explanatory models, what they experience and how they share it, and what will change in the future. Instead of prematurely knowing which path is the "right" one for clients, it is essential to always be open to new things in the encounter, to let oneself be surprised, to stay awake and attentive, to try out and experiment. As such a non-linear process, counselling is like a "dance of exploration and discovery that is constantly changing and transforming creatively" (Eberhart & Knill, 2010, p. 60).

In this respect, counsellors would not be knowledge experts but pure experts in shaping processes by creating play spaces in which even severe and complex topics can be creatively worked on together with pleasure and fulfilment so that something new and change can emerge. It is essential to observe both reality constructions and those of the client as contingent and constantly relativise them. Only in this way can one create cooperation in the sense of "play", as opposed to "game", which is about winning and losing or right and wrong, develop (cf. von Schlippe, 2008, p. 463).

However, it would be presumptuous to claim that process counselling can do without any knowledge. Developing expertise in a domain that has not been penetrated in some form and gaining a lot of experience appears to be an illusion. If we adopt the attitude of not knowing, this does not mean that we are suddenly blank slates. We cannot enter a vacuum. Nor do counsellors have to reinvent the wheel every time. Observation of reality always depends on the observer's perspective, and for counsellors, shaping this perspective's background by expertise and experiential knowledge.

"Thus, one can consider the fields of work of systemic individual, couple and family therapy as well as the setting of supervision as process-counselling 'playing fields' in their purest form. However, we should not conclude from this that a good systemic therapist or supervisor can do without knowledge – on the contrary. He needs a lot of psychological, communication-theoretical, therapeutic knowledge that underlies his process action. His provocative questions, the choice of methodology, and the respective foci in the counselling process based on a hypothesis formation that takes place 'in silence' within the counsellor's psychological system. Thus, systemic process expertise is ultimately also based on professional knowledge know-how as well as on broad experiential knowledge." (Barthelmess, 2016, p. 30)

"Man, sometimes it takes you a long time to sound like yourself." (Miles Davis)

Based on an intuitive mode of expertise formed on experience, the question of skill is therefore not off the table. However, experience seems to be a double-edged sword, especially for the practice of the counselling profession. Suppose it makes sense for successful counselling processes to accept each counselling process in its uniqueness to generate something new in creative interaction with clients. In that case, experience may prove to be an obstacle since a conservative characterises experience, i. e. it looks for proof and confirmation in what is already known and familiar.

"The reduction to the all too familiar simultaneously closes our view of the uniqueness of life processes. [...] But the fact that everyone is familiar with such situations shows how effective this mechanism is, which makes us search the world of experience primarily for regularities. Indeed, the same process that creates order and security – namely the reduction to familiar categories – is at the same time the gravedigger for creativity and change." (Kriz, 2004, p. 20)

Moreover, rich experience does not automatically lead to superior skill. The saying indeed goes that "experience is the best teacher". On the other hand, many years of experience does not necessarily guarantee extraordinary expertise. "Experience means nothing. You can also do your job badly for 35 years", Kurt Tucholsky once said.

Experienced counsellors, however, cultivate a way of dealing with their world of experience, we assume, which allows for the playful use of their patterns of experience and can nevertheless, or precisely because of this, release creative potentials. On the one hand, the confrontation with one's subjective theories, experiences, convictions, beliefs, etc., is the subject of training and further education in counselling. On the one hand, the confrontation with one's subjective theories, experiences, convictions, beliefs, etc., is the subject of further education and training in counselling, which in the best case continues periodically in the form of supervision or intervention.

Counsellors, therefore, develop a professional habitus that enables them to observe and relativise their reality constructs in the counselling process. On the other hand, the counselling setting is a particular form of social interaction that resembles a moratorium. In contrast to the situational logic of practice determined by pressure to act and urgency, the counselling setting offers a space for reflection and experimentation. They are given a different temporality with the possibility of postponement and delay. New perspectives can first be experienced and tried out without being exposed to the risk of the irreversibility of decisions made. Counselling, one could perhaps say, occurs in a slow, decelerated space in which pauses, hesitations, silences or even interruptions are possible, if not necessary. This creates repeated opportunities for counsellors to observe the process and themselves, become aware of their resonances and impulses so as not to fall into familiarity and thus remain present and attentive to the uniqueness of the situation. We cannot switch off our experiences, and they also determine what we perceive and how we observe. But the distancing step back and the consciously adopted attitude of not knowing can help put one's perspectives and experiences, the counselling knowledge, and emerging assumptions and hypotheses on hold.

This oscillation between distancing and being involved also seems possible for the counselling approach to intuition, i. e., the Dreyfus/Dreyfus model's expert level. To do this, we must first free ourselves from an everyday understanding of intuition as a quasi-mystical intuition, as an ability through which we have direct access to reality equipped mysteriously with a claim to truth that cannot be questioned.

Dreyfus and Dreyfus assume that intuition is not something inexplicably mysterious but something learned with their stage model. Intuition is ultimately the organic product of incorporated and encapsulated knowledge and experience. However, the crux with the incident described above arises again on the intuitive mode level. The difference is that one's access to the modalities of decisions and obstructed actions, so that plausible reasons and explanations cannot legitimise reflexive action. Like experience, intuition can be misguided and is thus no guarantee of goodness. However, if intuition can be learned, perhaps the perception of entering the intuitive mode can also be learned, so intuition and the situational-holistic function coupled to it could help counselling processes.

Schmid and Gérard, for example, assume a possible "intuition training". They define intuition from a systemic point of view as a "construction of reality" (Schmid & Gérard, 2008, p. 24), which is, therefore, initially neither "a seal of approval nor a disqualification" (ibid., p. 33). Schmid and Gérard describe the intuitive process as follows: "Intuitive control thus means neither control according to a different, better intelligence nor control that is thoughtless and uncontrolled in its motives and interests. Intuitive control means processing complex data into information that we could not process consciously and explainable. [...] The main achievement of intuition is thus the lightning-fast control of behaviour in complex situations" (ibid., p. 7). Since intuition can also be "misprogrammed" (ibid., p. 33), Schmid and Gérard emphasise "the need to purify intuition specifically through professional qualification" (ibid., p. 51). This purification cannot be done in a pristinely rational-analytical way. "Rather, scientific-methodical and insensate-intuitive procedures must be integrated into the process of intuition training. It transpires, for example, through circumstantial querying of the intuitions at work in professional situations, in supervision" (ibid.).

Jürgen Kriz goes one step further in his concept of order-order transitions. For him, intuitive moments seem to be indispensable in the counselling process, as only in this way can create strategies for the development of something new be set in motion. For the activation of creative resources, a moment of letting go of linguistic-abstract categories is needed, as these prevent the perception of the complexity and uniqueness of direct experience (Kriz, 2013, p. 203f). With the teleological principle of the sense-attractor, Kriz surmises that incipient orders can be grasped holistically at an early stage. It is not possible to verbalise when upsetting the stability of familiar patterns; the embryonic order will look akin to detail since it imposes itself somewhat diffusely and vaguely as a hunch, a "sense of possibility" (R. Musil). "From this perspective, intuition can thus be characterised as the facility to holistically grasp essential aspects of a developing or unfolding (or correspondingly transmuting) order. Which only later becomes plenarily describable analytically, at an early stage of development" (Kriz, 2001, p. 226). According to Kriz, teleological-imaginative approaches are categorically felicitous for promoting intuitive processes.

In contrast to orchestrating-determining processes oriented to past patterns, they have dynamic aspects. The path to realising imagined goals does not have to follow a linear, controllable course. But can develop through active experimentation, which ultimately sanctions ingenious access to different paths and possibilities (Kriz, 2013, p. 206). Against this background, Kriz also advocates that counsellors learn intuition so that creative processes for developing the new can emerge in the playful counselling process.

"For therapists, counsellors and coaches, promotion of their intuition aims at enabling them to recognise developments at an early stage through a holistic perception better than the rational-analytical view of the details would allow. [...] Therapists then develop the above-mentioned 'play-space' together with the patients, in which gives playful, artistic and creative space intuition to develop helpful imaginations." (ibid., p. 206f).

"It's not the note you play that's the wrong note – it's the note you play afterwards that makes it right or wrong." (Miles Davis)

Although the two intuition mentioned above concepts emphasise the learning of intuition and assume a consciously controllable use of intuitive processes in counselling, the idea of intuition still has something inexplicable. It remains questionable whether the term is suitable for describing the expertise of counsellors. Arist von Schlippe has rightly pointed out the dangers of an unreflected reference to the term intuition. The complementary communication situations in the counselling setting could easily lead to an abuse of power if counsellors were to refer to intuition in their approach since such decisions could no longer be refuted by argument. This is why von Schlippe pleads for abolishing the term in counselling (cf. von Schlippe, 2012).

Perhaps the term improvisation is a more appropriate way to describe what happens in the playful counselling encounter. We believe that the concept of improvisation can connect to the posture of not knowing. The frolicsome-ingenious processes of the counselling event can be described in a reciprocal-circular way. They were eschewing pitfalls resulting from an orientation towards person-bound, individual skills to expound counselling expertise. As with the concept of intuition, it is first necessary to abandon a mundane understanding of improvisation as an expression of inner genius or as a stopgap measure. Improvisation can then conceptualise as an "ephemeral art" (Meyer, 2005) characterised by a processual and eventful character. Meyer also emphasises the communicative and interactive aspects of improvisation.

"The individual enters into a dialogue with his environment in the form of communication and interaction. Demanding improvisation creating situations that provoke action in spontaneous, surprising and communicative tasks. Self-activity, communication, and interaction competence of the individual enable the unfolding of creative processes and challenge other people's reactions." (Meyer, 2005, p. 471)

Improvisation plays towards the heritage of displaying knowledge of the capriciousness, unplayability and unplannability of human encounters. With the possibilities that arise from the situation's circumstances. It resembles a "contingency unfolding game" (Bormann, Brandstetter & Matzke, 2010, p. 8). What improvisation is precisely, however, according to Dell, cannot be grasped, since as a performative act, it marks "precisely the difference between thinking and acting, between what is thinking on the one hand and what is acted out and felt on the other" (Dell, 2014, p. 6). "We can only circumscribe improvisation, only place ourselves in an attitude of readiness to improvise. Everything else is called forth by the situations and the resulting processes" (ibid.).

As an attitude, improvisation arises from "curiosity, flexibility and openness towards the other and the foreign" (Meyer, 2005, p. 470). Bertram describes the prerequisite for creative processes in a similar way: "It is an attitude that shows itself in the turning towards the open on a kind of fluid matrix of possibility between enthusiasm, curiosity, attentiveness and the desire to encounter, also with oneself. It is the non-linear, creative thinking and acting that understands how to navigate in open systems with multiple unknowns" (Bertram, 2014, p. 8).

The compatibility of an attitude described in this way with the systemic view and the perspective of not knowing, which is fundamental for counselling processes, seems to be given at this point. Playful encounters in counselling could thus be described as non-linear "trial movements" (ibid.), as the "trial displacement" (ibid.), as a game at the boundaries of the existing with the trial of their displacement in the rule enforcement. Counsellors and clients then improvise together with the clients' "material", for which, however, the clients are and remain experts. But the "material" of counsellors is also fed into this process because, in the counselling process, two (or more) psychological systems construct a social system, the counsellor-client system.

The improvisational attitude can then help counsellors to let go of their patterns or use them flexibly and variably, to let themselves be irritated and surprised, again and again, to give space to creative processes in the communicative-interactive counselling process. The skill of counsellors is then not based on the use of intuition, but in the shaping of methods based on the attitude of not knowing and an improvising attitude, so that the drifting together in the counsellor-client system can also take place playfully and joyfully.

"Anybody can play." (Miles Davis) – The playful encounter in teaching/learning processes

Counselling is not the only improvisation, and counsellors are not non-knowers. The depicted perspectives make it conceivable to manage the power to establish unconventionality, vulnerabilities and unknowns of social cooperations and encourage admittance to the perky snapshot of human experience, to the "salt in the soup." To use Arist von Schlippe's metaphor again. However, the soup's salting only becomes possible when fulfiling other components and framework conditions, when knowledge, tools, experiences and routines, etc., for making the soup are available. These can be analysed, described and prepared for teaching / learning processes.

The teaching of counselling, learning arrangements can be designed despite the general non-indestructibility of learners, through which favourable framework conditions for the creative acquisition of counselling expertise. Beyond the examination of declarative knowledge and the practice of methodological procedures, paving the way for proficiency. Beyond manualised processes through situated learning – experience-based and experience-oriented formats, self-reflection for subjective restructuring theories, etc.

But suppose the playful encounter is the essence of counselling processes, as it fills all other components with life. In that case, it seems worthwhile to us to also bring this liveliness into the teaching / learning process. For us, this also means, in the sense of the pedagogical double-decker, to exemplify and make it possible to experience what we believe is essential for counselling processes. It would then make sense to make the teaching-learning relationship playful for counselling teachers, meet the learners with the attitude of not knowing and an improvisational attitude, and recognise learners from the beginning as co-players in a joint exploration testing of new possibilities. The contingency and diversity of meaning of learning situations can thus be creatively explored and experienced in a playful space to finally test the connectivity and fit of new options for action, again situationally.

The design of this teaching-learning space and the provision of one's person as an object for observational learning can, of course, only ever be an offer; an offer that takes place in trust in the self-organisation of the learners, despite the unavoidable knowledge advantage of the teachers, as an encounter at eye level.

References

Barthelmess, M. (2016). Die systemische Haltung. Was systemisches Arbeiten im Kern ausmacht. Göttingen: Vandenhoeck & Ruprecht.

Bertram, U. (2014). Non-lineares Denken und Handeln entwickeln. Improvisationskraft, Erfindungsgabe und Probierbewegungen In praeview. Zeitschrift für innovative Arbeitsgestaltung und Prävention, No. 1/2014, 8–9.

Böhle, F. (2010). Erfahrungswissen und subjektivierendes Handeln – verborgene Seiten professionellen Handelns. In S. Busse, S. Ehmer [Eds.]: Wissen wir, was wir tun? Beraterisches Handeln in Supervision und Coaching (pp. 36–54). Göttingen: Vandenhoeck & Ruprecht.

Bormann, H.-F., Brandstetter, G., Matzke, A. [Eds.] (2010). Improvisieren. Paradoxien des Unvorhersehbaren. Kunst – Medien – Praxis. Bielefeld: transcript Verlag.

Busse, S., Ehmer, S. (2010). Vorwort. In S. Busse, S. Ehmer [Hrsg.]: Wissen wir, was wir tun? Beraterisches Handeln in Supervision und Coaching (pp. 7–13). Göttingen: Vandenhoeck & Ruprecht

Dell, C. (2014). Zum Begriff Improvisation. In praeview. Zeitschrift für innovative Arbeitsgestaltung und Prävention, No. 1/2014, 6–7.

Deutsche Gesellschaft für Beratung e. V. (2010). Essentials einer Weiterbildung Beratung/Counselling. http://dachverband-beratung.de/dokumente/DGfB_Weiterbildungsstandards_2010-03.pdf [25.6.2017].

Dreyfus, H. L., Dreyfus, S. E. (1987). Künstliche Intelligenz. Von den Grenzen der Denkmaschine und dem Wert der Intuition. Rheinbeck bei Hamburg: Rowohlt.

Eberhart, H., Knill, P. J. (2010). Lösungskunst. Lehrbuch der kunst- und ressourcenorientierten Arbeit. Göttingen: Vandenhoeck & Ruprecht.

Galdynski, K., Kühl, S. [Eds.] (2009). Black-Box Beratung: Empirische Studien zu Coaching und Supervision. Wiesbaden: VS Verlag für Sozialwissenschaften.

Gold, B. (2014 Professionalisierung von Coaching durch Experten-Novizen-Dialoge – Perspektiven aus der Expertiseforschung. In A. Ryba, D. Ginati, D. Pauw, S. Rietmann [Hrsg.], Professionell coachen. Das Fall- und Reflexionsbuch: Vom Erfahrungswissen zur Handlungskompetenz (pp. 12–29). Weinheim: Beltz Verlag.

Gruber, H., Ziegler, A. [eds.] (1996). Expertiseforschung: theoretische und methodische Grundlagen. Opladen: Westdeutscher Verlag.

Hargens, J. (2011). Aller Anfang ist ein Anfang. Gestaltungsmöglichkeiten hilfreicher systemischer Gespräche. 4. Auflage. Göttingen: Vandenhoeck & Ruprecht.

Hargens, J. (2016). Beraten lehren – oder: Wer ist denn kundig? In D. Rohr, A. Hummelsheim, M. Höcker [Eds.], Beratung lehren. Erfahrungen, Geschichten, Reflexionen aus der Praxis von 30 Lehrenden (pp. 38–46). Weinheim: Beltz.

Kaiser, H. (2006). Der Tacit Knowing View. Ein Vorschlag als Antwort fur die von G. H. Neuweg aufgeworfenen Fragen. www.hrkll.ch/typo/fileadmin/Texte/ILM/Der_Tactic_Knowing_View_fest.pdf [25.6.2017].

Kriz, J. (2001). Intuition in therapeutischen Prozessen. Systhema. No. 3. vol. 15, 217–229.

Kriz, J. (2004 Personzentrierte Systemtheorie. Grundfragen und Kernaspekte. In A. von Schlippe, W. C. Kriz [Eds.], Personzentrierung und Systemtheorie. Perspektiven für psychotherapeutisches Handeln (pp. 13–67). Göttingen: Vandenhoeck & Ruprecht.

Kriz, J. (2013). Kreativität und Intuition aus systemischer Sicht. In H. R. Fischer [Eds.], Wie kommt Neues in die Welt? Phantasie, Intuition und der Ursprung von Kreativität (pp.197–208). Weilerswist: Vellbrück Wissenschaft.

Meyer, K.-A. S. (2005) Improvisation als flüchtige Kunst und die Folgen für die Theaterpädagogik. Inaugural-Dissertation. https://opus4.kobv.de/opus4-udk/files/14/Meyer_Karl_2.pdf [23.6.2017].

Neumann-Wirsig, H. (2011). Jedes Mal anders. 50 Supervisionsgeschichten und viele Möglichkeiten. Heidelberg: Carl Auer Verlag.

Neuweg, G. H. (2004 Konnerschaft und implizites Wissen. Zur lehr-lern- theoretischen Bedeutung der Erkenntnis- und Wissenstheorie Michael Polanyis. 3rd ed. Münster/ New York: Waxmann Verlag.

Neuweg, G. H. (2015). Das Schweigen der Könner. Gesammelte Schriften zum impliziten Wissen. Münster/ New York: Waxmann Verlag.

Rohr, D., Hummelsheim, A., Höcker, M. [Eds.] (2016). Beratung lehren. Erfahrungen, Geschichten, Reflexionen aus der Praxis von 30 Lehrenden. Weinheim: Beltz.

Schiersmann, C., Weber, P. [Eds.] (2013). Beratung in Bildung, Beruf und Beschäftigung. Eckpunkte und Erprobung eines integrierten Qualitätskonzepts. Bielefeld: Bertelsmann Verlag.

Schmid, B., Gérard, C. (2008). Intuition und Professionalität. Systemische Transaktionsanalyse in Beratung und Therapie. Heidelberg: Carl-Auer.

Suzuki, S. (2001). Zen-Geist Anfänger-Geist: Einführung in Zen-Meditation. 10. überarb. Auflage. Bielefeld: Theseus.

von Schlippe, A. (2008). Systemische Praxis zwischen Handwerk, Kunst, Wissenschaft und Profession. OSC Organisationsberatung – Supervision – Coaching. 15(4). pp. 455–467.

von Schlippe, A. (2012). Intuition – Plädoyer für die Abschaffung eines Begriffes. In H. Molte, R. Schindler, A. von Schlippe [Eds.], Vom Gegenwind zum Aufwind. Der Aufbruch des systemischen Gedankens (pp.36–47). Göttingen: Vandenhoeck & Ruprecht.

Zwicker-Pelzer, R. (2010 Beratung in der sozialen Arbeit. Bad Heilbrunn: Julius Klinkhardt Verlagsbuchhandlung.

8 Research in Counselling

We need more research in counselling if we want to strengthen counselling as a profession and if we want to implement counselling in mental health systems (Schubert, Rohr & Zwicker-Pelzer, 2019; Bager-Charleson & McBeath, 2020). And the research should be multiple dimensional.

This chapter is a plea for mixed-methods research (MMR) designs in the field of counselling. Even if MMR is very elaborate, it is worth doing.

By way of example, I would like to briefly outline two of my projects, using MMR, in more detail: Exploratory Sequential Designs.

8.1 Mixed-Methods Research in our Marte Meo Project[4]

We want to remind you of the "Classification", the "five purposes for mixing in mixed-methods research:

1. ***Triangulation*** seeks convergence, corroboration, correspondence of results from different ways;
2. ***Complementarity*** seeks elaboration, enhancement, illustration, clarification of the results from one method with the results from the other method;
3. ***Development*** seeks to use the results from one method to help develop or inform the other method, where interpretation includes sampling and implementation, as well as measurement decisions;
4. ***Initiation*** seeks the discovery of paradox and contradiction, new perspectives of frameworks, the recasting of questions or results from one method with questions or results from the other method;
5. ***Expansion*** seeks to extend the breadth and range of inquiry by using different methods for different inquiry components" (Greene, 1989, S. 259; Greene, 2007)

[4] I thank my mentor Charles Deutsch, Harvard University, the Marte Meo Research Group, especially my wife Kathrin Meiners, also Sophia Nettersheim. This is an excerpt from Rohr, Nettersheim, Deutsch & Meiners, 2020)

Although at the beginning of mixed-methods research designs, qualitative and quantitative data were kept separate. They are considered distinct databases.

Mixed-methods research has five essential characteristics: the collection and analysis of both quantitative and qualitative data, the use of rigorous procedures in conducting quantitative and qualitative research, the integration of the findings, use of mixed-method designs and the use of conceptual framework (Creswell, 2017). By "Integration", we mean integrating quantitative and qualitative research through our research teams, philosophies, research process and research methods.

A mixed-methods research project provides more insight than qualitative or quantitative data alone by greater mining data depth. The different understanding from linking enables the databases to "talk" to each other. We can compare the two database results. Follow up quantitative results with qualitative data collection. Instead, first, explore qualitatively and then test it out quantitatively. Mixed-method designs can stand alone or combine with other frameworks.

Core Designs

There are three different core designs: convergent design, explanatory sequential design and explanatory sequential design. A plan's importance is: identifying theoretical framework, writing a mixed-methods question, and writing an excellent mixed-method study aim, composing the study using writing structure that matches the design, developing a joint display for integration, identifying the methodological/validity issues in design, drawing a diagram of configuration, identifying the type of mixed-methods design and creating an excellent mixed-methods title.

The **convergent design** qualitative interviews and analysis and quantitative survey and analysis stand alone in the first phase. Then they are merged and an interpretation follows. You should choose a convergent design when your mixed-method project intends to compare results, develop broader products, validate data, and build cases. It can be helpful when you need rapid data collection. It is also beneficial when you have equal emphasis on both quantitative and qualitative data.

The **explanatory sequential design** has three phases. In the first phase, the quantitative survey and analysis of the qualitative interviews and comment will be explained in the second phase. After the second phase, an interpretation follows.

The **explanatory sequential design** starts with collecting quantitative data through a cross-sectional web-based survey, which delivers numeric data. It follows an analysis of the data through data screening, providing descriptive statistics and factor loadings. In the case selection, an interview protocol development, 1 participant dorm will be selected and interviewed, which delivers an interview protocol.

The collection of qualitative data happens through documents and telephone interviews. It makes up the text and image data. Lastly, the qualitative data analysis follows a cross-thematic study and delivers a cross-thematic matrix and a visual model of multiple case analysis.

You should choose an explanatory sequential design when your mixed-method project intends to explain surprising, contradictory, outlier results or results that do not match theory or form groups/cases for further analysis. Other reasons could be when you have time to conduct your study in phases or emphasise starting a project from a quantitative perspective.

The third core design is the exploratory sequential design, which we selected.

Exploratory Sequential Design

We chose to employ an exploratory sequential design. As illustrated in Figure 6, in general, this design has three phases. In the first phase, interviews, observations and other qualitative methods are conducted and analyses made.

The second phase is the quantitative phase, which includes an instrument design or intervention design. Then follows a quantitative test of an instrument or intervention in phase 3, which builds up an interpretation. The analysis of qualitative data leads to the development of a quantitative device. "We can first explore qualitatively, and then test out the ideas quantitatively" (Creswell, 2017, p. 5).

Afterwards, quantitative data will be collected and analysed and an interpretation follows. You should choose an experimental sequential design when your mixed-methods project intends to build and test an intervention, instrument, survey, app or website or new variables. Other reasons could be when you emphasise starting your project qualitatively or when you have time to collect in phases over time.

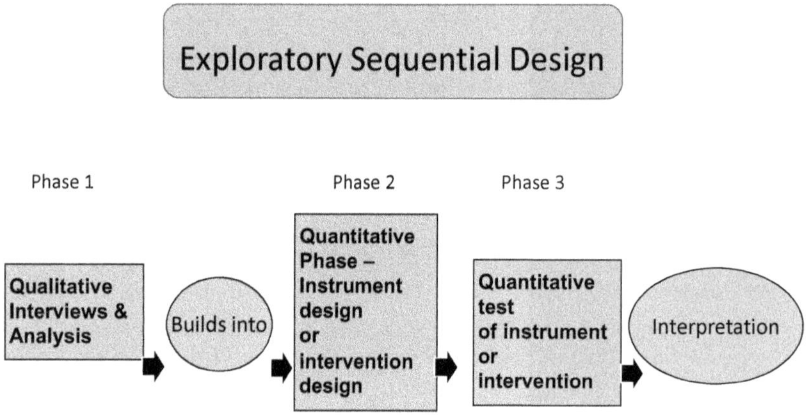

Figure 6: Exploratory Sequential Design (Creswell, 2017, p. 17[5])

An integrated exploratory sequential design (Creswell, 2017) seems to be best suited to our purposes. An exploratory sequential design enabled us to discover in detail how a selected group of experts and parents applied for the Marte Meo programme, and we then tested out the ideas culled from that process quantitatively with a large convenience sample.

The exploratory sequential design of the Marte Meo project has five phases as illustrated in Figure 7. A systematic literature review carried out in the first phase, which builds into qualitative interviews and analysis in the second phase. The third phase builds an analysis of videotaped observations. A quantitative phase with an online survey follows and in the last step follows an interpretation.

The staged qualitative research consisted of designing, conducting and analysing semi-structured interviews with parents and Marte Meo Counsellors and then using that analysis to inform the design,

[5] Not published PowerPoint slide within a webinar from John Creswell

the conduct and analysis of videotaped observations of everyday situations in day-care centres to examine the process and effects of Marte Meo interaction elements on children.

Combining these qualitative analyses then became the basis for developing an online questionnaire that could enable us to collect quantitative data on the current use of Marte Meo in practice by experts. As a result of this design, four phases of analysis will be carried out: after the two qualitative phases, after the quantitative phase and during the integration phase, which will connect the data strands and expand the initial qualitative exploratory results. This article reports the quantitative stage and the final integration stage of the research on the first stage.

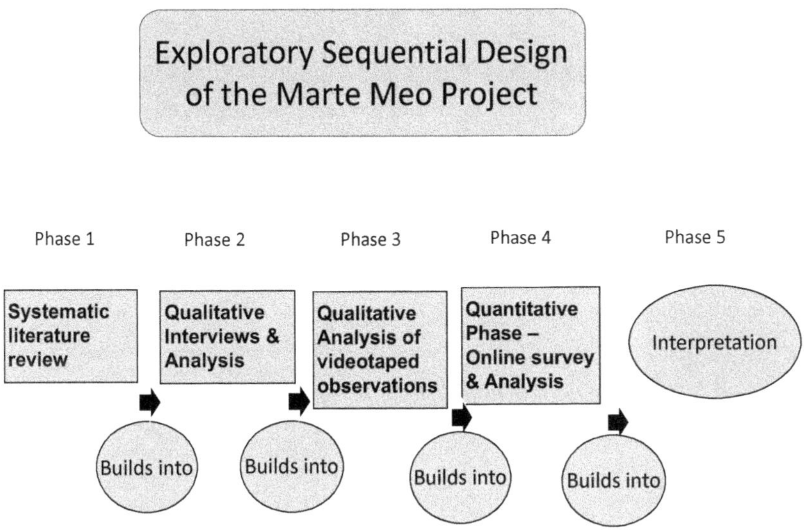

Figure 7: Exploratory Sequential Design of the Marte Meo Project

8.2 Mixed-Methods Research in our Genograms Project[6]

The second project is one concerning genograms. Genograms are an integral part of therapy and counselling.

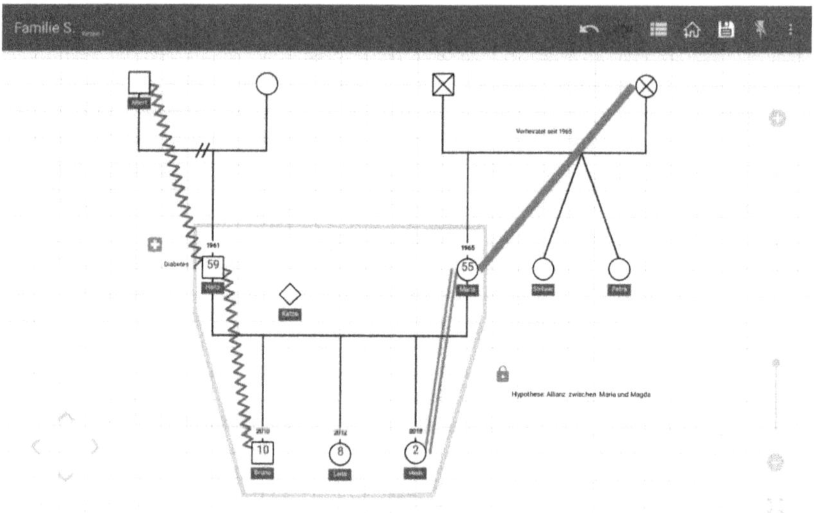

Figure 8: Example genogram created with the InGeno app.

The study investigated the meaning and functions of genograms in the professional practice of counsellors.

The article (Rohr et al., 2021) presents partial results of the research project InGeno, in which – based on the actual use of genograms to be researched – we are developing user-friendly software for genogram creation. One hundred eight counsellors took part in the quantitative online questionnaire study. The data were analysed descriptively and compared with the preliminary study's qualitative results by Rohr (2017), in which we analysed expert interviews on a similar question.

[6] This chapter is a translated short form from Rohr, Spath & Aschermann, 2021. Thanks to Ellen and Kristin.

Genograms are of central importance for those counsellors who use them in their counselling practice: they are an integral part of their counselling work, are used in a variety of counselling situations together with the clients and are further used and processed throughout the counselling process. In this context, genogram work fulfils various functions, such as gaining information about the clients, recognising transgenerational patterns and relationship dynamics, strengthening the clients' identity and uncovering their resources. The advantages and disadvantages of standardisation and creativity are discussed.

Overall, the present study confirmed and extended the results of Rohr (2017) to a large extent.

> "Genograms are visualisations of the bio-psycho-social situation of the family and enable clients to recognise patterns of behaviour – and thus to get to know themselves better" (Rohr, 2017, p. 9). They consist of objective data (analogous to the family tree) and subjective meanings. "The task in genogram work in the context of counselling and therapy is to work out the structures of the social matrix (the social field)." Further, Hildenbrand, a pioneer in the use of genograms in German-speaking countries, writes: "Instead, I separate between the given and the given-up in human action (Blankenburg, 1985) and find the actor in the distance between the two: The latter becomes an actor by making the given into the given up, i. e. by shaping his or her life" (2018, p. 26).

The article does not describe normatively and ideally how genograms 'should' be created. There is no single case study described, as this would not be helpful for our research questions. Our questions are discussed based on an elaborate research design. Based on the results we describe in this article descriptively: How do experienced counsellors and therapists 'actually' work with genograms, what advantages and disadvantages, limits and possibilities (modes of action) do they find?

The questionnaire used here was created, among other things, based on the evaluation of twenty qualitative expert interviews. It is part of the interdisciplinary research project "InGeno". A research team from the Department of counselling Research at the University of Cologne is developing a software (app) to create genograms and Computer Science Professor Dr Mario Winter, B.Sc. Sven Kullack and the Cologne University of Applied Sciences (cf. Rohr, 2017; Rohr et al. 2015).

Based on a systematic literature review (Cooper, 2017), our project provides a comprehensive overview of genograms' current research literature. In addition to a detailed account of developed extensions of the standard genogram for specific target groups and counselling settings, research findings on the utility of genograms in training and supervision and the need for discussing psychometric testing of genograms. The presented systematic literature review method aims to invite researchers to 'underpin' their future counselling and therapy research with this approach. In this case, it will inspire counsellors and therapists to test different extensions of genogram work depending on the target group and setting in practice.

The search on 05/09/2018 returned 348 hits. Thirty publications from other sources supplemented these. After removing duplicates, we checked the remaining 277 publications for thematic fit based on the titles or abstracts. Here, 112 publications were excluded as they did not fit in terms of content or were not available in English, German or Spanish. The remaining 165 publications were checked for their suitability in the full text. In this step, a further sixty publications were excluded because they did not contribute to the genograms' role in guidance practice.

The date of publication was not an exclusion criterion; also included were publications before 1990. A total of 105 publications were included in the systematic literature review and were analysed concerning their empirical content. The study d-The InGeno project pursues two overarching research questions: "How are genograms used in counselling and therapy?" and "How can a technical tool – or an app – support the use of genograms in the best possible way?". We address both questions with the help of mixed-methods research designs. As in the Marte Meo Project, we have chosen an "Exploratory Sequential Design" within the framework of a Complex Design. "We can first explore qualitatively, and then test out the ideas quantitatively" (Deutsch & Creswell, 2017, p. 5).

8.3 European Qualifications Framework (EQF) for Lifelong Learning – A current research project in Germany

I would like to conclude this chapter with an outlook on an elaborate research project which we carry out on behalf of the DGfB, the German National Association for Counselling (member of EAC and IAC). Together with Marc Weinhardt (Universität Trier), Cornelia Maier-Gutheil (Evangelische Hochschule Darmstadt), Tim Stanik (Hochschule der Bundesagentur für Arbeit, Schwerin) and Marc Höcker (Universität zu Köln und Universität Mainz) I will work on the development of a German qualifications framework for Counselling – in the context of the **European Qualifications Framework (EQF)**.

It is a particular challenge due to the specific conditions in non-formal learning. It requires a well-considered, staged and explorative approach because it is impossible to fall back on already established procedures for the allocation and reference competences of the DQR from other fields. In a first step, a multi-method approach triangulates a systematic literature review with a quantitative expert survey.

Here, the competencies and competence facets defined in the academic discourse and the competencies and competence facets depicted in guidance curricula are recorded to secure and further explore these in a Delphistu-die with one hundred experts' participation. The experts were selected in close consultation with the client to adequately reflect the guidance landscape's diversity and consider a cross-school perspective.

The Delphi study aims to check and supplement the literature review results and weighting concerning the Qualifications Framework for Counselling. It is to ensure that a methodically supported and intersubjectively comprehensible consensus is found within the member associations.

We will analyse parallel to this, procedures and instruments for establishing competencies, examinations and certification procedures of the member associations of the DGfB. Concerning their outcome and competence orientation to systematise their adaptation possibilities for the project context. Evaluating both partial studies' results (qualification framework for guidance and synopsis of competence assessment procedures). The context of qualitative group discussions with representatives of the member associations of the DGfB to derive proposals for certification criteria and practices and create acceptance for the project results across the member associations of the DGfB in the course of the project. The entire application's orientation follows a research concept oriented towards impact factors. It is thus natively connectable to competence-oriented discourses and aims at theoretical and empirical modelling of successful guidance actions.

8.4 Further literature that is highly recommended

At that point I want to recommend the following book:

> "Enjoying Research in Counselling and Psychotherapy: Qualitative, Quantitative and Mixed-methods Research." (Editors: Sofie Bager-Charleson, Alistair McBeath, 2020)

This textbook provides a guide to developing a rigorous and creative research-supported practice for students, practitioners, and researchers in counselling and psychotherapy. With an emphasis on critical thinking and "research mindedness", it introduces practical research skills and links them to self-awareness and critical reflection. Learning how to creatively and effectively use oneself in the treatment process is an essential component of therapy training. This level of self-awareness has long been a neglected area in research. With examples ranging from private therapeutic practice to related psychiatric research, each chapter combines how-to-do-it advice with illustrative real-life examples. The authors outline using a broad range of research methods, embracing Arts and RCT-based research, and covering qualitative, quantitative, pluralistic and mixed-methods approaches.

Sofie Bager-Charleson is Director of Studies on the MPhil / PhD in psychotherapy at the Metanoia Institute, UK, and a BACP and UKCP registered psychotherapist and supervisor. She chairs the research group "Therapists as Research Practitioners (TRP)" and is the co-founder of the annual Metanoia Research Academy for practitioners. Sofie's research focuses on psychotherapists' professional development, specialising in psychotherapy research, reflexivity, reflective practice, and personal development.

Alistair McBeath is a Doctoral Research Supervisor at the Metanoia Institute and the New School of counselling and psychotherapy, UK.

He is a Chartered Psychologist, and BACP and UKCP registered psychotherapist. Alistair considers himself to be a researcher-practitioner and is keen to promote this identity within the psychotherapy profession. He also works for an Edinburgh based therapeutic consultancy and is a member of the Editorial Board of the European Journal for Qualitative Research in Psychotherapy.

References

Cooper, H. M. (2017). Research synthesis and meta-analysis: A step-by-step approach (5th edition). Applied social research methods series: volume 2. Los Angeles, London, New Delhi, Singapore, Washington DC: SAGE.

Cresswell, J. W. (2017). Applying Core and Complex Designs. Webinar, MMRTP, May 5, 2017.

Moher, D.; Liberati, A.; Tetzlaff, J. & Altman, D. G. (2009). Preferred reporting items for systematic reviews and meta-analyses: the PRISMA statement. Annals of Internal Medicine, 151(4), 264-269. https://doi.org/10.1136/bmj.b2535

Rohr, D.; Nettersheim, S.; Deutsch, C.; Meiners, K. (2020): A mixed methods research study on the video-based Counselling method Marte Meo. Counselling and Psychotherapy Research Journal 2020; 00:1-13. https://doi.org/10.1002/capr.12380

9 Integrating research knowledge and awareness into Counselling and psychotherapy training: an apprenticeship model (John McLeod)[7]

Being a counsellor or psychotherapist is an activity that makes use of personal qualities and capabilities: emotional sensitivity, interpersonal skills, a sufficient sense of inner personal security, and an ability to offer care. It is not at all obvious that scientific research has much to offer, to people whose work involved offering counselling relationships to those who are experiencing problems in living. Even if it acknowledged that research evidence may have some relevance, it is still hard to know how to integrate that knowledge into practice. Research might be able to tell us about the likelihood that one intervention might, on the whole, be more effective that alternative strategy, for clients with a specific problem. Or it might tell us that establishing a collaborative connection, or alliance, between counsellor and client is a pre-requisite for effective help. But what does that mean in practice? Faced with the immediate reality of a person in distress, that research does not tell me what to do, right now. Research evidence needs to be balanced against many other factors, such as personal experience, intuition, client preferences, and cultural values.

In this chapter, I offer an overview of what I have learned about the type of research that might be relevant to the practice of counselling, and the ways in which counsellor and psychotherapist training programmes might support students to develop a positive and constructive relationship with research. I believe that this is an important issue, because research skills and awareness have the potential to both enhance and diminish the quality of service received by clients.

In the following sections, I offer a brief account of aspects of my personal journey, as a person, a counsellor and a researcher. This is then followed by a discussion of some suggestions for ways of including research skills and awareness in counsellor training programmes. I believe that these ideas can be best characterised as reflecting an "apprenticeship" model of learning. By this, I mean that research can

---

[7] published in D. Rohr, A. Hummelsheim and M. Hoecker (eds) (2016). Beratung lehren. Weinheim: Beltz.

be regarded as consisting of products or objects (such as articles, reports, conference presentations, measures, youtube videos, apps) that are made and used by people in collaboration with others in specific concrete situations. From this perspective, research consists of purposeful action to make things and tools that are created in workshops and distributed in markets.

A personal journey

I was one of the generation in Scotland, born within a decade of the war, for whom educational opportunity resulted in disconnection from cultural and class traditions. The first person from my family to attend university, I soon discovered that studying for a degree in mathematics gave me little satisfaction. Looking for alternatives within the university system, I discovered psychology. At that time, psychology was a broad social science discipline, which in a Scottish university also included the study of philosophy. So there were sources of meaning to be found.

Up to that point, I do not think that I had ever come across the idea or practice of psychotherapy. It was not a part of the social landscape where I grew up. Reading psychology, I began to be aware that, behind the science, there was something that was a bit strange, mysterious and scary. I read Freud, and Jung, and Laing. I attended an evening class on Transactional Analysis, and then had my first taste of therapy.

What then followed was the conventional academic path – a PhD, then a teaching job in a polytechnic. And through all of this time, more therapy, along with other personal development activities. It was not until I was in my mid-30s that I seriously considered that I could actually do this kind of work, that I could be a therapist. On the person-centred counsellor training programme that I completed, I was one of the youngest members of the group. In Britain, this was the general pattern. Until quite recently, people trained as counsellors after they had done something else – teaching, social work, nursing. It has only been in the last few years that young people have started to view counselling as a career that they might enter straight from school, or immediately following their undergraduate degree.

As a trained counsellor with a PhD, I soon found a job as a lecturer on a university Masters programme in counselling. Since, at that stage, I still had little experience as a therapist, I was allocated to teach the research methods part of the course, and ended up supervising most of the research dissertations. It was at this point that I made some important discoveries. I had been trained in person-centred counselling (Mearns & Thorne, 2013), which had been shaped by the research carried out by Carl Rogers and his colleagues in the 1950s. I do not recall any mention of research on the training course. At the time, this did not seem strange. The course was focused on the development of practical skills and self-awareness, so maybe there was just not enough time to look at the relevance of research. I already knew about the research evidence, in any case. But, as a new university lecturer in counselling in 1989, I began to see that in fact the whole of counselling and psychotherapy training in Britain was based on a model of experiential therapeutic learning that left little space for research.

Other discoveries followed. Not only was there little space for research skills and knowledge, but there was also a level of disdain or even hostility to the whole idea that research might be relevant to the unique, individual experience of therapy. In particular, there was a deep scepticism about the possibility that anything interesting could actually be measured. This last point created particular difficulties in relation to teaching the students. At that time, the counselling research textbooks that were available were all from the USA, and had been written for students who had already completed a psychology degree and were familiar with principles of experimental design and statistics. By contrast, only around 10% of my students had psychology degrees.

Much of my career, for the last 25 years, has been a response to the experience of trying to figure out what it was that might allow these students to appreciate the value of research. Then, as I became more involved in the counselling profession in Britain, I also became interested in the reasons for the institutional neglect of research within the professional community, and the types of strategies that might be adopted to remedy that situation. These interests resulted in books, involvement in committees and research conferences, editing a research journal, and co-authorship of a research training manual (McLeod, Elliott & Wheeler, 2010).

The broader context: the challenge of research-informed practice in Counselling and psychotherapy

Historically, training to become a counsellor or psychotherapist has focused on a number of core areas: therapeutic skills and interventions, therapist personal development and self-awareness, supervised practice, professional issues around boundaries and ethics, and the capacity to use theory to make sense of the therapeutic process and relationship. Alongside this practice-oriented curriculum, many training programmes also attempt to provide trainees with opportunities to develop research skills and knowledge. The most consistent and rigorous initiative of this kind has been the adoption, since the 1950s, of a "scientist-practitioner" model within counselling and clinical psychology programmes accredited by the American Psychological Association (APA, 1947; Howard, 1986) However, even within "scientist-practitioner" programmes that require students to take classes in research methods and carry out a research thesis or dissertation, it has been found that, after graduating, few practitioners read research articles, use research knowledge to inform their practice, or become involved in research projects (Cohen & Sargent, 1986; Morrow-Bradley and Elliott, 1986). A recent survey of psychotherapists in Britain carried out by Gyani et al. (2014) supports the general picture reported by Morrow-Bradley and Elliott (1986), that practitioners continue report that research has a limited relevance to practice, compared to other sources of knowledge such as supervision or experience with clients.

It is important to look closely at the findings of Cohen and Sargent (1986), Gyani et al. (2014), Morrow-Bradley and Elliott (1986), and other similar studies. Although these studies consistently show that therapy practice is not informed by research findings to any substantial degree, they also find that practitioners are, in principle, open to being influenced by research. Practitioner interest in research is reflected in the detailed reasons that they are able to offer, regarding the shortcomings of mainstream research methodologies in respect of capturing the complexities of real-life clinical practice (Gyani et al., 2015; Morrow-Bradley & Elliott, 1986). What seems to be happening is that therapists acknowledge the potential value of research, but are critical about the clinical and practical relevance of the type of research that is being carried out, and frustrated by the ways in which studies are written.

There have been many attempts to develop strategies to encourage counsellors and psychotherapists to engage with research evidence. In some therapy clinics and services, therapists are required to implement "evidence-based" approaches, and receive training and supervision to support them in the adoption of these methods (Cook et al., 2009; Edmunds et al., 2013). Another strategy has been to create Practice Research Networks (PRNs), in which practitioners work alongside university researchers to design studies, and collect data (Barkham, 2014; Koerner & Castonguay, 2015). Some professional associations, such as the British Association for Counselling and Psychotherapy (BACP) have invested in research support initiatives, such as publishing research journals, hosting conferences and training events, and offering a research consultation service to members. A further strategy has been to focus on primary training, with the intention of producing qualified practitioners who possess a positive attitude to research, and sufficient research skills and knowledge to use research findings to inform their practice.

From my perspective, all of these strategies are valuable and necessary. However, I believe that effective and inspiring research teaching, within the context of primary counsellor and psychotherapist training programme, represents a fundamental priority. If trainees have acquired research skills and awareness, they will be in a good position to take advantage of research opportunities, and research evidence, throughout their career. By contrast, if they have not acquired such skills and knowledge in primary training, they are unlikely to be able to find the time and resources to fill this gap, in the course of busy and demanding careers.

A particularly important contribution to understanding the ways in which research skills and awareness can be incorporated into the training of counsellors and psychotherapists, has been made by Charles Gelso and his colleagues at the University of Maryland in the USA. This team has conducted a series of studies into the characteristics of research training environments, within therapy training programmes, that produce constructive engagement with research following graduation (Gelso et al., 2013). The key themes that have emerged from these studies are that trainees are more likely to develop positive attitudes to research when:

1. Members of academic faculty function as models of appropriate scientific behaviour and attitudes, for example by talking about their own research projects;
2. Scientific activity is positively reinforced in the environment, both formally and informally;
3. Students are involved in research early in training, and in a minimally threatening way;
4. A range of approaches to research are taught and valued;
5. The importance of students looking inward for research ideas and questions is emphasized when students are developmentally ready for this responsibility;
6. Students are shown how research findings can be used to inform practice, by tutors who can describe their own personal and professional experience in relation to tis issue;
7. Students are taught during the latter part of their programme how research may be done in practice settings.
8. When carrying out their own research dissertation, the student is able to develop a relationship with their research supervisor that is characterised by rapport, being an apprentice to the supervisor, and identifying with the supervisor as a model.

Within my own work as a counselling trainer and tutor, I have found that the work of Gelso et al (2013) has helped me to understand what I can do, and what I should avoid doing, when designing research inputs. The following sections of this chapter offer an outline of how I have implemented these ideas within my own teaching practice.

Incorporating research skills and awareness into a counsellor training programme

I believe that research knowledge and awareness has the potential to make a meaningful and positive contribution to therapist development, in ways that enhance client outcomes. However, for this to take place, research-oriented learning opportunities for counselling and psychotherapy trainees need to be experienced by them as directly relevant to their primary goal of becoming competent practitioners.

At different universities and institutes where I have worked, I have had experience of delivering research training inputs that have varied in length and academic level. Some of these courses have functioned as stand-alone modules, with titles such as "Research methods in counselling". In other situations, research workshops have been incorporated into broader courses or modules on counselling skills, practice and theory. For example, a workshop in critically reading research papers can be used within a theory module, as a way of encouraging students to develop a questioning stance in relation to theoretical models such as CBT or psychodynamic. Within a counselling practicum course, a workshop on case study research can provide students with a deeper appreciation of what they might be able to achieve in the case study they are required to submit as their module assignment. In general, I have found that both stand-alone research modules, and workshops included in theory and practice modules, can be effective. Each of these strategies is associated with advantages and disadvantages. For example, a stand-alone module can offer students a more intensive experience of learning and reflecting on research issues. However, this learning may be perceived as separate from the practice of therapy. By contrast, workshops incorporated into other modules or courses, strengthens the connection between research and practice, but may run the risk of students gaining a rather fragmented and piecemeal understanding of research methods and findings.

My experience has convinced me that there are two key questions that need to be taken into consideration when planning research inputs for a therapy training programme: who, and when? I have worked in universities where research experts have been brought in to teach research to counselling students. This does not work. The lecturer may be a world expert on statistics, or qualitative methodology, but if he or she is not able to relate what they are saying to counselling situations and examples, most counselling students will not grasp the relevance of they have to offer. I would recommend that, as far as possible, research inputs should be delivered by research-active counselling and psychotherapy tutors. My other recommendation is that research inputs should begin early, so that students are encouraged to read research articles over the whole of their training. Inevitably, the main priority for students on counselling and psychotherapy programmes is to develop practical skills and theoretical knowledge that will enable them to cope with the terrifying reality of working with clients. I always acknowledge that practice is the priority, but advise students that if they read only one research article each week, by the time they come to do design and conduct their own research dissertation (or graduate), they will have sufficient knowledge to be research "connoisseurs" with a good appreciation of what research can offer them.

Core messages that I want students to hear

In practice, research classes tend to focus on specific research skills, such as conducting a literature review, using a statistics package, or analysing qualitative data. At the same time as addressing these specific skills, I take every possible opportunity to reinforce a set of core messages about the meaning of research in the context of therapy practice. Some of the key messages that I try to convey are:

There are many valid ways of knowing. I try to explain and demonstrate that research knowledge is a distinctive form of knowledge that sits alongside other forms of knowledge, such as practical knowledge, cultural knowledge, personal knowing, and theoretical knowledge. Being a therapist involves being able to draw on all of these sources of knowledge, in appropriate ways.

Research knowledge is provisional, incomplete and always developing. One of the advantages, as a teacher, of being able to drawn on one's own experience of doing research, is that I becomes much easier to communicate to students that research rarely leads to certainty. At the start of training, I offer students a map of the field of therapy research (McLeod, 2013) that, hopefully, makes it possible for them to begin to understand how and why certain research questions and ideas have been pursued in depth, while other important topics have been hardly investigated at all. This kind of mapping of the "big picture" of therapy research also enables reflection on the ways in which social, cultural, economic and political factors have shaped the research landscape.

Research skills and awareness can make an important contribution to therapist competence. When I am working with students, I am always trying to highlighting ways in which research knowledge can contribute to being a more effective practitioner. For example, using brief measurement scales to collect regular feedback from clients about the progress of therapy can lead to better outcomes. The use of specific therapy interventions, such as homework tasks or interpretation of transference, can be enhanced by reading about research into these methods.

Research engagement is part of reflexive life-long learning. Research knowledge and awareness plays a crucial role in life-long learning, by providing a basis for keeping in touch with recent developments in the field, and by enabling opportunities to contribute one's own ideas and insights through research involvement. On the whole, most therapists tend to be highly committed to life-long learning, in the form of making use of personal therapy at regular intervals over the course of their career. It is valuable for students to understand that their attitude to research, and use of research, is intimately connected to the kinds of issues that they explore in their own personal therapy. For example, most practitioners have a close interest in perhaps two or three areas of research, and "collect" knowledge around these topics. Other domains of research may be acknowledged as important in their own right, but are not so important at a personal level, and are treated more as background knowledge. Reflecting on the reasons why certain questions are personally fascinating (or become fascinating, or cease to be so) opens up valuable areas for self-exploration and development. Similarly, the experience of conducting research can represent a fertile source of personal development (Minichiello & Kottler, 2010).

Experiential learning: using research teaching to promote self-awareness, group cohesiveness and active curiosity

In order to engage the research imagination of trainees, it is essential to organise research learning opportunities that are interesting and personally involving. While it may be necessary to provide some conventional lecture-based teaching, as a means of introducing basic concepts, students are more likely to engage actively with research through direct experience of research processes. This direct experience is also relevant to broader self-development and self-awareness work that takes place in other parts of the training programme. For example, a workshop on conducting a research interview can stimulate valuable reflection on how the gender or personal style of the interviewer can influence the interviewee, or the similarities and differences between research interviews and counselling sessions.

The following paragraphs offer brief descriptions of some experiential exercises and workshops that I have used with groups of counselling/psychotherapy trainees.

Critically analysing a research paper. Students are asked to read a research paper, which is followed by a lecture that explores the way a typical research article is structured. They are then asked to read two further papers (one qualitative and one quantitative) and to make notes on what they perceive as methodological strengths of the study (what the researcher did that would convince a reader that the findings and conclusions of the paper are reliable and valid), and what the methodological weaknesses or limitations might be. They are told not to read any research methodology books, but to rely on their own judgement. Students then meet in groups of three or four to share their observations on each paper. Their conclusions are then discussed in a plenary with the whole class. What students learn from this is that they are capable of making sense of research papers, in ways that allow them to arrive at a balanced appraisal of the value of the paper. They gain confidence relation to on-going reading of research papers, and are encouraged to view further learning about research methods as a means of deepening and refining their understanding. This exercise also allows the tutor to make sure that students have read and reflected on at least three interesting research papers.

The experience of completing a measure. Students are invited to complete a standard outcome measure, in a mindful way, with awareness of the thoughts and feelings that arise during the process. They then make brief notes on their experience, and meet in groups of three or four to share their experience. The groups then report back in a plenary session of the whole class, and the tutor identifies themes in their shared experience, and uses their own observations as a means of talking about the ways in which measures are constructed, concepts of levels of measurement, norms, reliable and clinical change, reliability and validity, and how measures are used in therapy research and practice. This exercise can be a good way to introduce students to measures, such as CORE-OM or OQ, that they may come across in published articles or in their therapy practice. If there is sufficient time, it can be valuable to allow students to complete a range of measures, and compare different types of response formats and instructions. Completing scales allows students to have an insight into what it is like for actual clients to be asked to fill in a questionnaire, as well as allowing them more directly to reflect on their own personal issues. Once students have made friends with outcome measures, they may find it interesting and meaningful to learn about how quantitative data sets can be analysed using statistical packages, and also to read published articles that have used the kind of data which which they have become familiar.

Completing a qualitative mini-study. Counselling and psychotherapy trainees are often drawn to qualitative research, because it offers them a kind of narrative knowing that is relevant to practice. However, the field of qualitative research can also seem confusing, due to the complexity of methodological choices and epistemological positions that are available. I have therefore developed a workshop experience that allows students to complete a qualitative study in one day (or even, if time is tight, in half a day). I tell them that we are collectively going to explore the experience of depression/low mood, and how people deal with such with such episodes in their life. They are then provided with a brief outline of the procedure that we will follow. The class is divided into groups of around five members. Each group is given some time to develop an interview schedule. One person from the group then interviews someone from another group for 20 minutes, with the other members of their group as observers and note-takers. This continues until all participants have had an opportunity to be either an interviewer or an interviewee. The groups then have some time to analyse the main themes that have emerged in the interview, and also to reflect on the experience of being an interviewer and being an interviewee. I am available for consultation during any of these phases of the workshop. The whole group then reconvenes, and each small group presents their findings. What always emerges is that even this rather limited "mini-study" has generated a rich understanding of the experience of low mood and how people cope with it in everyday life. In the final stage of the workshop, I make connections between what the group has discovered, and the literature on qualitative methodology. Following the workshop, students are invited to read some published studies on recovery from depression, in order to learn about how "professional" researchers have handled the kinds of methodological issues that they encountered during the workshop (and to compare their findings with the results of these published studies). This workshop has the potential to open up many areas of self-awareness and personal development that are relevant to the process of becoming a therapist, including the experience of collaboration with other group members, the impact of asking questions in different ways, and the process of self-disclosure.

Case study analysis using HSCED. Case study research is highly relevant to therapy training, because most counselling and psychotherapy training programmes require students to submit at least one detailed case study based on their own practice. If students are encouraged to read research-based case studies, they can develop a deeper appreciation of they ways in which case material can be analysed and reported. Learning about case study research can also give students the confidence to write about their own cases, later in their career. In terms of learning about research methodology, the recent development of "systematic" case study inquiry, emphasises the collection of rich case data, from qualitative sources, such as interviews, as well as quantitative measures (McLeod, 2010). Analysing this type of data requires students to reflect on the strengths, limitations, and different contributions of qualitative and quantitative methodologies. Hermeneutic Single Case Efficacy Design (HSCED; Elliott, 2002, Elliott et al., 2009) is a structured approach to case study data analysis, in which small teams of researchers work independently to generate alternative analyses of the same case material. In workshops, my colleagues and I have invited students to conduct HSCED analysis of real-life case data from a client within our own research programme. This type of learning is both enjoyable for students, as well as giving them an opportunity to reflect on key questions around the process and outcome of therapy, in addition to exposure to issues concerned with research methodology. Further information on this mode of research teaching can be found in McLeod et al. (2015) and Thurston et al. (2015).

These examples of teaching research through experiential learning illustrate some of the possibilities that emerge when research is viewed as an adjunct to counselling, rather than as a completely separate type of activity. These workshop ideas can be modified and adapted, depending on the aims and philosophy of the training programme, and the time available. Ideas for other workshops and exercises can be found in McLeod, Elliott and Wheeler (2010).

An important theme which consistently emerges in these workshops, concerns the topic of ethical dilemmas in research (Danchev & Ross, 2014; Sieber & Tolich, 2013). Counselling and psychotherapy trainees are usually highly aware and sensitive around ethical issues such as avoidance of harm, and maintenance of boundaries, as a result of their involvement in clinical work. In my experience, it is not a good use of time to give lectures on research ethics, to these students, because they are already familiar with ethical principles. Exploring ethical issues in the context of actual research examples and data, is a more meaningful and effective means of learning about this area.

What do students need to know?

In any counselling or psychotherapy training programme, there is always pressure on time – there are many topics that need to be covered and skills that need to be developed. It is therefore important to be clear about the priorities for research teaching. My own position is that I am mainly interested in preparing students to be informed consumers and readers of research products, such as journal articles, and that the main aim of my research teaching is to enable them to be "literate" in respect to a core set of methodologies that they are likely to encounter over the course of their professional career.

It is valuable to focus on developing skills and awareness in relation to core methodologies, in the context of research projects and dissertations that can be completed within the time available to them as trainees. In my experience, many counselling and psychotherapy trainees are over-ambitious in relation to the research they carry out, and end up using unproven or complex methodologies that lead to frustration and unpublishable findings. The publishability of research is a significant factor, because it is only by completing the process of creating a knowledge "product", all the way through to the publication or dissemination stage, that students can learn about the compromises and realities associated with the way that research is socially constructed and managed.

I suggest that it is possible to identify five types of research "product" that are achievable by trainees at Masters or Doctoral level, and that allow opportunities to develop essential research skills:

- a publishable literature review;
- qualitative, interview-based study of the client / therapist experience of an aspect of therapy;
- quantitative, practice-based outcome evaluation;
- autoethnographic inquiry into personal experience;
- systematic, multi-method, single case study.

Practical guidelines for carrying out these types of research, can be found in McLeod (2014).

Learning how to conduct study based on a well-understood and widely-used methodological approach, provides a basis for going on, at a later stage, to carry out more complex research. For example, some trainees who carry out grounded theory interview-based studies may become interested in the role of language in interaction, and move on to develop skills in Conversation Analysis, narrative analysis, and similar language-focused qualitative methodologies. Trainees who are exposed to practice-based outcome research, arrive at an appreciation of how quantitative measures work in practice, and may then wish to become involved in a randomised trial study.

The process of learning about these core methodologies need not necessarily be linked to the completion of a dissertation or thesis. For example, autoethnographic research can be used as a way of deepening the process of personal development. Trainees on most programmes are required to write a case report on their work with a client – this can be used as an opportunity for collecting and analysing case study data, and reading case study articles. Where possible, I encourage students doing research projects to form research peer support groups, in which different members are using different methodologies. They are therefore in a position to offer support and challenge to colleagues who are doing a type of research that contrasts with their own personal experience.

Conclusions: research teaching as a form of apprenticeship

For participants in counselling and psychotherapy training programmes, learning about research can become a way of strengthening professional competence and self-awareness, and a means of accessing ideas from the international knowledge network that exists beyond the boundaries of their training community. Where possible, this chapter has pointed out examples of training practices and strategies that have the potential to awaken the research imagination of trainees. It is certain that there are many more examples of research training ideas, that have been developed by groups of tutors, that have not been published or disseminated. There are also many stories that might be told by trainees, about ways in which research skills and knowledge have made a positive contribution to their practitioner journey. It would be helpful for all of us if more of these stories could be shared.

Returning to my own story, I believe that the approach to research teaching that I have tried to develop, has been accompanied by an increasing awareness of the importance of understanding the ways in which knowledge is socially constructed and controlled. It seems to me that at least some of the resistance that therapists have exhibited in relation to research, can be seen in a positive light, as a (largely unconscious) effort to resist the tendency in our culture to regard universities as the places where knowledge is created, and university faculty as individuals who are the holders of that knowledge. The movement in the direction of defining research as an expert and specialist form of practice, has resulted in a major explosion of research knowledge over the past 100 years, in all aspects of life. What is perhaps not sufficiently appreciated, is that this has come at a cost. Because university-based research is generally organised into "disciplines", such as psychology, sociology, economics and so on, it has become increasingly difficult to tackle real-life problems that cut across discipline boundaries. In addition, the power and authority invested in university researchers has resulted in a lack of critical appraisal, within the public as a whole, of the knowledge they generate.

These issues are very apparent within the field of research in counselling and psychotherapy. For example, although therapy is influenced by social and economic factors, almost all research concentrates only on psychological variables. Similarly, the academic knowledge produced by researchers is given priority over the practical knowledge of those who provide services. For example, because it is very hard to carry out controlled and rigorous outcome research on open-ended long-term therapy, most outcome research has largely focused on short-term, time-limited therapy. As a result, evidence-based guidelines recommend that short-term, time-limited therapy is advisable, because there is more evidence that it is effective. At the same time, most therapists know that, while short-term, time-limited therapy can be valuable for some clients, there are also people who can only be helped by offering them the possibility to continue for as long as they need.

I have come to realise that there is an older tradition, based on the creating and transmission of practical knowledge through apprenticeship learning in collaborative workshop environments (Lave and Wenger, 1991; Sennett, 2008). What this tradition tells us, is that some very good things can happen when learning is taken out of the classroom, and instead is organised around making things that have a clearly-understandable practical purpose. The research process, and knowledge itself, becomes a form of dialogue, conversation and joint action, grounded in relationship. Viewed from this perspective, I believe that research begins to make sense to counselling and psychotherapy trainees and practitioners, and to become satisfying and even enjoyable. The task of resistance then becomes the responsibility of the tutors who are facilitating research training, in respect of negotiating with their universities and institutes to enable the creation of appropriate learning communities within which this kind of work can take place.

References

APA Committee on Training in Clinical Psychology. (1947) Recommended graduate training program in clinical psychology. American Psychologist, 2, 539–558.

Barkham, M. (2014) Practice-based research networks: Origins, overview, obstacles, and opportunities. Counselling and Psychotherapy Research, 167–173.

Cohen, L. H., Sargent, M. H. and Sechrest, L. B. (1986) Use of psychotherapy research by professional psychologists. American Psychologist, 41, 198–206.

Cook, J.M., Schnurr, P. P., Biyanova, T. and Coyne, J.C. (2009) Apples don't fall far from the Tree: Influences on psychotherapists' adoption and sustained use of new therapies. Psychiatric Services, 60, 71–676.

Danchev, D. and Ross, A. (2014) Research Ethics for Counsellors, Nurses and Social Workers. London: Sage.

Edmunds, J.M., Beidas, R.S. and Kendall, P.C. (2013) Dissemination and implementation of evidence-based practices: training and consultation as implementation strategies. Clinical Psychology: Science and Practice, 20, 152–165.

Elliott, R. (2002) Hermeneutic Single Case Efficacy Design. Psychotherapy Research, 12, 1–20.

Elliott, R., Partyka, R., Wagner, J., Alperin, R., Dobrenski, R., Messer, S.B., Watson, J.C. and Castonguay, L.G. (2009) An adjudicated Hermeneutic Single Case Efficacy Design study of experiential therapy for panic/phobia. Psychotherapy Research, 19. 543–557.

Gelso, C. J., Baumann, E. C., Chui, H. T. and Savela, A. E. (2013) The making of a scientist–psychotherapist: the research training environment and the psychotherapist. Psychotherapy, 50, 139–149.

Gyani, A., Shafran, R., Myles, P. and Rose, S. (2014) The gap between Science and Practice: How therapists make their clinical decisions. Behavior Therapy, 45, 199–211.

Gyani, A., Shafran, R., Rose, S. and Lee, M.J. (2015) A qualitative investigation of therapists' attitudes towards research: horses for courses? Behavioural and Cognitive Psychotherapy, 43, 436–448.

Howard, G. (1986) The scientist-practitioner in Counselling psychology. The Counselling Psychologist, 14, 61–105.

Koerner, K. and Castonguay, L. (2015) Practice-oriented research: What it takes to do collaborative research in private practice. Psychotherapy Research, 25, 67–83.

Lave, J. and Wenger E. (1991). Situated Learning: Legitimate Peripheral Participation. Cambridge: Cambridge University Press.

McLeod, J. (2010) Case Study Research in Counselling and Psychotherapy. London: Sage.

McLeod, J. (2013) An Introduction to Research in Counselling and Psychotherapy. London: Sage.

McLeod, J. (2014) Doing Research in Counselling and Psychotherapy. 3rd edn. London: Sage.

McLeod, J., Elliott, R. and Wheeler, S. (2010) A Training Manual in Research Skills and Awareness for Counsellors and Psychotherapists. Lutterworth, UK: British Association for Counselling and Psychotherapy.

McLeod, J., Thurston, M. and McLeod, J. (2015) Case study methodologies. In A. Vossler and N. Moller (eds) The Counselling and Psychotherapy Research Handbook. London: Sage.

Mearns, D. and Thorne, B. (2013) Person-centred Counselling in Action. 4th edn. London: Sage.

Minichiello, V. and Kottler, J.A. (eds)(2010) Qualitative journeys: student and mentor experiences with research. Thousand Oaks, CA: Sage.

Morrow-Bradley, C. and Elliott, R. (1986) Utilization of psychotherapy research by practicing psychotherapists. American Psychologist, 41, 188–197.

Sennett, R. (2008) The Craftsman. London: Allen Lane.

Sieber, J. E. and Tolich, M. B. (2013) Planning Ethically Responsible Research. 2nd edn. Thousand Oaks, CA: Sage.
Thurston, M., McLeod, J. and McLeod, J. (2015) How to use case study methodology with single client therapy data. In A. Vossler and N. Moller (eds) The Counselling and Psychotherapy Research Handbook. London: Sage.

10 'Transcultural Counselling', Racism, Power, and Discrimination

10.1 Preface

> "The concept of 'culture' is gaining in significance within the discourse of counselling and psychotherapy, as a means of making sense of the ways in which shared identities and behaviours are constructed and maintained." (West & McLeod, 2003, p. 83)

I want to start this section with a reference to a publication: a special edition of "Counselling and Psychotherapy Research – Linking research with practice" (CPR): Culture and Therapy (2003). To arouse your curiosity, I have quoted a few passages from the Introduction to the Theme Section by West, William and McLeod, John (2003) 'Cultural landscapes in counselling and psychotherapy': Laungani reflects that, for him, the result of 30 years of living in England and engaging with English culture has been that:

"When I am in India, I am accused of being too English (whatever that means) and in England, when the English can bring themselves to express an opinion, I am accused of being 'too Indian' (whatever that might mean). I am thus in a no-win situation" (Laungani, 2001, p. 21). He offers a metaphor of the turtle: the shell is our cultural heritage – destroy the shell and you destroy the turtle. How many clients share this dilemma, this painful exposed sense of dislocation, of not belonging? How well prepared are therapists to respond to such issues?

In its first three years, *Counselling and Psychotherapy Research* has published a steady stream of papers concerned with the impact of cultural factors on the therapeutic process. Ryden and Loewenthal (2001) described the struggle of lesbian clients to discover whether their therapist under- stood their world. Tuckwell (2001) analysed the complex dynamics and avoidances that occur in the interaction between therapists and clients who are culturally/racially different. Cornforth (2001) explored the ways in which cultural assumptions and realities are conveyed both in, and beyond, language. Engaging in counsellor training is typically experienced in terms of entering a different culture: Fetherston (2002) deconstructed this experience from the point of view of a visitor from social science; Hill (2002) investigated the role of community meetings in constructing the microculture of training. Millar (2002) evaluated the effect of counselling within the occupational culture of the police service.

The publication of *Multicultural Counselling* (Palmer, 2002) has made available a valuable collection of papers concerning theory, practice and research in culture-focused therapy. *Racial Identity, White Counsellors and Therapists* (Tuckwell, 2002) has provided a powerful, research- based text, which invites practitioners to reflect on the implications of their racial identity." (West & McLeoad, 2003, p. 84)

10.2 Introduction

Counselling has to deal with 'Transculturalism', Racism, Power, and Discrimination. Those ethical topics can not be the focus of this book. But in this book, we have to discuss if there are different ways of counselling in other European countries, about differences and similarities in 'Culture'. We have to be aware of stereotypes. Counselling always has got a political dimension. E. g. we must take a clear stand concerning right-wing parties gaining influence in many European countries.

We have to be very careful not to reproduce social injustices and discrimination in counselling settings themselves. Racism is one form of discrimination. At the same time as this book is published, I am publishing a book concerning 'Racism and Counselling' (Gold, Weinberg & Rohr, 2021). Because of this, I will point out this topic briefly.

I want to begin with the preface from Prof. Eia Asen (London). He is German, but he is living and working in London for almost 40 years. His international perspective is very interesting for this book, too:

"The systematic disadvantage and marginalisation of people constructed, perceived and labelled as 'Other' has been dubbed Institutional Racism (McPherson, 1999) in the UK for over two decades: this is the collective refusal of an organisation to provide appropriate professional services to people on the basis of their perceived 'culture' and/or origin. Institutional racism manifests itself in discriminatory practices, attitudes and patterns of behaviour in which prejudice, ignorance and racist stereotyping are usually unwittingly reproduced, leading to the devaluation of people who are located by the local majority society outside its own 'white normality'. People of colour and black people as well as people who are read as Muslim are particularly affected by such experiences of discrimination. They are not only exposed to the racist structures of organisations such as the police, teaching institutions or the health system, but similar racist structures are also reproduced in the context of counselling.

This may seem surprising at first glance, as counsellors in particular believe in their self-assessment that they have a special understanding and tolerance for different cultural values and perspectives. But it takes more than that, especially when it comes to working as white counsellors with Black clients and clients of colour. Here it is important to reflect on the often invisible socially powerful and racist structures and the counselling models influenced by them and their limited applicability. White counsellors should understand that many models are actually 'WEIRD'. The acronym WEIRD (Henrich et al., 2010) stands for "Western, Educated, Industrialised, Rich and Democratic". One could add another W (for "White"), but then the acronym would be even more 'weird' or WWEIRDer. What is this about? It's about the fact that much psychological research routinely assumes that its findings are broadly representative, even though 96% of the subjects – and the majority of the researchers – are from Western countries, which are home to only 12% of the world's population. Thus, most current counselling approaches are informed by this 'Eurocentric' (and North American) research and findings, and they reflect scientific power structures that are also racialised.

Institutional racism can be found everywhere and of course in counselling practice. I vividly remember the two-day anti-racism training with a follow-up six months later that took place more than 20 years ago in the London clinic I was running at the time. Everyone attended, including housekeeping, cleaning, administration, secretaries and counsellors. It was a shock for all of us to discover the unconscious racism in our assumptions and practices – a truly depressing yet educational experience. We now saw the 'whiteness' of all staff and the total absence of Black counsellors in our team as evidence of institutional racism in our clinic. So we immediately began to recruit new staff who represented the heterogeneity of the people in our service districts. We embarked on a very important shared and mutual teaching and learning process in which we engaged with systemic, critical of racism and transcultural content. We started asking self-reflective questions such as: what stereotypes and prejudices are powerful in my mind? How do these influence my counselling practice? How might they affect those seeking advice? What ideas did I learn about others at school and in my family of origin? Am I aware of my own social position and privileges and how might these influence my counselling interventions?

Our increasingly heterogeneous team sent an important signal to our clients – and also to other clinics and organisations. And we experienced daily that learning critical of racism is best done in heterogeneous and multi-professional teams. Thus, we often became aware of previously unnoticed racist issues and as an institution we had to find new ways to deal with specific racist situations, e. g. when a client refused to be treated by a Black therapist. Our clinic decided a year later to offer counselling training through the university with a central focus on race and culture. Other counselling training institutes also included race and culture centrally in their curricula, not as a one-off 'ethnic hour addition', but as an integral part of counselling training in every hour of training. Even today, there are no training courses in the UK that do not have 'race and culture' as a central part.

And yet counsellors have to be on their guard every day: racism is like a virus against which you have to inoculate yourself regularly. Unfortunately, there is never immunity, although it is easy to forget how endemic and actually ineradicable this virus is. Although I have been working at the Anna Freud Centre for seven years now, it was the murder of George Floyd and the newly revived 'Black Lives Matter' movement to examine the institutional racism of our clinic, which in the past was primarily psychoanalytically oriented. This led to the decision in the summer of 2020 that each of the nearly 300 staff and employees was required to attend anti-racism training organised by the institution. I say this self-critically and as I write these lines I ask myself why this happened only now and what my own responsibility is and was for this omission. And I realise what the authors of this book emphasise again and again: Racism works as a permanent power structure in the entire social system and consequently also in many everyday situations.

In the USA and Great Britain, counsellors and therapists have been dealing with "multiculturalism" and corresponding culturally competent and sensitive approaches for more than 40 years (e. g. Monica McGoldrick et al., 1982; Celia Falicov, 1983). In these countries, "intercultural competence" has been important and in demand for decades and fully integrated into teaching programmes. For at least 20 years, Anglo-Saxon counsellors have also explicitly addressed institutional racism and its impact on practice. Teaching counsellors of colour and Black teaching counsellors teach in training institutes and are strongly represented at this level, thus influencing teaching and learning. In Germany, the field of "intercultural counselling" in the counselling field started to develop two decades ago (cf. e. g. El Hachimi & v. Schlippe 2000; Hegemann & Salman, 2001), but terms like 'culture' or 'religion' have mostly replaced 'race' and the specific focus on 'culture' has meant that racism and implicit power relations have been and are only marginally addressed. A systematic and at the same time systemic examination of racism as a special form of discrimination is, as far as I know in the German, the French, the Austrian, the Polish, the Spanish (and others) counselling scene, long overdue.

This is the focus of this chapter, namely to bring in perspectives critical of racism and thus to make an important contribution to filling the yawning gap in work contexts. E. g. Counsellors in Germany – which truly also has a colonial history, albeit a different one than the UK – should be encouraged to consider racism as a socially powerful construction – with very concrete and real effects! – in their counselling work and in supervision. This chapter is written from a white perspective and is primarily aimed at white counsellors who want to engage with and critique power and racism in relation to their own counselling work. We want to show how important it is to reflect on one's own positionality and especially to be aware of one's own white privileges in order to balance the power relations a bit, at least in the counselling setting. But we also emphasise how important it is that in training contexts, and in the academic study of counselling, the examination of whiteness is included as a central element.

In this way, counsellors can critically reflect on their own positioning and entanglement within these power relations and thus concretely integrate a critique of power and racism into their work and contribute to making social power relations visible."

I thank Eia for his 'English' – or international – perspective and want to point out that the following is from my German perspective:

In the last few years people who are discriminated against in Europe have intensified enormously. Both acts of racist violence and the existence of public racist statements – not least on the part of various political actors – have increased significantly. The worldwide protests as part of the Black Lives Matter movement following the murder of George Floyd (May 25, 2020) brought the often ignored racist police violence into focus again and point to the consequences of structural racism. Simultaneously, it is racially motivated, physical violence and intentionally discriminatory behaviour that shapes many people's lives. The effects of (un)conscious attitudes and internalised images also have an enormous impact on social and individual life. Racial discrimination is also expressed through everyday actions, ways of thinking and behaviour.

The section sees itself as an approximation regarding the merging of counselling with perspectives that are decidedly critical of power and racism.

Above all, this applies to the context of Counselling, as this is the only way to take people with their own racism experiences seriously. Make the (psychological and physical) effects of racism visible in scientific or practical discourse. Second, all human beings are part of a social balance of power. White people benefit – usually subconsciously – BIPoC (Black, Indigenous, People of Colour) accordingly are confronted with the adverse effects. The social system is characterised in most European countries by a multidimensional power structure or social hierarchy that act in a discriminatory manner as structural violence (cf. Galtung, 1975, p. 12 ff.). In addition to other relevant power structures such as the classical or (hetero/cis) sexist, the racist power structure represents an essential dimension. Thirdly, and as a result, positioning of racism and other forms of discrimination on supposed social or political "fringes" is rejected because it makes it difficult, if not impossible, to reflect upon one's entanglement in precisely those power relations.

Against this background, the question arises where counselling in theory and practice offers connection possibilities, but where there are also contradictions to power and racism criticism and where counselling runs the risk of reproducing racism itself.

This section's primary aim is for *white* Counsellors to deal with criticism of power and racism concerning their work and to critically question the certainties and methods they have come to live by against this background.

The written content in this chapter is mainly from a white perspective. We have endeavoured to use information from individuals who have experienced racism in their lives. However, we're conscious that those people may write from a privileged role. Even so, inadvertent internalised thought can be reproduced. In particular, the relevance of dealing with the racist power structure and one's privileges as *white* Counsellors is seen as crucial here and should be emphasised.

10.3 Discrimination – what is it?

> "People are not discriminated against because of their gender, belief, race, language, homeland, origin, orientation or disability. They are discriminated against because society is structurally racist, sexist, trans, homophobic and hostile to disabled people."
> Sibel Schick (2020)

A look at the specialist literature reveals many different definitions for the term discrimination. This is mainly due to the various (research) perspectives that can be taken when dealing scientifically with discrimination. These include a sociological, a social psychological or a legal one. The definitions also differ in their complexity, which means taking into account different practice areas.

Access and entry into these multi-layered mechanisms of action can be made more accessible. Pates, Schmidt and Karawanskij (2010, p. 255) understand discrimination to mean "that a person treats worse than others because they are assigned to a certain group or have a certain characteristic". Hormel and Scherr (2010, p. 7) give the following definition: "Discrimination usually includes statements and actions that direct against members of certain social groups with a degrading or disadvantageous intention".

The combination of these two definitions results in three critical aspects of discrimination.

First, discrimination is about unequal treatment or disadvantage. Second, it manifests itself in language as well as in behaviour and concrete actions. Third, it affects people perceived as belonging to certain social groups, regardless of whether they are members of these groups or identify themselves as such or not.

Scherr, El-Mafaalani and Yüksel (2017, p. Vi, emphasis in the orig.) expand these definitions and aspects by adding

> (...) Discrimination here not only a consequence of disadvantageous actions, which are based on stereotypes but as a complex social phenomenon that has become historical, social conditions, institutionally solidified expectations and routines, organisational structures and practices as well refer to discourses and ideologies.

10.4 Racism and 'Culture'

> "The noble word culture takes the place of the frowned upon expression race, but remains a mere cover image for the brutal claim to rule." Theodor W. Adorno (1975, pp. 276f.)

Many people speak of racism only when attitudes, statements or unequal treatment refer to concepts of biological or genetic categorisation of people, i. e. to the construction of human 'races'. Categorisations and attributions based on so-called 'culture' and/or 'religion' therefore evade the suspicion of being racist for many.

In general, biologistic 'race theories' are officially discredited in Europe after the Second World War. But this does not mean that people are no longer divided into groups according to racist ways of thinking and acting, given different values and accordingly treated unequally (Shooman, 2012, p. 53). It is noticeable that in many lines of argument, the reference to so-called 'culture' has taken the place of 'race'. The basis for racism is, therefore, "a determining concept of culture" in which "defined cultural-territorial units [...] are homogenised as 'cultural groups'" (Friedrich, 2019, p. 306).

As already described, racialisation processes – naturalisation, homogenisation, polarisation and hierarchisation – also occur here. In the literature, the reference to 'culture' is represented with different terms, for example, as new or neo-racism, as cultural racism or as "racism without races" (Balibar, 1990). Biskamp (2017, p. 274) clarifies that there is still a focus on differences generated by external ascriptions concerning 'culture'. Their so-called 'culture' will continue to be created and maintained constructs that are supposed to distinguish people from one another.

For example, in connection with racism, ostensibly biological distinctions are no longer used to justify discrimination and violence but supposedly insurmountable and rather cultural differences. At first, it is not immediately visible to what extent this is associated with a hierarchisation of the 'cultures'. The focus is on a supposedly irreconcilable difference in traditions and ways of life. Also, there is an emphasis on the destructive effects that would result from the coexistence of 'mixing' of so-called cultures (Balibar, 1990, p. 28). This can currently be seen clearly in the area of anti-Muslim racism, which comes to light, for example, in debates about the headscarf or the construction of mosques (cf. Shooman, 2011, 2012; Attia, 2017). Especially regarding this context, Balibar updates and emphasises in a recent interview (Beckmann, 2018):

> "What worries me is that we experience racism that can even do without race. [...] The everyday object of hate is Islam, or it is the Muslims. This shows that racism is repeatedly modernising, and even if its biological variant no longer catches, it returns as cultural racism. Religion is taken as a substitute to maintain racist thinking."

Here, too, it is essential to clarify that religious affiliation can be a category assigned by other people and does not have to correspond to actual religious affiliation. Outward characteristics, such as names and accents, are decisive for these assignments, which in turn refers to the continued existence and updating of underlying biological concepts. Shooman (2012, p. 55) speaks of a "racialisation of Muslims", which she also identifies in various studies on Muslims in Europe, since contact with 'Europeans' is often determined there as a measure of integration and "explicitly postulates an antagonism between being *Muslim* and being *European*" (Emphasis in the original). Such a research perspective negates European Muslims or Muslim Europeans' existence, thereby reinforcing a widespread everyday understanding of these categories and making the naturalisation of 'culture' regarding the category 'Muslim' clear.

Another example of the fact that biological-racist concepts continue to use under the guise of 'culture' is the theming of sexuality, which often occurs in marking and describing BIPoC. Sexuality – a topic that is already very related to physicality and understood in this way – has always been an integral part of racist categorisations. For example, the degree of civilisation from a colonial-racist perspective was tied to the (granted) ability to control and self-control (cf. Castro Varela & Mecheril, 2016, p. 11).

Even under the formulated 'cultural' omens, a "sexual threat staging" takes place, which, as in biological racism, addresses the sexuality of those marked as *other* and describes them as a threat (Mecheril & van der Hagen-Wulff, 2016, p. 121, Emphasis in the original). In the context of anti-Muslim racism, then only 'Muslim men' or marked as such and not *white* European men in their self-image are "sexist and raping" (Castro Varela & Mecheril, 2016, p. 10). If *the* 'Muslim women' addressed or marked as such, (cultural) racism and sexism often go hand in hand and strong, empowered, and emancipated women are not made visible in this discourse.

As shown with the help of the different examples, the naming of 'culture' as a distinguishing feature is essentially not about the critical detachment and distancing from biological-racist concepts. Nor about a differentiated examination of 'culture' (including the 'own'!) in itself, but rather about maintaining and legitimising racist ways of thinking and acting and corresponding power relations – while at the same time denying them.

If we speak of racism in this section, it explicitly refers to concepts of both biological racism and cultural racism in their interweaving.

10.5 Transcultural Approaches from a Racism-Critical Perspective

The background of the realities in a heterogeneous society, so-called 'transcultural' or 'intercultural' ideas, approaches regarding counselling developed in European countries (e. g. Hegemann and Oestereich, 2009; Abdul-Hussain & Baig, 2009; Pirmoradi, 2012; Nazarkiewicz & Krämer, 2013).

This should help work in counselling situations with people who have a *different* cultural background 'and / or the Counsellor inside' as culturally *Others* are perceived. Different cultural factors often play a role here: For example, whether people come from a collectivist or individualistic 'culture', how they feel about equality and sexual or gender diversity, and whether they are religious or not.

Racism, discrimination and the corresponding balance of power are mentioned differently in these approaches. Some seem to be of only marginal importance; for others, they play a more critical role. For example, Nazarkiewicz and Krämer (2013, p. 25) speak of a "transcultural approach". In this sense, "[reflects] transcultural work [...] power relations, their influence on the development of identity and the social positioning of individuals [...]" (ibid., p. 25). Nazarkiewicz (2016) suggests replacing the term "interculturality" with that of "cultural reflexivity". Pirmoradi (2012, p. 51 ff.) also refers to postcolonial approaches in his book on 'intercultural' family therapy and counselling.

However, 'intercultural' often thought of as the pivotal factor in how a person frequently views corresponding customers through a 'filter', much less perceived as independent. There can be a reluctance to use 'intercultural' because it is going hand in hand with sincerely naming racism and discrimination conditions that impact counselling contexts. Cognisance is the supposedly homogeneous 'cultures' that meet (seemingly on an equal footing) and among which there is a need to mediate.

The narrowing to 'culture' in 'transcultural' approaches is the associated construction of and preoccupation with constructed *others,* as well as the lack of attention to social power relations which have already been reflected on and criticised in various places, especially in the area of pedagogy and educational work (Mecheril, 2010; Foitzik, 2010; Brunner & Ivanova, 2015).

One keyword is "intercultural competence [...], whereby this – in accordance with the current discourse on migration and interculturality – is often interpreted as the ability to act successfully with cultural foreigners" (Brunner & Ivanova, 2015, p. 21). Here it is all about "the knowledge of cultural differences and similarities, which are to Professional [...] embraced to prevent intercultural conflicts and to face them" (Mecheril (2010) also criticises this perspective by referring to three things:

First, offers on 'intercultural competence' primarily address members of the dominant society. This reproduces the description of them as acting persons (subject) and the image of the marginalised as non-acting or passive persons (object) (ibid., p. 16 ff.).

Secondly – despite theoretical assertions of an open and non-static concept of culture – in practice, we work with images that are unambiguous in terms of culture and that link culture directly with ethnicity or nationality (ibid., p. 19 ff.; Brunner and Ivanova 2015, p. 21f.). Thus reproducing images and attributions and determining affiliations from a powerful position.

Thirdly, Mecheril (2010, p. 25) criticises a "technological exploitation tendency", which reflected in the fact that "acquired 'competences' [...] are a guarantee of successful action in intercultural situations" (Brunner & Ivanova, 2015, p. 22). However, other factors, such as situational contexts or non-cultural aspects, are neglected.

'Intercultural' approaches run the risk of being reshaped by 'culture', losing sight of other perspectives and contexts of reasons and consequently reproducing ascriptions and power relations. This also applies to the context of counselling, which does not seem to be sufficiently the case so far. As shown, the exact reproductions which is carried out by people who are socialised in *white and are* contrary to the development of cooperation: counselling relationships and the claim to enlarge the scope for action and possibilities.

Kunze (2018, p. 45 ff.) suggests three "comprehension slides" for counselling contexts. In addition to the "psychological context of meaning" (ibid., p. 48) as the first understanding film, he explicitly distinguishes the "cultural context of meaning" (ibid., p. 50) from a "social context of meaning" (ibid., p. 54). As the second and third comprehension slide. In this way, he also determines a place on the theoretical or model level where the discussion about social power should occur. Simultaneously, working with the understanding film "cultural contexts of meaning" must not lead to counselling with this continuing – now theoretically and qua model legitimised and not reflecting other processes – making clients as powerful as others (cf. Oberzaucher-Tölke, 2014, p. 99). Because this is also easier and more connected than dealing with, for example, one's racism on the level of the understanding film "social contexts of meaning", and this runs the risk of functioning as a pseudo-reflective fig leaf.

We notice the Counsellors' self-reflection mirror as a fundamental component for counselling critical of power and racism. In the context of 'culture' and in the course of 'intercultural' approaches, a fundamental questioning of the same and a "continuous self-reflection of the Counsellors and therapists concerning their personal and professional characteristics as well as their social positioning, which cannot separate from each other" is required (ibid. 2018, p. 663). Self-reflection of the Counsellors is a fundamental component for counselling that is critical of power and racism.

10.6 Components of training standards that are critical of power, discrimination, and racism

Against the background of what has currently been said plus the demand for the professionalisation of counselling, we call for the inclusion of power, discrimination, and racism criticism as essential components in Counsellor training. Both in the area of "theory and methodology" as well "self-development".

Initiatives are underway to implement joint certification on a national, European and international level. The undertaking of understanding shared content and quality standards is taking place in the various umbrella associations (e. g. the European Association for Counselling (EAC), the International Association for Counselling (IAC) and the European Association for Psychotherapy (EAP) working collectively. This could be an excellent time to implement criticism of power and racism in curricula.

Curricular criticism of power and racism is, for example, linked to content on power in counselling situations (cf. Levold, 2016, p. 110ff.), but would explicitly consider social power relations. Here, too, the considerations of Nazarkiewicz (2016, p. 28f.) deal with different questions in the context of training and the reflection of individual counselling situations: Which images, stereotypes, and prejudices are influential in my head? How do they influence my (intuitive) reactions to Counsellors and their statements? Which images are caused by specific characteristics, and how does this influence my counselling? What impressions did I learn about others in my family of origin, in kindergarten/daycare, school, etc.? In the context of 'migration', 'culture', 'gender' etc., am I ready to question my interpretations and 'truths'? Do I take the Counsellors' perceptions seriously? Have I left the definition power to the Counsellors (both externally and for myself)? From which social position do I formulate my questions and choose interventions? Am I aware of my privileges, and what effects do they have on the counselling situation?

Finally, it should be pointed out at this point that, in addition to specific advice-related events/training/workshops in this context – depending on social positioning – also on approaches of *critical whiteness* (e. g. Eggers et al., 2017; Tißberger, 2017) or empowerment (eg Hamaz u Ergün-. Hamaz, 2013; Can, 2013; Doğmuş should be made in 2017) to provide a basis for a powerless and racism critical to creating controversy.

10.7 Conclusion and Outlook

> "I wish you – and me – that you can replace the word guilt with responsibility." (Tupoka Ogette 2019, p. 89)

When looking to the future and how to handle power, discrimination, and racism in counselling contexts, this sentence is of great importance. As could be shown based on the debates in this section, the implication of power- and racism-critical perspectives is necessary for both the theory and practice of counselling. From a *white* perspective, the focus should not be on one's feelings of guilt and shame but rather on recognising racism as a social balance of power and the assumption of responsibility for one's actions.

In this field, Counsellors must therefore be willing to break away from the "illusion of competence" of having general knowledge of those marked as *other* (cf. Mecheril et al., 2011, p. 36). This is the only way to consider the central stance that people can be understood as experts in their realities of life. It is also necessary to recognise consultants and specialists' knowledge and expertise with racism and actively do something from a *white* position to increase their visibility. This can only succeed in the long term if people with the appropriate experience and perspectives are listened to seriously and their privileges are shared (power-sharing).

As shown, there are also contradictions and pitfalls, for example, in the attitude of neutrality / impartiality, which require a further discussion that is critical of racism.

The explanations given here on a practice that is critical of racism are only the first application-oriented steps. For this reason, this section should be understood as an invitation to open the field of counselling for further reflections critical of racism and discrimination.

The question of what role counselling can play in strengthening "transformation potentials" and in supporting "empowerment processes", as described by Velho (2016, p. 205), should also be investigated.

Finally, it is crucial for a practice critical of power and racism that counsellors know about social racism and discrimination relationships and critically reflect their position and entanglement within these power relationships. To consider this necessity, the curricular inclusion of explicit racism and discrimination- critical content in training would be a first important step in the counselling community. In this way, Counsellors, institutes and associations could take on social responsibility in the context of racism.

References

Abdul-Hussain, S. u. S. Baig (Hrsg.) (2009): Diversity in Supervision, Coaching und Beratung. Wien (facultas.wuv).

Attia, I. (2017): Diskursverschränkungen des antimuslimischen Rassismus. In: K. Fereidooni und M. El (Hrsg.): Rassismuskritik und Widerstandsformen. Wiesbaden (Springer VS), S. 181–192.

Balibar, É. (1990): Gibt es einen "Neo-Rassismus"? In: É. Balibar u. I. Wallenstein: Rasse, Klasse, Nation. Ambivalente Identitäten. Hamburg (Argument), S. 23–38.

Beckmann, A. (2018): Sozialforschung. Wie sich der Rassismus modernisiert hat. Köln (Deutschlandradio). Verfügbar unter https://www.deutschlandfunk.de/sozialforschung-wie-sich-der-rassismus-modernisiert-hat.1148.de.html?dram:article_id=413731 [01.05.2020].

Biskamp, F. (2017): Rassismus, Kultur und Rationalität. Drei Rassismustheorien in der kritischen Praxis. In: PERIPHERIE 37 (2), S. 271–296. Verfügbar unter https://doi.org/10.3224/peripherie.v37i2.07 [11.03.2018].

Brunner, M. u. A. Ivanova (2015): Praxishandbuch Interkulturelle LehrerInnenbildung. Impulse – Methoden – Übungen. Berlin (Wochenschau).

Can, H. (2013): Empowerment aus der People of Color-Perspektive. Reflexionen und Empfehlungen zur Durchführung von Empowerment-Workshops gegen Rassismus. Berlin (Senatsverwaltung für Arbeit, Integration und Frauen).

Castro Varela, M. d. M. u. P. Mecheril (2016): Die Dämonisierung der Anderen. Einleitende Bemerkungen. In: M. d. M. Castro Varela u. P. Mecheril (Hrsg.): Die Dämonisierung der Anderen. Rassismuskritik der Gegenwart. Bielefeld (transcript), S. 7–19.

Doğmuş, A. (2017): Empowerment im Lehramtsstudium. In: K. Fereidooni und M. El (Hrsg.): Rassismuskritik und Widerstandsformen. Wiesbaden (Springer VS), S. 771–788.

El Hachimi, M. u. A. v. Schlippe, (2000): Therapie und Supervision in multikulturellen Kontexten. In: System Familie 13: 3–13.

El-Tayeb. F. (2017): Vorwort. In: M.M. Eggers, G. Kilomba, P. Piesche, P. und S. Arndt (Hrsg.): Mythen, Masken und Subjekte. Kritische Weißseinsforschung in Deutschland. 3. Auflage. Münster (Unrast), S. 7–10

Falicov, C. (1983): Cultural Perspectives in Family Therapy. Rockvill, Maryland (Aspen).

Falicov, C. (1983): Cultural Perspectives in Family Therapy. Rockvill, Maryland (Aspen).
Nghi Ha, K. (2017): Macht(t)raum(a) Berlin – Deutschland als Kolonialgesellschaft. In: M.M. Eggers, G. Kilomba, P. Piesche, P. und S. Arndt (Hrsg.): Mythen, Masken und Subjekte. Kritische Weißseinsforschung in Deutschland. 3. Auflage. Münster (Unrast). S. 105–117
Fischer, G. (2009): "Eine ganz hinterhältige Art von Trauma". Kölnische Rundschau 10.03.2009.
Foitzik, A. (2010): Die Normalität des Rassismus in interkultureller Bildungsarbeit. Reflexionen eigener Praxis. In: A. Broden und P. Mecheril (Hrsg.): Rassismus bildet. Bildungswissenschaftliche Beiträge zu Normalisierung und Subjektivierung in der Migrationsgesellschaft. Bielefeld (transcript), S. 265–285.
Friedrich, S. (2019): Rasse. In: B. Gießelmann, R. Richterich u. B. Kerst (Hrsg.): Handwörterbuch rechtsextremer Kampfbegriffe. 2. Auflage. Frankfurt am Main (Wochenschau), S. 301–313.
Galtung, J. (1975): Strukturelle Gewalt. Beiträge zur Friedens- und Konfliktforschung. Hamburg (Springer VS).
Hamaz, S. u. M. Ergün-Hamaz (Hrsg.) (2013): Empowerment. Berlin (Heinrich-Böll-Stiftung). Verfügbar unter https://heimatkunde.boell.de/sites/default/files/dossier_empowerment.pdf [23.08.2019].
Hegemann, T. u. R. Salman (Hrsg.) (2001): Transkulturelle Psychiatrie: Konzepte für die Arbeit mit Menschen aus anderen Kulturen. Bonn (Psychiatrie Verlag).
Hegemann, T. u. C. Oestereich (2009): Einführung in die interkulturelle systemische Beratung und Therapie. Heidelberg: (Carl-Auer).
Henrich, J., S. Heine a. A. Norenzayan (2010): Most people are not WEIRD In: Nature 466: 29.
Hormel, U. u. A. Scherr (2010): Diskriminierung. Grundlagen und Forschungsergebnisse. Wiesbaden (Springer VS).
Levold, T. (2016): Macht. In: T. Levold u. M. Wirsching (Hrsg.): Systemische Therapie und Beratung. Das große Lehrbuch. 2. Auflage. Heidelberg (Carl-Auer), S. 110–114.
McGoldrick, M., J. K. Pearce a. J. Giordano (1982) (Hrsg.): Ethnicity and Family Therapy. New York (Guilford Press).
McPherson, W. (1999): Stephen Lawrence Inquiry Report. London (H.M.O. Publ.).
Mecheril, P. (2010): "Kompetenzlosigkeitskompetenz". Pädagogisches Handeln unter Einwanderungsbedingungen. In: G. Auernheimer (Hrsg.): Interkulturelle Kompetenz und pädagogische Professionalität. Wiesbaden (Springer Fachmedien), S. 15–34.
Mecheril, P. (2011): Wirklichkeit schaffen: Integration als Dispositiv. In: Aus Politik und Zeitgeschichte 61 (43/2011): 49–54. Verfügbar unter http://www.bpb.de/system/files/pdf/P6W6D1.pdf [19.08.2019].

Mecheril, P. u. K. Scherschel (2011): Rassismus und "Rasse". In: C. Melter u. P. Mecheril (Hrsg.): Rassismuskritik. Band 1: Rassismustheorie und -forschung. 2. Auflage. Schwalbach/Ts (Wochenschau), S. 39–58.

Nazarkiewcz, K. (2016): Kulturreflexivität statt Interkulturalität. Re-thinking cross-cultural – A culture reflexive approach. In: Interculture Journal 15 (26): 23–31.

Nazarkiewicz, K. u. G. Krämer (2013): Interkulturell, multikulturell, transkulturell: Kultur(en) in Begleitprozessen systematisch berücksichtigen. In: KONTEXT 44 (1): 22–39.

Oberzaucher-Tölke, I. (2014): "Der andere Patient" – die Konstruktion kultureller Differenz in der Psychotherapieaus rassismuskritischer Perspektive. In: Psychologie und Gesellschaftskritik, 38(2), 91–102.

Ogette, T. (2019): Exit Racism, rassismuskritisch denken lernen. Münster (UNRAST).

Pates, R., D. Schmidt u. S. Karawanskij (Hrsg.) (2010): Antidiskriminierungspädagogik. Konzepte und Methoden für die Bildungsarbeit mit Jugendlichen. Wiesbaden (VS).

Pirmoradi, S. (2012): Interkulturelle Familientherapie und -beratung. Eine systemische Perspektive. Göttingen (Vandenhoeck & Ruprecht).

Scherr, A., A. El-Mafaalani u. G. Yüksel (Hrsg.) (2017): Handbuch Diskriminierung. Wiesbaden (Springer VS).

Shooman, Y. (2011): Keine Frage des Glaubens. Zur Rassifizierung von 'Kultur' und 'Religion' im antimuslimischen Rassismus. In: S. Friedrich (Hrsg.): Rassismus in der Leistungsgesellschaft. Analysen und kritische Perspektiven zu den rassistischen Normalisierungsprozessen der "Sarrazindebatte". Münster (Ed. Assemblage), S. 59–79.

Shooman, Y. (2012): Das Zusammenspiel von Kultur, Religion, Ethnizität und Geschlecht im antimuslimischen Rassismus. In: Aus Politik und Zeitgeschichte (16–17/2012): 53–57.

Tißberger, M. (2017): Critical Whiteness. Zur Psychologie hegemonialer Selbstreflexion an der Intersektion von Rassismus und Gender. Wiesbaden (Springer VS).

Velho, A. (2016): Alltagsrassismus erfahren. Frankfurt am Main (Peter Lang).